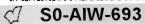

MY KOREA

MY

KOREA

TRADITIONAL FLAVORS, MODERN RECIPES

HOONI KIM

WITH AKI KAMOZAWA

Photography by Kristin Teig

W. W. NORTON & COMPANY
Independent Publishers Since 1923

Copyright © 2020 by Hooni Kim
Photographs copyright © 2020 by Kristin Teig

For information about permission to reproduce selections from this book, write to
Permissions, W. W. Norton & Company, Inc., 500 Fifth Avenue, New York, NY 10110

For information about special discounts for bulk purchases, please contact
W. W. Norton Special Sales at specialsales@wwnorton.com or 800-233-4830

Manufacturing by Transcontinental Printing
Book design by James Casey
Production manager: Anna Oler

Library of Congress Cataloging-in-Publication Data

Names: Kim, Hooni, author. | Kamozawa, Aki, author. | Teig, Kristin, photographer.
    Title: My Korea : traditional flavors, modern recipes / Hooni Kim with Aki Kamozawa,
    photography by Kristin Teig.
Description: First edition. | New York, NY : W. W. Norton & Company, 2020. | Includes index.
Identifiers: LCCN 2019057930 | ISBN 9780393239720 (hardcover) |
    ISBN 9780393634532 (epub)
Subjects: LCSH: Cooking, Korean. | Cooking, American. | LCGFT: Cookbooks.
Classification: LCC TX360.K6 K56 2020 | DDC 641.59519—dc23
LC record available at https://lccn.loc.gov/2019057930

W. W. Norton & Company, Inc., 500 Fifth Avenue, New York, N.Y. 10110
www.wwnorton.com

W. W. Norton & Company Ltd., 15 Carlisle Street, London W1D 3BS

1 2 3 4 5 6 7 8 9 0

To my wife, who shows me every day what it means to be good.

To our son, Sean, who gives us so much joy in life.

And to my mother, whose infinite love gave me the strength to disobey her.

CONTE

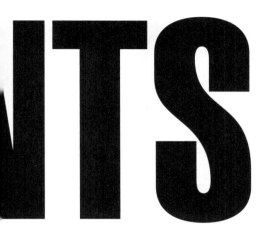

INTRODUC

TION

I experienced what would become my first "taste memory" when I was four or five years old. I was visiting my maternal grandmother in the city of Busan in South Korea, a bustling metropolis crowded with restaurants and with vendors hawking street food. My cousins took me to a small food cart in one of the endless alleys in the neighborhood. There was a knot of people gathered around it, young and old, jostling for space.

A woman was cooking on an enormous makeshift flat-top grill, and the strong, savory, spicy aroma wafting toward me pulled me forward. She was using a huge wooden spatula to move around small white oblong-shaped pieces of rice cake and thin triangular pieces of fish cake that were smothered in a glistening, bright red gochujang sauce. This was *tteokbokki*, a popular street food loved by Koreans everywhere.

My cousins paid the woman 10 Korean won (the equivalent of one penny) and I was given a single toothpick and the chance to spear either a piece of rice cake or one of fish cake. I went for the steaming-hot soft, and chewy rice cake. As I took my first bite, the powerful flavors of the gochujang sauce hit me all at once: spicy, tangy, sweet, and salty. The combination of slightly sweet, tender rice cake and rich, vibrant sauce struck the perfect balance. I had never eaten anything like it before and it was almost violently good—the flavors felt like they were punching away at my palate, in the best way. I was hooked. Tteokbokki (page 289) was the first food to make it on the "must-eat" list that I later developed for my annual trips to Korea.

My second "taste memory" was *gim* (laver, or dried seaweed). Thanks to the popularity of Japanese cuisine, many people in the US are familiar with nori, the laver used to make sushi rolls and hand rolls. More recently, Korean seasoned seaweed snacks made with gim have also become popular in the States. You can see little kids running around in New York City playgrounds and eating these crisp pieces of seaweed, which are considered healthy by their moms and nannies. Even my neighborhood supermarket carries gim snacks.

As addictive as those packaged seaweed snacks can be, their flavor pales in comparison to gim that is toasted and salted at home. When I was a child, I thought gim was the best-tasting *banchan* (side dish) on the table, and I would tell everyone that the gim was all mine, off limits to my older cousins. There is a delicate crispy texture to gim that is freshly toasted, which puts it on a whole new level.

It's quite easy to prepare gim at home. Lightly brush freshly pressed sesame or perilla oil on the sheets of seaweed and then toast it over an open flame (or simply toast it in a pan). Sprinkle a little salt on top and serve immediately. Once you taste this crackly gim wrapped around warm, freshly made rice, the memory will stay with you forever, as it did for me.

Gim was always my favorite food to eat when I visited my paternal grandmother, who lived on the distant island of So An Do, my late father's birthplace. So An Do is a tiny island off the southernmost tip of the Korean peninsula, located in South Jeolla Province. All the people on the island are descended from five original families of settlers. It still feels like a small village, and everyone is like family. Even today, when I visit So An Do, villagers will greet me as "Jun-Ho's son" rather than using my name.

When I visited So An Do as a young child, each household not only grew its own vegetables and raised its own livestock, it also dried its own Korean red chili peppers to make *gochugaru* (red chili flakes) and made its own *jangs* (Korean fermented bean pastes or sauces). Families prepared their own gim as well, harvesting the seaweed from the ocean that surrounded them. Being in So An Do was like going back in time to a different era, when people were directly connected to the land and the sea. Everything we ate there was precious. Food was not purchased; it was harvested or homemade. Everyone appreciated how much time, effort, and care went into growing, catching, and reaping the food, because they did it themselves. The food was necessary for survival, yes, but it was much more than that. It was truly a labor of love and, as such, invaluable.

But the trip to So An Do was very difficult. Coming from the modern comforts of London, I hated the long, arduous journey. When I was a child, it took three whole days to get there from the UK, where we lived at the time. My mother and I would transfer from plane to plane to bus to taxi to ferry and, eventually, to a rickety twelve-foot-long wooden boat for the thirty-minute boat ride to my late father's home.

I dreaded the lack of modern bathrooms and air-conditioning. There was only one store on the entire island, and it housed the sole telephone for the community. Nevertheless, I knew the importance of making that trip, year after year. My father, who had passed away when I was two years old, was my grandmother's only child, and I was her sole grandchild. While I don't remember my father, I remember how much my grandmother doted on me. She would hold my hand, crying, while I slept, watching over me all night long and remembering her own son.

As I grew older, I learned to appreciate all the foods that So An Do had to offer. At every meal, I enjoyed the homemade kimchi and jangs, just-laid eggs, vegetables from the backyard garden, and seafood caught by my uncles. Every ingredient was so fresh and delicious. As much as I'd originally dreaded the long, exhausting trips to So An Do every year, that dread slowly transformed into anticipation of the vivid flavors that I would get to eat once I arrived.

During high school and throughout college, I visited the city of Seoul almost every summer. My list of "must-eat" Korean foods grew exponentially. Grilled short ribs marinated in soy, *yangneom galbi* (page 129), were one of my favorites. Tender pieces of garlicky short ribs were grilled over an open charcoal fire. The fattiness of the beef and the sweetness of the marinade contrasted beautifully with the crispy char and the slightly bitter, smoky flavor the meat developed as it cooked. The best parts are always the chewy bits that cling to the bones. I discovered spicy stews like *kimchi jjigae* (Aged-Kimchi Stew, page 198), *sundubu jjigae* (Spicy Soft Tofu Stew, page 202), and *mae-un tang* (Spicy Fish Bone Stew, page 201), which had so much depth of flavor that they screamed for a chilled shot of soju (the traditional Korean liquor made from sweet potatoes) to wash them down. During this time, I fell in love with more than Korean food; I fell in love with the whole experience and culture of Korea itself.

KOREAN FOOD IN THE US

My mom and I moved from London to the United States when I was around nine years old. As a Korean American living in New York, I grew up eating the food of the city's Koreatown. What I found there was a far cry from the luscious ingredients we ate in So An Do and the vibrant street foods I had enjoyed in Busan. However, it did serve as a reminder of the food from Korea, and I would find myself back there again and again. Many of my friends would also frequent Koreatown, and, like me, they constantly complained about the quality of the food. Still, we would inevitably be drawn back to that single block of 32nd Street off Broadway. Looking back, I realize that the main draw of Koreatown was the atmosphere and the sense of belonging I felt there. The hustle and bustle, the loud voices speaking in Korean, the throngs of people there on a Saturday night, and the smell of kimchi and doenjang all transported me back to my visits to Korea. Surrounded as I was by people who looked like me, it was easy to forget for a moment that I was a minority.

Although the food served in Koreatown was a shadow of what I had tasted in Korea, it was cheap, servings were generous, and the restaurants were open twenty-four hours a day. Some of the best times I had in my twenties were in Koreatown. We would stay up all night long, until the dim glow of dawn slowly began to dispel the haze of an alcohol-fueled night and overtake the bright neon signs of 32nd Street. We would spend the evening moving through multiple restaurants, bars, and *noraebangs* (Korean karaoke joints), counting each place as Koreans are wont to do, as *il-cha, yi-cha, sam-cha,* and *sa-cha.* Il cha was the first place, where we would meet for dinner. Yi-cha was the second stop, at a restaurant or bar where we would drink. Sam-cha would be our third stop, singing at a noraebang. Finally, sa-cha would be our final destination, another restaurant where we could start eating again to cure our hangovers. It's not unusual for Koreans to excitedly say, "Let's go to yi-cha!" before dinner is even over—a sure sign that the night is just getting started and will last into the wee hours of the morning.

We drank Korean alcohol, constantly clinking our glasses together to *gunbae* with each other. It gave us a feeling, however fleeting, of kinship, of family. All it took was one night in Koreatown together to bond us; regardless of ethnicity, in that moment of camaraderie we were all Korean.

Having spent so much of my youth in Koreatown, I understand the feeling of being transported by where you are and what you eat to a different time and place—despite the fact that the food there lacked any real flavor. True, complex flavors come with time, effort, attention to detail, and, most important, from using the best ingredients that you can lay your hands on.

When I was in my twenties, I ate food containing MSG, preservatives, pesticides, growth hormones, antibiotics, and other such chemicals with abandon. White Castle sliders, Doritos, instant ramen, buckets of KFC—I could eat anything I wanted as often as I wanted, and it never affected me. Who cared if there was MSG in it? The food was cheap and it hit the spot. The first few bites would give me a burst of umami, which triggered cravings for more, and I would invariably eat too much. How often have you started eating a bag of potato chips that taste so mouthwateringly good that after a while you find yourself unable to stop, even though you're full?

As I entered my thirties and then my forties, things began to change. I started to notice my body's response when I ate processed foods or the food at cheap restaurants: difficulty digesting, inflammation, lethargy, excessive thirst, and even migraines. The same holds true for most people I know above the age of forty. The symptoms may vary from person to person, but once you hit a certain age, your body starts to send you clear signals. My body was trying to tell me something, and I began to listen.

Many people today, including some in the food industry, believe that MSG is identical to naturally occurring glutamates and hence safe to consume. But MSG is made via a chemical synthesis in a laboratory setting; it is not naturally occurring, although it may be derived from natural ingredients. Naturally occurring glutamates are always bound to a protein. The glutamates in MSG are synthetically isolated from their proteins and then artificially reattached to sodium in order to stabilize them. So there is a difference. The human body is used to naturally occurring glutamates and digests them easily, but we don't know exactly how the body digests commercially manufactured MSG. One theory holds that because the glutamates in MSG have been isolated from their natural protein, your body is unable to regulate the amount of this MSG in the bloodstream, and it may reach toxic levels.

I'm not a scientist, so I have no proof of any long-term damage that MSG inflicts on our bodies. But as a chef, I've been taught, and I continue to teach my cooks, that there are no shortcuts to achieving maximal flavor. You need to start with fresh, delicious, high-quality ingredients and bring out their flavors slowly, over time, using your culinary skills. There are naturally occurring glutamates in seaweed, mushrooms, tomatoes, and meats, and the process of fermentation allows natural glutamates to develop in jangs, cheeses, and other fermented foods. These are all flavorful ingredients and products that our bodies are meant to eat and can easily digest. To me, MSG is nothing but a shortcut. It is a way of cheating to create the illusion of flavor in cheap, unhealthy ingredients, and it goes against the very foundation of Korea's culinary traditions, which are deeply rooted in nature and the idea of food as medicine. I never use MSG in my kitchens. I believe that we owe it to our customers to be honest in our cooking and to take the time, effort, and devotion necessary to create real flavor.

TRADITIONAL KOREAN INGREDIENTS

As with any other cuisine, the quality of the ingredients is of the utmost importance in Korean cooking. Jangs make up the core flavor profile of the cuisine. Because traditionally every Korean household and restaurant made their own jangs each year, the sauces were inherently artisanal and differed from place to place. Jangs were so important and so fundamental to the well-being of a household that Koreans still have a saying that if your jangs go bad, your household will have bad luck that year. The restaurant kitchens that made the best jangs produced the best food. The same dish served at two different restaurants could vary greatly because, in addition to the style or personality of the chef and his choice of ingredients, the flavor of their own jangs made their food unique.

Nowadays it's difficult for people to make their own jangs, particularly in an urban environment. The biggest obstacle is finding the space to make and store the jangs, because they need to be outside, exposed to sunlight and wind. As a result, many of the jangs eaten in Korea today are commercially produced, although you can still find quite a few traditionally made jangs that are sold in stores. Mass-produced jangs aren't based on the time-honored methods of fermentation. They rely on shortcuts to quickly ferment the jang, which results in flavors that lack depth and complexity. There are none of the distinctive flavor differences that make Korean food unique. Unfortunately, many of the restaurants in Korea and pretty much all of them here in the United States use commercial jangs, and it shows in the quality of their food.

Because traditionally made jangs are naturally fermented, their flavors never stop changing. Just as wine is alive until it turns to vinegar, the complex flavors of a jang evolve as it ages, as it oxidizes. Jangs can be aged for even longer than many wines, taking years for the flavors to develop. Even the salts used for seasoning jangs (and kimchi as well) are traditionally aged for two or more years.

A long fermentation process is key to developing the complex flavors. Jangs were traditionally fermented outside in large clay pots, or *jang-dok*, that are porous enough to allow the jang to breathe. At dawn every morning, Korean housewives would painstakingly wipe down every single pot to rid it of any impurities that might have come out through the porous walls, resulting in a cleaner jang. Each traditionally made jang has a unique flavor due to the various bacteria that cause the fermentation to begin, the quality of the soybeans used, the salinity differences between the jang at the top and bottom of the jang-dok, and variations in sunlight or climate, including the humidity of a particular season.

Many of the essential flavors of Korean food are developed through the preservation and aging of fresh ingredients that are harvested at the peak of their season. Various ingenious preservation techniques, fermentation among them, are used to deepen the intensity of the ingredients and make them more complex. Drying concentrates the flavor of vegetables, meat, fish, and seafood and extends their shelf life. Salting and dehydrating seafood turns up the volume of its delicate sea flavor. Pickling enriches the flavors of vegetables as well as creating a crunchy texture and a savory taste.

The final, and most important part of Korean food, as any Korean mother will tell you, is the concept of cooking with *jung sung*—to cook with heart and devotion. The result is the Korean food that I crave, the cuisine that I aspire to serve in my restaurants, and the flavors that I hope to share with you through this book.

Picking and tasting lettuces in a
garden on Jeju Island.

DANJI

I was always interested in food, but when I was young, it was mostly in terms of the pleasure of eating it. I was your typical Asian student, excelling in math and science, but I didn't have a passion for anything in particular. During my college years, my mother steered me toward medicine so I acquiesced. Little did I know that I would hate the hospital environment, which I only discovered two years into medical school. I was so depressed by the negative energy there that I became sick. I started getting headaches and ulcers, and I took a year off to recover. I decided to use the time to learn how to cook by attending The French Culinary Institute (now the International Culinary Center) in SoHo.

The nine-month program was the perfect length for my "sabbatical," and it would allow me to go back to medical school when the program was over. While attending culinary school, I was encouraged to *stage* (work as an unpaid intern) at local restaurants. My first stint was at Tocqueville in Union Square, under chef Marco Moreira, and then I worked at Cru under chef Shea Gallante. As I trained at these restaurants, my culinary skills grew in leaps and bounds, and I realized that I had finally found my passion.

After graduating from culinary school, I interned at what I considered to be the best restaurant in New York City, Daniel. I was supposed to be there for two months and then return to medical school, but after two weeks, the executive chef, Jean-François, offered me a full-time job. My decision not to go back to medical school devastated my mother, who refused to speak to me for over a year, but I knew that I aspired to become a chef, and taking that job was the easiest decision I ever made.

Working at Daniel was like going through culinary boot camp. Unlike most fine dining restaurants, Daniel is huge. Serving more than three hundred guests a night with precision at the highest levels of fine dining is something that, even today, almost no other restaurant is able to pull off. I worked eighty to ninety hours a week, usually six but sometimes seven days straight, and every minute was spent aiming for perfection. The team of chefs and cooks paid meticulous attention to detail to create each dish and time them all just right to bring them together for each table.

The French chefs at Daniel, starting with Daniel Boulud, took a huge amount of cultural pride in their food, in French flavors, presentations, and cooking techniques. They were like Olympic athletes competing as part of the French national team every night. Watching and learning from them, I realized that just wanting to cook delicious food was not enough to make me the chef I aspired to become. I needed my own identity. I wanted to cook Korean food with the same pride in it as the French chefs at Daniel. I wanted to cook the food of my own heritage.

My plan was to train under a respected Korean chef at a high-quality Korean restaurant. Sadly, there weren't any in NYC or anywhere else in the United States at that time. The closest thing I could find was the best Japanese restaurant in the city and, arguably, in the country. So I left Daniel to work at Masa under chef Masa Takayama. (Masa was then, and still is, the most expensive restaurant in New York City.)

Masa's kitchen had a completely different style from that of Daniel. The sounds of the kitchen were subdued in comparison and the approach to cooking was very Japanese. Daniel's kitchen was loud, with cooks shouting instructions in French all the time. At Masa, no one yelled except the chef. At Daniel, we cooked for several hundred guests every night; at Masa we cooked for fifty on a busy day. I learned a whole new range of cooking techniques and discovered a whole new set of ingredients, flown in daily from Japan.

Japanese cooking required even more precise knife skills than French, and there were different knives for specific tasks. For example, we would use a *deba* knife for cleaning fish, a *usuba* knife for cutting vegetables, and a *yanagi* knife for slicing raw fish. I learned about preparing ingredients I would never have otherwise been able to work with unless I lived in Japan. But I also recognized many ingredients from my childhood eating adventures in Korea.

Somewhat surprisingly, I cooked a lot of Korean food at Masa. We had family (staff) meal three times a day, and it was the line cooks' responsibility to make those meals. Chef Masa loved Korean food and was always asking me to make his favorite Korean dishes, which included *mae-un tang* (Spicy Fish Bone Stew; see page 201), *doenjang jjigae* (Fermented-Soybean Stew, see page 205), and *kimchi jjigae* (see page 198).

So it was at a Japanese restaurant that I learned how to cook Korean food. Since I was Korean American, everyone assumed that I could already cook Korean food, but I had never actually done so. I spent a lot of time during my off hours doing research and hunting for recipes. I must have cooked over fifty different versions of Masa's favorite Korean dishes, always trying to improve upon them. The staff at Masa consisted of ten other talented chefs who generously offered their thoughts, opinions, and critiques of each dish I created. This was incredibly valuable feedback. More than half of the menu at my first restaurant, Danji, stemmed from the family meals I cooked at Masa. My Bulgogi Sliders (page 142), Mae-un Tang (Spicy Fish Bone Stew, page 201), Eun-dae-gu Jorim (Soy-Poached Black Cod, page 177), and Fried Chicken Wings with Two Sauces (page 296) are based on the recipes I created back then.

As a cook, you learn so much by cooking a chef's food in his restaurant. You learn about his techniques, his seasoning, his flavor combinations, his values, and his overall philosophy. However, eventually, if you are a good cook, cooking someone else's food isn't enough anymore. If you have a creative personality, there is no place for your own ideas when you are cooking under a great chef. You cannot add anything to his dishes; the best line cook or sous chef is merely an extension of the chef. If a cook wants to be creative, his only choice is to cook his own food, and the only way to do that professionally is to become a chef. I wanted to cook Korean food, and I wanted to cook my own food. So I knew I had to open my own restaurant.

I opened my first restaurant, Danji, in 2010. In contrast to the huge jang-doks that were traditionally used to store jangs and kimchi all year round, a danji is a small clay jar that holds traditional ingredients and food for daily use. I named my restaurant Danji because the space was tiny. At 700 square feet, it was all I could afford in Manhattan. I invested all the money I had, and when that wasn't enough, I borrowed from the bank and from my family, which motivated me to work very hard. Failure never even crossed my mind. I was too busy working day and night to think about any dire possibilities.

When I opened Danji, one of the best pieces of advice I received was that the restaurant should be a reflection of me, of my own personality as both a Korean American and a New Yorker: so much so that close friends would be able to recognize it as Hooni Kim's restaurant the moment they walked in the door, even if I wasn't there. I considered every detail, from the type of flooring, the chairs, and the size of the bar to the stereo and the music, all the way down to the color of the bathroom door handle. Danji represented my taste in music, my style in décor, the type of service I wanted to receive in a casual restaurant, and the Korean flavors I liked to eat.

The first menu you create in your own restaurant has to illustrate who you are as a chef. For me, it was very important that I establish credibility by cooking authentic traditional Korean dishes. No matter what cuisine you specialize in, you must have first mastered the classics. There can be no interpretation, no fusion, no modern takes on any cuisine until you truly understand and embrace its foundations. With the traditional section of my menu, I wanted to show that I could create the best versions of classic dishes without dumbing down the flavors or taking shortcuts. Alongside those traditional dishes, though, I also wanted to use creative flair to apply Korean flavors to my favorite foods from my youth, from White Castle sliders to Buffalo wings. These dishes comprised the modern section of the menu. That balance of traditional and interpretive Korean food was the statement I wanted to make. This was Hooni Kim's Korean food.

HANJAN

After several years of receiving great reviews, accolades, and even a Michelin star—a first ever in the world for a Korean restaurant—I began traveling to Korea multiple times a year. Each time, I would visit the countryside and stop at food markets in different areas to learn more about Korean ingredients. I love to eat at the restaurants in the markets that serve all of the vendors, because they are always the best way to learn about any cuisine.

The more I visited Korea, the more my menu at Danji began to shift toward the traditional. Unfortunately, our tiny kitchen was so limited that there wasn't enough space to accommodate many of the ideas I wanted to embrace. There was no room for fermenting or pickling. Our walk-in fridge was too small to store everything that would need aging. There wasn't enough prep space for larger quantities of ingredients. In short, it was very hard to expand the traditional Korean side of the menu. Danji's kitchen just wasn't designed to do that.

Danji in Hell's Kitchen, New York City.

Hanjan in the Flatiron District, New York City.

So I decided to open another restaurant. The inspiration for this restaurant was not my background or my interpretation of Korean dishes, as at Danji. It was traditional, authentic, old-school Korean food. I named it Hanjan. In Korean, *hanjan* literally means "one drink," but of course, saying "Let's go and grab a drink" never actually means just one. The word evokes the social, communal drinking culture of Korea. It is the start of a night of laughter and heartfelt conversations with friends, sharing in joy and sharing in heartache. Hanjan embodies the ambience and camaraderie that come with sharing food and drink in Korea.

There is a whole category of Korean foods called *anju* that you eat while having drinks. Although nowa-days American-style bars that serve only minimal bar snacks are catching on in Korea, traditionally in Korean culture, drinking and eating are always tied together in a communal way, so you never drink alcohol without food and you never drink alone. While anything can become an anju in a pinch, there are certain foods that pair exceptionally well with traditional Korean alcoholic beverages such as soju, makgeolli (unfiltered rice beer), and rice wine. Thus, the drinking culture of Korea opens up another whole world of food. With Hanjan, I wanted to introduce New York City to this drinking culture and to the Korean drinks and anju that are an inseparable part of it.

One of my favorite things to do in Korea is to visit the *pojang machas* on the streets of Seoul late at

(Left to right): Storefront of my favorite spicy rice cake restaurant, Ppalgan Tteokbokki, in Haeundae, Busan. Grilling meat at a Korean bbq restaurant. Wando, my father's hometown.

night. These are pop-up street bars that serve all sorts of delectable anju dishes, ranging from the exotic, such as live baby octopus, to the familiar, such as *pajeon* (scallion pancakes). Koreans are generally big drinkers, and pojang machas used to be the place to go after a long night of drinking when regular brick-and-mortar establishments were closed. They were places where salarymen would grab a last one for the road. At one time, pojang machas were found in any neighborhood alley, but now, alas, they can only be found in certain neighborhoods. They are worth visiting if you are willing to search them out.

Anju is comfort food, food that modern Koreans eat in market restaurants or at pojang machas after a long day of work. It is the food and drink that their parents and generations before them also enjoyed. That was the food that I wanted to cook. So Hanjan's first menu included very traditional dishes such as Pajeon (Scallion Pancakes, page 285) and Dubu Kimchi (Warm Tofu with Kimchi and Pork Belly Stir-Fry, page 278). These dishes were the very best versions of what I had tasted in Korea. During the years since Danji had opened, I had become so much more Korean, and for my second restaurant, my inspiration was all from Korea.

Hanjan provided me with the space I needed to develop a larger menu of traditional Korean dishes. Pickling, fermenting, and the prep work involved for these require a lot of space. It was such a relief to have a walk-in refrigerator that was four times bigger than my first one. Even in regular Korean households, it is not uncommon to have two or three refrigerators: one for kimchi, a main refrigerator, and, sometimes for larger families, another refrigerator, along with a separate stand-alone freezer. The amount of preserved foods and other ingredients that need to be stored for long periods of time is enormous.

I was very happy with Hanjan, and I was proud of what I had accomplished, and it showed in the food. We were given two stars in a glowing review by Pete Wells, the *New York Times* restaurant critic, who called me "the leading interpreter of Korean food in New York."

MY FOOD, MY KOREA

As a Korean chef, I think constantly about Korean food and its place in America's culinary culture. The food I serve stays true to authentic Korean flavors. While I offer creative nontraditional Korean food at Danji, I do not dilute or use substitutes for any ingredients that are integral to the flavor profile of traditional Korean dishes. I do apply more sophisticated culinary techniques than would normally be used by a mother or grandmother in a traditional Korean kitchen, but these techniques are intended to support and enhance the texture and sophistication of the original dishes, never to interfere with the authentic flavor. I use the highest-quality ingredients I can get my hands on, free of pesticides, hormones, antibiotics, and preservatives. Nowhere else will you find a casual Korean restaurant that uses ingredients on par with those used at Michelin three-star restaurants. My food is what you might get from a Korean grandmother if she went to culinary school, interned at high-end Michelin restaurants, and settled in New York City (and perhaps had an addiction to White Castle sliders).

Today in the US, many up-and-coming chefs of Korean heritage are gaining recognition through fusion interpretations of Korean food rather than adhering to traditional versions. And many famous non-Korean chefs are now incorporating Korean ingredients into their menus. There is nothing wrong with making a paella accented with kimchi or a risotto flavored with doenjang. Creative uses of Korean ingredients here can only help Korean food become more mainstream and familiar, and it is great to see how far Korean food has come in the States. But I do not believe in watering down the unique flavors of traditional dishes because of the misconception that Korean flavors have to be muted in order to appeal to the American palate: for example, using Japanese miso instead of a traditional doenjang or making kimchi without garlic so the smell is not as pungent. Traditional Korean food in its purest form can be delicious to everyone if prepared correctly.

This cookbook is a gathering of recipes that I have developed over the years at my two restaurants. They epitomize my views on traditional Korean food, current interpretations, and future extrapolations. I hope that as you cook your way through these recipes, you will get a true sense of Korean food as I see it. This is my food based on my love for Korea and all of the things it brings to the table.

T

IE KOREAN PANTRY

There are now Korean supermarkets in most major US cities that sell all of the ingredients required to make any of the recipes in this book. H Mart has stores in eleven states and they also sell online (hmart.com). You can also check out your local Asian supermarkets. Chinese and Japanese supermarkets carry many of the Korean ingredients I call for, or their equivalents. Kim'C Market (kimcmarket.com) and Gotham Grove (gothamgrove.com) sell amazing high-end artisanal jangs, oils, and vinegars that I highly recommend. WooltariUSA (wooltariusa.com) has great gochugaru. And Amazon offers many Korean ingredients.

As you will see, many of the staple ingredients in the Korean pantry are dried, fermented, or heavily salted, so they have a very long shelf life if stored properly. This also means that even if you don't have a Korean supermarket in your city, you'll be fine if you stock up once in a while online or when you can make a visit to an Asian market.

There are a few key ingredients that I keep in my pantry at home: the basic jangs (doenjang, ganjang, and gochujang), ingredients for dashi (dashima, dried shiitake mushrooms, and dried anchovies), gochugaru, kimchi, sesame oil, and garlic. They form the foundation for many of the recipes in this book.

Most of the fresh vegetables and meats called for in the recipes can be purchased at any market, although I always recommend organic and/or local produce when possible. It's more flavorful, contains more nutrients, and is better overall for your palate and health. Unfortunately, most Asian supermarkets do not carry much organic or local produce. So I hit the farmers' market or Whole Foods first and then head to the Asian supermarket for everything else I need. When you are shopping at a Korean supermarket, I recommend having a copy of this list for reference purposes.

Jookjangyeon jang farm near Pohang, South Korea.

(1) Doenjang, (2) ganjang, and (3) gochujang are the three primary ingredients in Korean cooking. All fermented, and pretty salty, they are used to season and flavor dishes of all kinds. In the old days, every Korean family made its own jangs, which would determine how deliciously the family would eat for the coming months or even years. You could consider these three jangs the equivalent of the French "mother sauces," from which every other sauce is derived. Bottom line: If you have access to high-quality ganjang, doenjang, and gochujang, you'll be able to cook amazing Korean food.

DOENJANG (FERMENTED SOYBEAN PASTE)

Doenjang is a fermented soybean paste that at first glance may appear similar to Japanese miso. However, doenjang is created through a more complicated process. Traditionally in Korea, it is made by sculpting cooked soybeans into small blocks called *mejoo* and hanging them from a wall, bound with stalks of rice straw, for several weeks. The contact with the straw encourages the growth of *Bacillus subtilis*, a type of probiotic bacterium. The mejoo blocks are then placed in large clay jars, covered with a solution of water and salt, and left to ferment. After a week or so, the blocks break down and separate into a top layer of doenjang and bottom layer of ganjang (Korean soy sauce). The doenjang and ganjang are then transferred to separate jars and left to ferment further, for a minimum of three months and sometimes up to several years, depending on the maker. With age, the flavors of both the doenjang and the soy sauce become more complex and deep. At Danji and Hanjan, we typically use doenjang that has been allowed to naturally ferment for three to four years, from the artisanal brand Jook Jang Yeon.

Because of its natural fermentation, doenjang has the same sharp, funky smell as a strong cheese, such as Raclette, Époisses, or Taleggio. Just as you might come to associate the stink of a Raclette with its wonderful creamy flavor, once you have tasted a good doenjang stew, you will think only of its nutty and earthy flavor when you get a waft of its potent scent.

Naturally fermented artisanal doenjang is salty, concentrated in flavor, and full of healthy probiotics for a healthy gut microbiome. Mass-market doenjang tends to be less salty and sweeter, and because it is not natu-rally fermented, it will not have the probiotic bacteria. I implore you to use artisanal doenjang if at all possible. When making Doenjang Jjigae (Fermented-Soybean Stew, page 205) using artisanal doenjang, some people will rest the stew anywhere from 30 minutes to several hours after cooking before they serve it. As it rests, the initial sour acidic flavor will disappear and it will become sweet, nutty, and full of umami. With commercial doenjang, there is no transformation from acid to sweetness, and it can be consumed right away.

Buying: Admittedly, artisanal doenjangs are not easy to come by in the US, but it is worth the time and effort to find them. Korean markets sometimes carry a few different artisanal jangs, and Kim'C Market and Gotham Grove usually have some in stock. If you happen to live in the NY/LA/Atlanta areas, some markets there sell local homemade doenjang. The brand we use, Jook Jang Yeon, makes doenjang, ganjang, and gochujang using traditional methods. You can find it in selected supermarkets and online at kimcmarket.com. If you can't get artisanal doenjang, I recommend the Sempio brand. It is fairly delicious and relatively easy to find. You can easily determine whether the doenjang you buy is artisanal or mass-produced by the price, as artisanal can be up to three times more expensive, and by reading the ingredient list: commercial doenjang often contains wheat.

Storage: Keep doenjang in its plastic container or in a glass jar in your refrigerator for up to 12 months.

Use: Doenjang is most commonly used to add flavor to stews (jjigae). It is also the main component of Ssamjang (page 57), a sauce that is eaten with Korean barbecue and added to lettuce wraps.

GANJANG (KOREAN SOY SAUCE)

Ganjang, Korean soy sauce, is used to season food as Western cooks use salt, and it adds umami and deep flavors to almost every Korean dish. It is traditionally made only with soybeans, salt, and water, and does not contain wheat. Traditional or artisanal Korean soy sauce is highly fermented, and while similar to Japanese and Chinese soy sauces, has a richer, tangier flavor.

Buying: Generally, ganjang falls into three different categories: *guk-ganjang* (or *chosun-ganjang*), *jin-ganjang*, and *yangjo-ganjang*. Guk-ganjang is the lightest in color and very salty. It is typically used to season soups and stews. Jin-ganjang is aged guk-ganjang. It is darker in color, sweeter, and less salty. Yangjo-ganjang, which is made with wheat, is similar to Japanese soy sauce. In the supermarket, you will find many different types of ganjang created by large ganjang companies. It can get confusing because the traditional labels are not regulated or certified, so labels can be misleading. The array of different ganjangs has become so vast that even Koreans can have trouble determining which ganjang pairs properly with each dish.

For the recipes in this book, I recommend either jin-ganjang or yangjo-ganjang (along with salt for seasoning, if necessary); I advise you to steer clear of guk-ganjang, as it is very salty. You may encounter other specialized ganjangs, such as *mat-ganjang* (*mat* means flavor in Korean), which usually have added MSG. I don't use these.

Sempio is a popular commercial Korean soy sauce, and it is available in most Korean markets. There are versions of low-sodium Korean soy sauces, but I don't use them. If you cannot find a Korean brand, you can substitute Japanese soy sauce, as the flavors are similar.

However, please note that all Japanese soy sauces except tamari contain traces of wheat. My go-to Japanese brand is Yamasa Marudaizu.

Storage: Ganjang should be stored in your pantry.

Use: Ganjang is used for seasoning and to add flavor and umami to many dishes.

GOCHUJANG (FERMENTED RED CHILI PASTE)

Gochujang is essentially a mix of fermented soybean powder, gochugaru, and sweet glutinous rice paste, making it deliciously sweet, spicy, and funky all at once. To me, gochujang epitomizes the essence of Korean flavors. It is bold and aggressive, and when it is used in Korean dishes, it becomes the main flavor profile. These days, I see a lot of bottled gochujang-based hot sauce in the US market. I think the manufacturers want us to use it as an all-around condiment, as you would use Sriracha. But in Korea, gochujang is rarely used as a condiment. Maybe you'll see it as a dip for dried seafood/jerky and bibimbap. Otherwise, it is used only in recipes that highlight its flavor. It's a complex ingredient that shines when used properly, not meant to be squeezed onto leftover Chinese takeout.

Buying: High-quality traditionally made gochujang is difficult to find in the US, but artisanal doenjang producers often make gochujang too. Find one and you will generally find the other. Again, Kim'C Market and Gotham Grove usually stock artisanal gochujang and doenjang. Some Korean supermarkets sell artisanal gochujang; look for Jook Jang Yeon or, in New York City and LA, gochujang from local Korean farmers. Chung Jung One offers a very good mass-produced version called Sunchang. It is the most popular brand in Korea and has been for years.

Storage: Gochujang should be stored in the refrigerator after opening.

Use: Gochujang is used in many dishes for its spicy and pungent character. It is very difficult to make a subtle gochujang dish. You can neutralize it slightly by adding sesame oil or even mayonnaise, but, ultimately, it is the strongest, most assertive ingredient used in Korean cooking.

GOCHUGARU (KOREAN RED CHILI FLAKES)

Gochu means pepper and *garu* means flakes, hence gochugaru: Korean red chili flakes made from sun-dried red chilies. Coarsely ground gochugaru is used in recipes for everyday dishes and kimchi. Finely ground gochugaru is used to make gochujang (see above) and certain thick sauces like the one used for Tteokbokki (Spicy Rice Cakes, page 289). Sun-drying concentrates the flavor of the chili peppers, similar to how Italians sun-dry tomatoes. Gochugaru chilies have a rounded sweetness and spiciness, a balance that distinguishes them from most other chilies, which are usually either one or the other.

Buying: Gochugaru can be found at any Korean market. You will sometimes see *chung-yang* gochugaru, a really spicy version. If you like your food quite spicy, you can substitute chung-yang gochugaru for 10 to 20 percent of the amount of gochugaru called for in the recipe. The best-tasting gochugaru is made from Korean chilies. Be sure to check the origin of the pepper in the ingredient list, as some Korean brands use chilies from China or Mexico. Brands that use Korean chili peppers (NH and several others) are only available at Korean supermarkets, and they cost five to eight times as much as those made from Chinese or Mexican peppers. To me it's worth it, because these peppers are sweeter and have more depth and flavor. If you cannot find gochugaru made from Korean chili peppers, use the Tae Kyung brand from China. I would not recommend substituting other chili pepper flakes, as Korean gochugaru's flavor is very distinctive. The heat level of the chili peppers varies from season to season and crop to crop, so some batches may be more intense than others.

Storage: Gochugaru should be stored in a cool, dry place. If you will be storing it for longer than a month, I suggest you put it in the freezer, where it will keep for up to one year. You can use it directly from the freezer.

Use: Gochugaru is used to spice up food; you can bet most spicy foods in Korea are red because of gochgaru and gochujang. Gochugaru is used in kimchi and gochujang, supplying a sweet and spicy balance of flavors. Due to the seasonal variance in the heat of the peppers, the kimchi and other foods that I make at Danji and Hanjan can be quite spicy or fairly mild. Although consistency of flavor is important in a restaurant, I believe that cooking with what nature gives you is more true to the spirit of cooking Korean food than always striving for a uniform flavor profile.

KOREAN CHILI PEPPERS

Korean chili peppers are called *put gochu* when they are still green. Chilies that have ripened and turned red are called *hong gochu*. The red chili peppers are just a hint sweeter than the green ones. I use the green chilies in recipes where I want a fresher flavor, but the red peppers make a bright, beautiful garnish. Korean chili peppers provide a wonderful balance of spice, acidity, and sweetness, and they brighten up heavier, earthier dishes. As with jalapeños and other chilies, their heat level can vary. Taste a small piece before using, and if they are too spicy, you can remove the seeds and veins to lessen the heat.

The types of chili peppers I like to use: (1) Long hot green pepper, (2) Korean chili pepper, (3) gochugaru, (4) Holland red pepper.

Buying: Look for Korean chili peppers at Korean markets. If you can't find them, you can substitute other long hot chili peppers.

Storage: Wrapped in a dry paper towel, the peppers can be kept in your refrigerator for 5 to 7 days.

Use: Korean chili peppers add a kick to any dish.

DASHIMA (DRIED KELP)

Dashima (its Japanese name is *kombu*) is dried kelp that's thicker than miyeok (see below); it comes in pieces about 12 inches wide and 4 to 5 feet long. It has a rich, salty taste and adds umami to any dish. Dashima is a versatile ingredient that harmonizes beautifully with other ingredients, making it an essential part of my pantry.

Buying: The best dashima is thick and large, sold folded and wrapped in plastic. I suggest you buy a 1-pound bag because the best dashima is found in larger packages that will keep the pieces intact. Feel for thickness; the thicker the seaweed, the deeper the flavor. Most Asian markets carry dashima; in Japanese markets, look for kombu.

Storage: Dashima can be stored in a cool, dry place in an airtight container for up to 6 months.

Use: Dashima is most commonly used to make Dashi (page 189), but it is also used to deepen the flavors of other broths and soups. You can even make a banchan from a piece of dashima right after it has been used to make dashi by cutting it into small bite-sized pieces and seasoning it with soy, sugar, and rice vinegar to taste. Or deep-fry small pieces of dashima and sprinkle sugar on top to make crispy, addictive chips that will taste like flavor bombs in your mouth.

MIYEOK (DRIED SEAWEED)

Miyeok is thinner and more delicate than dashima. It is commonly known by its Japanese name, *wakame*. It is very flavorful and has a silky, slippery, soft texture that feels wonderful in your mouth. Miyeok has a subtle aroma of the sea, similar to dashima, and its delicate texture matches its soft flavor.

Buying: You can find miyeok/wakame in most Korean and Japanese supermarkets, usually side by side with the dashima. Since these seaweeds are sold in clear packages, they can easily be distinguished by their size and thickness even if the packages are not marked.

Storage: Miyeok can be stored in a cool, dry place in an airtight container for up to 6 months.

Use: Miyeok is used mostly in soups, but I also use it in my Seaweed Sashimi (page 87).

GIM (NORI)

Gim is the thinnest of the three seaweeds Koreans use in cooking. You probably know gim as nori, the thin sheets of dried seaweed used to wrap sushi. Koreans use it the same way for wrapping gimbap, Korean-style sushi rolls containing egg, pickled radish, carrots, spinach, and some kind of meat. It's also served as a banchan, brushed with oil, toasted, and seasoned with salt (see page 12), and packages of seasoned gim snacks are available in most Korean groceries. Gim is delicious and goes with any meal that is served with rice.

(Top): Dashima (left), Gim (right).

(Bottom): Two types of Miyeok.

Buying: The best-quality gim come from Wando, a small island on the southwestern tip of Korea near my father's birthplace. You will be able to see on the package if the gim is from Wando. Although I prefer buying untoasted gim and toasting and seasoning it myself, there are many good brands that are already brushed with sesame oil, toasted, and seasoned; some versions use olive oil or perilla seed oil instead of sesame oil, and salt levels can vary. You can also find individual one-meal packages of gim, already cut to bite size, that contain 10 to 12 pieces of seaweed.

Storage: Once you've opened the package, gim will stay fresh and crisp for 2 to 3 days if stored airtight in a cool, dry place.

Use: Gim is a popular and easy banchan.

DRIED SHIITAKE MUSHROOMS

Dried shiitake mushrooms are quite different from fresh shiitakes because the drying process brings out amazingly deep umami flavors. Earthy, rich, and complex, they will add a savory note to any dish.

Buying: Dried shiitakes can be found in any Korean, Japanese, or Chinese market. I recommend buying them vacuum-packed, because these retain their flavor better. The rounder the shape of the mushroom caps, the better the flavor.

Storage: The mushrooms can be stored in a cool, dry place for up to 3 months, wrapped well or sealed in an airtight container.

Use: Dried shiitake mushrooms are mostly used to make Dashi (page 189).

DRIED ANCHOVIES

Koreans usually use anchovies dried, rather than fresh or cured. Cured anchovies have that pungent, fishy taste that most Americans are familiar with, but fresh ones have a more subtle sea flavor. As the fresh fish dry, their flavor, especially in the skin and bones, deepens and intensifies. Anchovies range from about half an inch to 3 inches in size. In Korea, the larger ones are most often used for stock; the bitter-tasting heads and black digestive tracts should be removed before using them. The smaller ones can be left intact, because their heads and digestive tracts aren't big enough to affect their flavor much. Make sure the anchovies you buy are fully dry and the edges are sharp. If they are not, you can dry them out further in the sun for about an hour, a tip that I got from Maangchi, the famous Korean YouTuber and cookbook author.

Buying: In Korea, there are markets that sell dozens of types of dried anchovies sorted according to size, color, origin, and method of catch. The best ones are about 3 inches in length and shiny silver, with straight bodies. In the US, look for frozen dried anchovies, which keep their freshness the longest. Dried anchovies come in a variety of packages, from quite small to very large. The freshest ones will be silver or white with a slight sheen; older dried anchovies will be yellowish. Tong Tong Bay is a reliable brand in the US that sells both small and large dried anchovies.

Storage: Store dried anchovies in the freezer for several months.

Use: Koreans use dried large anchovies in dashi, soups, and stews. They are subtle enough to be eaten, once defrosted, on their own, and they are often served as an anju, or snack, with beer or soju, accompanied by gochujang and mayo. (This is such a basic snack that on Korean TV, characters who are poor or lonely will often be shown forlornly eating dried anchovies and drinking soju.) Small dried anchovies are also used for banchan. They can be sautéed in oil, with either a sweet or a spicy seasoning, as in my recipe for Myulchi Bokkeum (Sweet Crispy Baby Anchovies, page 79).

ANCHOVY SAUCE

Korean anchovy sauce is similar to Thai and Vietnamese fish sauce, but it is much more concentrated in flavor and extremely salty. It is made by curing and fermenting fresh anchovies in salt, then cooking and straining the liquid.

Buying: You can buy bottled anchovy sauce at most Korean markets; if you have any trouble finding it, substitute Thai or Vietnamese fish sauce—but double the amount that the recipe calls for. Unfortunately, I have yet to find a Korean anchovy sauce in the US that does not contain MSG, so I often use Red Boat Fish Sauce, sold at Whole Foods. It is 100-percent natural. Chung Jung One is a good brand of anchovy sauce available in all Korean markets, and Three Crabs Brand is a delicious Vietnamese fish sauce sold in most Asian supermarkets.

Storage: Bottled anchovy sauce will keep for 1 to 2 years in your pantry.

Use: Anchovy sauce is used mostly to season kimchi and banchan. It is also added to soups and stews to give them a rich umami taste.

Dried shitake mushrooms (above); dried anchovies (below).

SALTED SHRIMP

Salted shrimp is heavily salted and fermented small white shrimp. It is a uniquely Korean ingredient, used mainly for kimchi and occasionally to season stews and meats. The brine is also used in cooking or as a dipping sauce. There is a long tradition in Korean cuisine of heavily salting and fermenting various types of seafood, such as squid, fish, and oysters, especially in the South Jeolla region.

Buying: If you live in a big city, you may be able to find a small mom-and-pop market in Koreatown that sells homemade salted shrimp free of additives or preservatives. Otherwise, salted shrimp are available in most Korean supermarkets, in either the kimchi section or the refrigerated fish section. Read the labels, because the mass-produced brands can contain a lot of MSG and preservatives.

Storing: Salted shrimp can be stored in your fridge for up to 3 months. Make sure to keep the jar tightly sealed to prevent the pungent aroma from escaping.

Use: Because salted shrimp are a great catalyst for fermentation, they are most often used to make kimchi. I prefer to puree my salted shrimp before using them in kimchi so they dissolve into the vegetables more easily. Salted shrimp are also served as a dip served alongside pork dishes such as grilled pork belly barbecue and traditional bossam, boiled pork belly.

RICE

Rice is key in providing a counterbalance for the strong, spicy, and pungent flavors of Korean foods. When preparing a Korean meal, it is easy to overlook the importance of rice. Freshly made rice that is prepared with care is something special. Rice that has been sitting in the rice cooker all day long or that has been microwaved doesn't have the aroma or the special texture that make it so delicious. You may be surprised to find how much freshly made rice can elevate a meal.

Rice is served with every Korean meal except when noodles are part of the menu. Koreans usually eat medium- or short-grain rice, which contains more starch than the long-grain rice used by the Chinese, Thai, and Vietnamese.

I recommend Tamaki Gold short-grain white rice for most of the recipes in this book. This is the rice most sushi chefs in the United States use. It has great flavor and is quite moist, and the plump grains hold their shape well. Make sure to rinse it well before cooking, because it contains a lot of loose starch that would make your cooked rice gummy and too sticky. At home, I serve my family Tamaki Haiga. It is a milled short-grain white rice with the rice germ still intact, giving it a more robust texture than regular white rice, where the rice germ has been removed. It is slightly grayish and is more nutritious than other white rices. Haiga rice also contains less starch than regular white rice, so you don't need to rinse it as much before cooking.

The only other type of rice called for in this book is sweet glutinous rice. You can use any brand of sweet glutinous rice available at your market.

Buying: Short- and medium-grain rice can be found in any Korean, Japanese, or Chinese market. It's important to choose rice that was harvested recently, because old rice will have dried out, and its brittle kernels won't cook as well. Look for a sticker that reads "New Crop." This is freshly harvested rice that will have more moisture and be more delicious.

Storage: Rice can be stored in a cool, dry place for 6 months or more.

Use: Most Korean food is strongly seasoned because it will be served with unseasoned rice. One of the reasons why I (and most Asians) season well when cooking is that we learn at a very young age to select the right amount of banchan to eat with every bite of rice. With Korean food, you're always adjusting the ratio of rice and banchan when you eat so that you can find your own sweet spot in terms of seasoning. This constant practice of finding equilibrium helps me with finding that perfect balance when I'm cooking and seasoning my food with salt and soy sauce.

NOODLES

The recipes in this book use five different kinds of Korean noodles: dangmyeon, naengmyeon, somyeon, jajangmyeon, and maemilmyeon. As you've probably realized, *myeon* is Korean for noodles.

Dangmyeon: Dangmyeon noodles are made from sweet potato starch. They are used for Japchae (Sweet Potato Noodles, page 260), a quintessential Korean noodle and vegetable dish. They are like glass noodles or vermicelli—very thin and translucent, with a stretchy, chewy texture. They don't have much flavor on their own, but they are excellent at absorbing flavors from other ingredients. Dangmyeon are sold dried in clear cellophane packages. I like the Wang brand, because these cook faster than other brands, usually 6 minutes or less in boiling unsalted water. Dangmyeon can be stored for up to 6 months in a cool, dry place.

Naengmyeon: These noodles are made mostly from buckwheat flour, with a bit of wheat or potato starch mixed in to give the dough some elasticity. They are generally served cold. In Korea, restaurants specializing in these noodles have large machines that shape the

Salted shrimp (above); short-grain white rice (below, top); short-grain Haiga rice (below, bottom).

(Top to bottom): Dangmyeon;
naengmyeon; maemilmyeon;
somyeon; jajangmyeon.

dough into noodles and express them directly into boiling water to make à-la-minute naengmyeon. I recommend the Chung Soo brand, available in most Korean supermarkets. These come with an instant soup packet, which I strongly suggest you avoid. It has an artificial flavor, and the result will be nothing like that of real Mul Naengmyeon (Buckwheat Noodles in Chilled Broth, page 242).

Maemilmyeon: Maemilmyeon (*soba* in Japanese), buckwheat noodles, are made from a mix of 70 to 80 percent buckwheat flour and 20 to 30 percent wheat flour. The wheat flour gives the pale gray noodles a gently elastic texture and softens the bitter notes of the buckwheat flour. Because of their robust grain flavor, maemilmyeon are served with stronger sauces, usually based on soy sauce. I like the Sukina brand, which can be found in Korean, Japanese, and Chinese markets. The noodles take 6 to 7 minutes to cook. They should be stored in a cool dry place.

Somyeon: Somyeon (*somen* in Japanese) are thin wheat noodles served in delicate broths or alongside strongly flavored dishes. On their own, they don't taste like much more than flour and water. Packaged dried somyeon are sold in Korean, Japanese, and Chinese markets. I like Pulmuone organic somyeon, which are slightly chewier than other brands. Dried somyeon noodles take only about 2 minutes to cook, so be careful not to overcook them. They should be stored in a cool, dry place.

Jajangmyeon: Also made from wheat flour and water, jajangmyeon are much thicker, heartier, and more elastic than somyeon noodles. Jajangmyeon are best paired with an assertive sauce such as jajang (black bean sauce) or gochujang (fermented red chili paste). They are sold both fresh and dried. The fresh noodles take 3 to 4 minutes to cook, the dried 6 to 7 minutes. These are specific to Korean cuisine, so your best bet is a Korean market, or shop online at hmart .com. I prefer fresh jajangmyeon from Pulmuone,

which you can find in most Korean markets. If you can't find the fresh noodles, Wang makes a nice dried version. Store fresh noodles in your refrigerator, dried noodles in the pantry.

TTEOK AND MOCHI (RICE CAKES)

Tteok are white rice cakes, traditionally made by pounding a dough made of steamed rice powder until it becomes soft and chewy, that are used in savory cooking. When you're not in the mood for noodles or regular rice, tteok provides a nice alternative. Its neutral flavor and chewy texture work well in stews and soups, as well as stir-fries. Mochi, Japanese rice cakes that tend to be softer and more pillowy, are typically used in desserts.

Buying: Look for tteok in the frozen section of Korean or Asian supermarkets. Or, if you're lucky, your local Korean market will make fresh tteok every day and sell them at room temperature. Mochi, which are used in Korean, Japanese, Chinese, and Taiwanese cuisine, can be found in any Asian market. They will probably be in the sweets section, packaged in plastic and sold at room temperature.

Storage: Fresh tteok must be cooked the same day or frozen for later use. Frozen tteok can be kept in your freezer for up to 1 month; defrost them overnight in a bowl of cold water in the refrigerator. Mochi can be stored in a cool, dry place until their expiration date.

Use: Tteok are a favorite Korean ingredient in part because they are so affordable. They are the main ingredient in tteokbokki, the spicy rice cakes sold at Korean street food carts for $3 to $4 a serving. They are also added to soups and other traditional dishes in Korean restaurants. I like to use mochi as a garnish for Patbingsu (Shaved Ice with Sweet Red Beans, page 338).

(Top to bottom): Tteokbokki tteok;
tteok guk tteok; mochi (see page 41).

TOFU

Called *dubu* in Korean, tofu is made from the "milk" of ground soybeans. The traditional way to make tofu involves using millstones to extract the milky liquid from soybeans and heating it with a natural coagulant from the sea called nigari, then pressing the curds to achieve the desired texture. These days, you can buy good-quality soymilk and use nigari for a quick 15-minute steam to create a lovely soft and silken tofu; see page 67.

Buying: I highly recommend the Banrai brand of soymilk, which can be found online and at select markets. It is soymilk created specifically for making tofu, not for consumption on its own. The regular soymilk found in your neighborhood supermarket is not ideal for making tofu. Instead, buy unadulterated soymilk at an Asian supermarket. Nigari is usually found in Japanese markets, or online.

I recommend making your own tofu because it is so simple, and you can control its texture. However, if you do buy tofu, I recommend the House brand, which is available in most Asian markets.

Storage: Freshly made tofu can be stored covered in airtight plastic wrap in the refrigerator for up to 3 days. The texture will become denser as it gets older. Store-bought tofu should be immersed in cold water and covered in plastic wrap. It will hold until the expiration date stamped on the container.

Use: There are four different types of tofu used in Korean cuisine:

Firm: This tofu has the densest texture. Traditionally it's used to make a simple panfried tofu banchan that is served with a dipping sauce. But I think soft tofu is better for that dish, because the firm tofu is too tough.

Soft: This type of tofu, which is less dense than firm tofu but still somewhat firm, is mostly used in stews. You can also panfry cubes of soft tofu—if you are gentle.

Silken: Silken tofu is smoother and softer than soft tofu and has a silky texture, hence the name. This is my favorite kind of tofu to use in stews, such as Kimchi Jjigae (Aged-Kimchi Stew, page 198) and Doenjang Jjigae (Fermented Soybean Stew, page 205).

Extra soft: This type of tofu, called *sundubu* in Korean, is used exclusively for sundubu jjigae, a traditional tofu stew (see Spicy Soft Tofu Stew, page 202). It is meant to break up very easily, so don't worry when it falls apart as you are cooking.

**Tofu (left to right)—
firm; soft; silken; extra soft.**

Scallions (top to bottom)—1-inch
batons; hairy: thinly sliced.

Its different textures and neutral flavor make tofu a versatile ingredient. I love adding it to strong-flavored dishes, as well as serving it on the side. Because it has little flavor of its own, it is receptive to different sauces and many different flavor profiles. And because it is made from soybeans, which are the main ingredient in ganjang and doenjang, it pairs wonderfully with these.

SCALLIONS

I use scallions, also known as green onions, quite often in my recipes. I love their fresh, oniony flavor, and the way they give earthy or spicy dishes a lightness that balances the stronger flavors and textures.

Buying: You can find scallions in any supermarket. They tend to be more flavorful during the warmer months. The scallions in Korea and Japan are much thicker than those in the US. I prefer the flavor of these thicker scallions, so look for *dae-pa* if you're at a Korean market, or *Tokyo-negi* at a Japanese market. Scallions should be washed well before using, because dirt can be found between the layers. If they are not organic, I suggest adding 2 tablespoons baking soda to a large bowl of water and soaking the scallions for 15 to 20 minutes to rid them of most of the pesticides; make sure you rinse them well afterward to get rid of the alkaline flavor. A soaking in alkaline water is actually a good practice for any fresh fruits and vegetables that are not organic.

Storage: After washing them, you can store scallions in your refrigerator wrapped in a dry paper towel and then a plastic bag for up to 3 days.

Use: Many of the recipes in this book call for thinly sliced scallion rounds. I prep them using a technique I learned at Masa. First slice the scallions (both green and white parts) as thin as possible, using the "long slicing" method: This means that you use your knife to slice back and forth across the vegetable rather than chopping up and down. It's important that your knife be sharp, so it can do all the work for you. Avoid putting pressure on the scallions while slicing, which would cause them to become slimy. Transfer the sliced scallions to a colander set inside a bowl in your sink and run cold water over them for 5 minutes to wash away as much slime as possible. Drain the scallions thoroughly, then put them on a clean, dry kitchen towel, wrap them in the towel, and squeeze them as dry as possible. Spread the semi-dried scallions on a dry paper towel and allow them to air-dry for 10 minutes, then store in the refrigerator in a covered container lined with a paper towel. When you are ready to use them, the scallions will be fluffy and light. I use this garnish so often it reminds me of an old-school Italian chef and his chopped parsley. These scallion rounds can be used everywhere: in stews, marinades, and soups.

PERILLA LEAVES

Perilla leaves are spade-shaped bright-green leaves that have a fresh, grassy flavor with notes of mint, basil, and anise. They are absolutely delicious and boost the Korean flavor of any dish. However, their taste can be quite aggressive, so use them judiciously. Perilla leaves can lighten hearty dishes and add complexity to simpler, lighter flavor profiles. Although the leaves resemble the Japanese shiso leaf, they taste much stronger, and shiso leaves do not make a good substitute.

Buying: You can find fresh perilla leaves at Korean markets and, occasionally, in Chinese supermarkets. They are sometimes mislabeled as sesame leaves there.

Make sure you wash perilla leaves very well before using them. I would absolutely use the baking soda method described in the section on scallions above, since perilla leaves are sprayed with lots of pesticides because they are a favorite snack for insects.

Storage: Perilla leaves can be stored in a plastic bag in the fridge for up to 3 days.

Use: Perilla leaves are used frequently as a finishing herb, to give hearty stews an aromatic herbal touch. They are also used as a wrap, along with lettuce, in traditional Korean barbecue.

KOREAN PEARS

Korean (or Asian) pears differ from Western pears in texture, flavor, and appearance. Similar in shape to apples, they are large and round and have pale yellow-brown skin with white flesh. They are sweeter than Western pears but ever so slightly acidic. They are extremely juicy, with a texture reminiscent of watermelon. Korean pears are my favorite fruit, and I like to use them as much as I can in Korean cooking when some sweetness is needed, as in Yangnyeom Galbi (Soy-Marinated BBQ Beef Short Ribs, page 133), Galbi Jjim (Braised Beef Short Ribs, page 135), Bulgogi Sliders (page 142), and Ganjang Gejang (Soy-Marinated Raw Blue Crabs, page 84). In Korea, the best pears come from the southwestern city of Naju and can grow as big as a cantaloupe in size. The best Korean pears in the US come from California.

Buying: You can find Korean or Asian pears in Asian markets and some supermarkets in the fall and winter. They can be difficult to track down in the warmer months, but it is getting somewhat easier to locate them out of season because they are now grown in Chile and other parts of South America and exported to the US.

Storage: Korean pears can be stored in the fridge for up to 2 weeks.

Use: Korean pears work well in marinades for meats because their high sugar content adds sweetness and

their acidity breaks down the fibers, working as a meat tenderizer. When processed in a food processor, they become a loose puree that is easy to add to sauces. If you can't find Korean pears for a puree, kiwis, which also act as a natural sweetener and meat tenderizer, are a good substitute; strain out the seeds before using the puree.

MU (KOREAN RADISH) AND DAIKON (JAPANESE RADISH)

These two radishes are very similar and can be used interchangeably in most of my recipes. Mu, or Korean radish, is thick, short, and stout, like a football; daikon, or Japanese radish, is longer and thinner. Mu resembles red radishes in flavor and texture, and the flesh is slightly more watery and spicy than that of daikon, which is similar to a turnip. I love making soup with these radishes because they become wonderfully soft when fully cooked, and their sweet but earthy flavor enhances the broth.

Buying: Daikon is widely available in American markets, but you will need to visit a Korean market to find Korean radishes. The best season for Korean radishes is fall and winter, though they may be found year-round. During the warmer months, buy the heaviest, most dense radishes you can find. Lighter radishes will have air pockets at their core, making them less crunchy.

Storage: Korean radishes and daikon can be stored in your fridge for up to 1 week.

Use: It is very difficult to differentiate between these two radishes when they are cooked, so they can be used interchangeably in cooked preparations. For kimchi, however, Korean radishes maintain a crisper, crunchier, fresher texture through the fermentation process, so I recommend using them.

(Clockwise from top left): Korean pear; Korean mu radish; perilla leaves; daechu.

47

DAECHU (JUJUBES)

Called jujubes in the US, these small stone fruits are sometimes referred to as Chinese or red dates. Koreans use jujubes that are partially dehydrated and have the texture of Fig Newton cookie filling. They are about the size of a chestnut, though a little more oval in shape, and bright or dark red. Jujubes add subtle sweetness to medicinal or restorative dishes such as *samgyetang*, a traditional herb-infused chicken soup.

Buying: Partially dried jujubes are available in Korean and Chinese markets and most Asian supermarkets. They are found in either the fresh or dried vegetable section.

Storage: Jujubes keep for several weeks in a cool, dry place or for a few months in the freezer.

Use: In Korea, jujubes are most commonly used to brew tea. They make a nice addition to a cheese plate or to sweet and savory dishes such as Galbi Jjim (Braised Beef Short Ribs, page 135). They can also be eaten raw, skin and all, as a snack or as a sweet, jammy dessert.

RICE VINEGAR

Made from fermented rice, this vinegar is used widely in Korean, Japanese, and Chinese cooking. It has a mellow, slightly sweeter flavor and lower acidity than most other vinegars. I believe that rice vinegar works better in Asian cooking than wine-based vinegars because of its lower acidity.

Buying: Rice vinegar is found in any Asian market as well as in the Asian food aisle of most grocery stores in the US. My favorite is the Japanese brand Mizkan. Avoid very cheap rice vinegars; they tend to have an artificial sourness rather than a natural fermented-rice one.

Storage: Rice vinegar can be kept in a cool, dry place for up to 6 months.

Use: Rice vinegar is used in sauces and dressings and as a seasoning in many dishes.

SAKE

Because it is harder to find Korean rice wine in the US, I use sake, Japanese rice wine, in my recipes. Sake pairs very well with Japanese and most other Asian cuisines. Today you will find high-quality sakes in many NYC restaurants that offer fine wines. It has a delicate rice flavor that may be very dry or floral, depending on the producer, and an alcohol content of 17 to 20% ABV. For cooking, I like a very dry sake that neutralizes as soon as the alcohol burns off, leaving just a sweet, mellow taste of rice behind. Any sake will taste a lot sweeter after the alcohol has burned off, so using a dry sake for cooking is important, or the wine will add too much sweetness to your finished dish.

Buying: Unless you're cooking a dish where sake is the base flavor, any affordable bottle of dry sake will do. I usually use Sho Chiku Bai, which is produced in Berkeley, California. Depending on state laws, it can be found in supermarkets or the local liquor store.

Storage: Once the bottle is opened, sake will be good for a few weeks in the fridge for cooking, but only for a few days for drinking. If you've burned off the alcohol in your sake (a step called for in several of the recipes in this book), it should be used within 3 days.

Use: Sake is used in the kitchen for sauces and marinades. Once you've finished cooking, enjoy sipping some chilled sake alongside the finished dish.

MIRIN

Mirin (*mat-sool* in Korean) is a Japanese sweet rice wine often used in Japanese and Korean cooking to enhance sweetness and flavor. There are several types of mirin, which have different concentrations of alcohol and MSG contents. The cheapest mirins are low in alcohol (less than 1.5% ABV, to avoid the liquor tax) and are full of MSG. A natural and true mirin, called *hon-mirin* in Japanese, is about 14% ABV and contains no MSG. These mirins tend to be harder to find. Eden Organic makes a widely available mirin that is naturally brewed from rice and contains no added MSG or sugar; it is nonalcoholic.

Buying: I use Ohsawa Organic Genuine Mirin, which can be found online. It has zero MSG but does contain alcohol, which may need to be burned off before using (the individual recipes specify this when necessary). If you can't get your hands on real mirin, look for Eden Organic Mirin at Whole Foods and other supermarkets.

Storage: Once a bottle of mirin has been opened, it must be stored in the refrigerator with the lid tightly sealed. It'll be good for up to 4 weeks, but the older it gets, the duller the flavor will be.

Use: Mirin is used mostly in sauces and marinades.

SESAME OIL

The strong, nutty scent of toasted sesame oil is distinct and arresting; as with truffle oil, once you've smelled it, you will never mistake it for anything else. For more subtle dishes, the oil should be used sparingly, as its fragrance can overpower delicate aromas or flavors. In dishes made with Korean jangs, its boldness makes it the perfect oil to stand up to and balance out the deep, intense flavors. Sesame oil, or, to be more specific, toasted white sesame oil, is made by slowly toasting white sesame seeds and then pressing the oil out of them. It takes time, because the seeds must be toasted in small batches to ensure even browning. The quality of a sesame oil is determined by the quality of the sesame seeds, how well the seeds were toasted, and how recently the oil was pressed. Today only a few companies still take the time to make sesame oil the traditional way. I've been told that many companies press the oil out of raw seeds and then add artificial smoke flavor. Both types of oil will smell nutty and delicious, but only authentic toasted sesame oil retains the nutty taste of the toasted seeds; sesame oil made with artificial smoke has a slightly bitter aftertaste and none of the inherent nuttiness that makes the oil so special.

Buying: Freshly pressed sesame oil is found in food markets all over Korea, where small vendors make it in small batches. These oils usually cost $10 to $20 per 375-ml bottle. Here in the US, Nong Hyup brand, found in some Korean markets, retails for over $40 a bottle. Some larger Korean supermarkets also sell freshly pressed sesame oil. It's one of those things in life that I feel is totally worth the price. If you don't have access to high-quality sesame oil, though, Sempio and Kadoya make acceptable mass-produced versions.

Storage: Once opened, a bottle of traditionally made sesame oil can be stored in the refrigerator for up to 1 month. Mass-produced sesame oil will keep for up to 3 months in the fridge. The cold temperature both preserves the flavor and prevents the oil from becoming rancid. After removing the bottle from the fridge, warm it for a couple of minutes with your hands and then shake well before using.

Use: Sesame oil is used to finish many different Korean dishes, as well as in dressings.

TOASTED SESAME SEEDS

Sesame seeds, which come from the flowering sesame plant, have a slightly nutty flavor and a pleasantly chewy texture. In Korea, the toasted seeds are mostly used to make oil but are also added to various dishes for their nutty aroma and flavor.

Buying: Toasted white sesame seeds are sold in all Asian markets in packages that range in size from 10-ounce jars to 5-pound bags. I recommend buying 1-pound vacuum-packed bags of seeds, which will remain fresh longer.

Storage: After opening the package of seeds, wrap it tightly in plastic wrap and freeze for up to 6 months. Because they are dry, the seeds will not clump when frozen and so can be used directly from the freezer.

Use: Toasted white sesame seeds are used to garnish many dishes, adding both flavor and texture. To make the seeds even more aromatic, toast them again right before you use them: Heat them in a small skillet over a low flame, constantly shaking the pan so they don't burn, for about 5 minutes; this will bring out the oils in the seeds and make them much more delicious.

SALT

I recommend that everyone cook with mountain salt from the Himalayas or Andes. They are the purest, naturally occurring salts that you can buy and they are the salts that I use in my kitchen at home. Mountain salts can be found in textures ranging from a fine powder to coarse grains. I prefer to cook with the medium-coarse salts.

Toasted sesame seeds.

Doenjang fermenting inside a
jangdok covered with lotus leaves
to prevent overdrying.

FUNDAMENTAL SAUCES AND CONDIMENTS

The sauces and condiments in this chapter are building blocks. I consider them pantry items because they keep for a long time in the refrigerator. They are very versatile and can be used in many different dishes beyond the recipes in this book. For instance, Pajeon Sauce (page 59) can be used as a dumpling sauce or as a dipping sauce for tofu, or to dress vegetables. You could add some to your Chinese takeout if it's a little bland. Or, instead of your usual tomato and meat sauce for your baked ziti, try the BKO (Bacon Kimchi Onion) Sauce (page 60). It's fantastic! Once you have these in your own kitchen, you will find many different applications for them, so be creative and have fun cooking with them.

Jangdoks in the backyard of a house in Jeju, Korea, filled with doenjang, gochujang, and ganjang.

(1) Scallion Dressing, page 59;
(2) Ssamjang, page 57; (3) Chojang,
page 58; (4) Pajeon Sauce, page 59;
(5) BKO Sauce, page 60;
(6) Spicy Mayo, page 61.

SSAMJANG
쌈장

Makes 1 cup

5 tablespoons doenjang (Korean fermented
    soybean paste)

3½ tablespoons gochujang (Korean red chili
    paste)

4 garlic cloves, minced

1 tablespoon minced onion

2 tablespoons toasted sesame oil

1 tablespoon toasted sesame seeds

1½ tablespoons sugar

2 tablespoons toasted and coarsely chopped
    walnuts

3 scallions, thinly sliced, rinsed, and dried as
    directed on page 45

Ssamjang is a Korean condiment used mostly in recipes that involve wrapping meat in lettuce or cabbage leaves. *Ssam* means to wrap, and *jang* is the broad term for all Korean fermented pastes or sauces, such as doenjang (fermented soybean paste), gochujang (red chili paste), and ganjang (soy sauce). A traditional ssamjang recipe includes both doenjang and gochujang.

In most ssamjangs, the flavors of the jangs tend to be overpowering. In my recipe, I balance the assertive, earthy jangs with a bit of brightness. Doenjang, by its nature, is aggressively salty and not particularly sweet, but here, the addition of onions, garlic, and sugar balances out the saltiness. Nuts and seeds give the ssamjang a crunchy texture and a nutty flavor. The flavor of a well-rounded and balanced ssamjang is strong but not overpowering. It will mask any inherent bitterness in your vegetables and enhance their natural sweetness. Ssamjang is my favorite dip for raw vegetables, and I always have a jar in my fridge at home.

Combine all the ingredients in a bowl and mix well. Use immediately, or store for up to 3 months in a tightly sealed container in the refrigerator.

CHOJANG
초장

Makes 2 cups

¼ cup mirin

1 cup gochujang (Korean red chili paste)

½ cup toasted sesame oil

2 tablespoons sugar

½ cup rice vinegar

½ teaspoon minced ginger

5 garlic cloves, minced

Chojang is tangy, salty, spicy, and sweet all at the same time, with a very long finish thanks to the gochujang, its main ingredient. It is typically served as a condiment or dipping sauce, along with soy sauce, when eating raw fish (hwe). Koreans prefer their hwe to be as fresh as possible, resulting in a chewy texture that is unlike that of Japanese sashimi, where the fish is rested so the texture becomes soft. For that reason, chojang is usually the condiment of choice for Korean hwe; the flavors last longer in your mouth than soy sauce, lingering for the entire time that you are chewing the fish.

Combine all of the ingredients in a bowl and whisk until well blended and emulsified. Use immediately, or store for up to 1 month in a tightly sealed container in the refrigerator.

SCALLION DRESSING

Makes about ½ cup

¼ cup soy sauce

1 tablespoon water

1 teaspoon sugar

1 tablespoon gochugaru (Korean red chili flakes)

1 tablespoon toasted sesame oil

2 tablespoons rice vinegar

1 tablespoon mirin

1 teaspoon toasted sesame seeds

This versatile dressing has a classic Korean flavor profile. It is used to dress the scallions for Danji's Bossam (Braised Pork Belly, page 145) and my Beef Brisket Bulgogi Sliders (page 142). It pairs especially well with other aromatics too, such as onions and garlic chives. It will add a Korean accent to a simple green salad, or you can substitute it for the sauce in the Bibimbap (Rice with Beef and Vegetables, page 217).

Combine all the ingredients in a bowl and mix well. Use immediately, or store for up to 2 weeks in a tightly sealed container in the refrigerator. Stir the sauce well before using, because the sesame oil will separate and rise to the top as it sits.

PAJEON SAUCE

Makes 1 cup

2 tablespoons water

2 tablespoons rice vinegar

6 tablespoons soy sauce

1 tablespoon gochugaru (Korean red chili flakes)

2 garlic cloves, minced

¼ teaspoon minced ginger

1 teaspoon toasted sesame oil

This bright, vinegary sauce works wonderfully with pan-fried or deep-fried battered foods, including dumplings. The acid in the sauce cuts through the richness of these foods while adding more flavor. You can serve it as a dipping sauce or drizzle it over the dish. I prefer to offer it as a dipping sauce in individual small bowls on the side because that allows diners to "double dip," giving them control of the seasoning of their food.

Combine all the ingredients in a bowl and mix well. Use immediately, or store for up to 2 weeks in a tightly sealed container in the refrigerator. Shake or stir well before using.

BKO (BACON KIMCHI ONION) SAUCE

Makes 3 cups

1 pound bacon, cut into ¼-inch dice
1 large onion, cut into ¼-inch dice
1 pound kimchi, cut into ¼-inch dice

BKO is a condiment that I created at Danji. It has only three ingredients but delivers an exciting kick of flavor: the salty, smoky taste of the bacon; the sweetness of the onion; and the sour, spicy kimchi. It's a key ingredient in several of my recipes, including Spicy Pork and Gochujang Bolognese Noodles (page 262) and Golbaengi Muchim (Spicy Whelk Salad with Soba Noodles, page 167). It can also be stirred into fried rice or used as a topping on pizza, or even on nachos with melted cheese. A grilled cheese sandwich stuffed with BKO is awesome! I serve it at Danji as a topping on French fries for a kimchi-inspired poutine. We don't eat bacon in Korea, so obviously BKO is not traditionally Korean, but it is a great example of the philosophy behind Danji, where I use familiar American ingredients to enhance traditional Korean flavors.

Put the bacon in a medium skillet set over medium heat and cook, stirring often, for 10 minutes, or until the fat has rendered and the bacon is just beginning to brown. Add the onions and cook for about 5 minutes, stirring, until they become tender and translucent. Add the kimchi, increase the heat to high, and cook for about 10 minutes, stirring often and being careful not to let the mixture stick to the bottom of the pan and scorch, until the liquid has evaporated and the mixture is dry. The vegetables should be soft and the consistency should be that of a thick meat ragu or chili.

Use immediately, or let cool and store for up to 1 week in a tightly sealed container in the refrigerator.

SPICY MAYO

Makes 1½ cups

1 cup mayonnaise
3 tablespoons Sriracha
1 tablespoon soy sauce

Versions of spicy mayo are found in a variety of cuisines and dishes these days. I've seen it in tacos, bahn mi (the Vietnamese sandwich), and burgers, as well as on corn on the cob. The Japanese love putting it on almost everything on a late-night menu! I slather it on my Beef Brisket Bulgogi Sliders (page 142), and at home I put it anywhere I'd use regular mayo but want to add a slight spicy kick, such as with fried calamari or in egg salad.

Put the mayonnaise, Sriracha, and soy sauce in a small bowl and whisk to blend. Stored in a covered container or a plastic squeeze bottle in the refrigerator, this will keep for up to 4 weeks.

BANCHAN

No Korean meal is complete without banchan, the numerous small dishes that are served with rice on every table. Banchan are an integral part of Korean cuisine, and I think it is one of the reasons Korean food is so popular all over the world.

Everyone has their favorite banchan. It might be savory and sweet Kong Jaban (Stewed Sweet Black Beans, page 73) that glisten with a syrupy sheen. Or perhaps steaming-hot soft, slippery Gyeran Jjim (Steamed Egg Custard with Salted Shrimp, page 89). Or it might be crunchy Kong Namul (Spicy Bean Sprouts, page 126), which bring great texture to a meal. As everyone is sharing the banchan, you can pick and choose which dishes to eat and personalize your meal according to your own preferences. There are no real rules when it comes to banchan. You just eat what you want, when you want, mixing and matching as you go.

The category of banchan is broad and diverse. In a restaurant setting, banchan are the small complimentary side dishes served alongside the entrée. At home, pretty much everything other than the rice is considered banchan. Because every meal typically includes a nice spread of banchan, it is normal for a Korean household to keep large quantities of certain banchan in the fridge to put out with every meal. These banchan are called *mit banchan*, or lower banchan. They are generally fermented or preserved dishes that will keep for a long time. As such, they reflect the culture of preserving foods for consumption throughout the winter, when it was hard to obtain fresh food. Having a bunch of mit banchan in the fridge is a great way to ensure you can always put together a quick meal on a busy weeknight.

Mit banchan include dishes such as Sigeumchi Namul (Spinach with Sesame, page 127), Mu Mallengi Muchim (Spicy Dehydrated Korean Radishes, page 115), various types of kimchi (pages 96 to 109), and Myulchi Bokkeum (Sweet Crispy Baby Anchovies, page 79). Larger meat or fish dishes and stews such as Galbi Jjim (Braised Beef Short Ribs, page 135), Eun-dae-gu Jorim (Soy-Poached Black Cod with Daikon, page 177), and Doenjang Jjigae (Fermented Soybean Stew, page 205) are prepared on a daily basis to serve as the main banchan of the meal.

Banchan are a key element of the communal aspect of Korean culture. Other than everyone's individual bowls of rice and soup, everything on the dining table is shared. Eating from the same bowl of stew, the same plates of banchan, sharing the tastes and flavors of the meal, gives us a sense of togetherness and builds a bond. Eating together in this manner will bring you a little bit closer to the friendly, familiar culture of Korea.

The banchan recipes in this chapter are my favorites to make at home, but we also serve them time and time again at Danji and Hanjan. While many Korean banchan have strong marinades and sauces that can easily overpower the main ingredients, these recipes allow the ingredients to shine. While a few of these recipes require advance planning, many are quick and easy to make, so I encourage you to try as many as you can and find out which are your favorites.

You will notice that in most of the banchan, kimchi, and muchim (quick-pickled) recipes, I do not indicate the number of servings. Traditionally, all banchan are made in large batches and enjoyed for several days. For a family of 4, a quart of any banchan should last for a few days. If you are cooking for only 1 or 2 people, I suggest you reduce the banchan or muchim recipes by half so that you can be sure that these will keep fresh in the fridge.

One important thing to keep in mind is that most of the vegetables used for banchan have specific seasons when they are at their peak. For instance, in Korea, cabbage kimchi was traditionally made only once a year, in the winter, when cabbage and radish were at their sweetest and the cold weather ensured prime conditions for fermentation. Villagers would come together to make enough kimchi for everyone to last at least until the following summer. This communal kimchi-making event was referred to as *gimjang*, and after the kimchi was divided up, it was stored away, usually buried underground so the temperature was kept constant and above freezing, to be eaten little by little each day. When the supply of kimchi ran out (generally by the summer), muchim, simple quickly pickled vegetables, were made with summer crops such as cucumbers, lettuce, scallions, and chives.

These days in the US, we are able to get cucumbers from Mexico in winter and Napa cabbage from California in summer. But this well-traveled produce does not taste as good as seasonal local vegetables, so I suggest you manage your expectations if you decide to ferment or cook with them. These out-of-season vegetables tend to be full of preservatives because of their long travel time. You should definitely wash them well before using. My recommendation is to shop at your local farmers' market and ask which vegetables are best at the moment. Buy those, and then use one of my recipes/techniques to make your own seasonal banchan. It's what I do.

HOMEMADE TOFU WITH PERILLA SOY SAUCE
두부 (Dubu)

Serves 4

Tofu
4 cups unadulterated soymilk
24 to 32 grams (0.8 to 1.1 ounce) liquid nigari
    (see headnote)

Perilla Soy Sauce
½ cup sake
½ cup soy sauce
1 tablespoon rice vinegar
½ teaspoon minced garlic
4 perilla leaves, thinly sliced

1 tablespoon toasted sesame seeds, for garnish
Scallions, thinly sliced, rinsed, and dried as
    directed on page 45, for garnish (optional)

Traditionally making Korean tofu was a laborious process involving the use of millstones to grind soybeans to extract the soy "milk." Then the soymilk was steamed with a natural coagulant and pressed to achieve the desired texture. These days you can buy unadulterated soymilk in Asian supermarkets, which means making your own tofu is much easier than you might think. Homemade tofu has a wonderful fresh flavor and soft texture that you don't get with tofu that has been sealed in a package for weeks, so I highly recommend that you try this recipe. All you need is soymilk and nigari (and a digital scale—it's difficult to measure the small amount of nigari called for any other way).

The better the soymilk, the better the tofu. I use Banrai soymilk, which is specifically intended for tofu-making. Generally, any nigari you find in a Japanese supermarket will work; you can also order it online from Amazon and other sources. You only need a small bottle (1 ounce) for this recipe. You can adjust the amount of nigari up or down, depending on how firm you like your tofu. I wouldn't use less than 18 grams (0.6 ounce) of nigari, or the tofu will take much longer to set or not set at all.

Because tofu has such a mild flavor, I like to accentuate it with a strong sauce. The one I usually make includes perilla leaves, one of my favorite herbs. (Perilla is a summer crop, so the leaves are at their most flavorful during the warmer months.) If you can't find perilla, you can substitute a generous amount of thinly sliced scallions that have been rinsed in cold water and thoroughly dried (see Scallions, page 45). The sauce is salty from the soy sauce

(recipe continues)

but not overpoweringly so, because there is an equal amount of sake that gives it some sweetness and bright acidity, all elevated by the pungent, earthy aroma of the perilla.

The recipe below produces a silky, creamy tofu that is completely different from packaged silken tofu, no matter the brand. We're talking soft, smooth, and so fluffy and light that it just slips down your throat, with the fresh, vivid sweetness that comes from good soymilk. Note that this tofu will stay pillowy and soft only for the first day it is made. As you keep it in the fridge, the tofu "sets" and becomes denser. It is perfectly good to eat for up to 3 days after it's made, but make sure it is in a tightly sealed container, because tofu will pick up other aromas very easily.

Put the soymilk in a nonreactive 9-by-5-inch loaf pan. Add 24 grams of nigari for a softer texture, or up to 32 grams of nigari for a firmer texture, and mix gently with a spoon to blend.

Cover the loaf pan with plastic wrap. Place a small rack in the bottom of a stockpot or other pot large enough to hold the loaf pan, so the pan will not touch the bottom of the pot. Put the loaf pan on the rack and add enough water to the pot to come up to the level of the soymilk, then remove the loaf pan from the pot. Cover the pot with a lid or aluminum foil and set it over medium heat. Bring the water to a very gentle boil. Place the loaf pan with the soymilk on the rack and re-cover the pot. Adjust the heat as necessary to maintain a gentle boil and boil for 10 minutes. You can check by looking out for a light but steady stream of steam escaping from the pot. Turn off the heat and let the tofu rest for 15 minutes. It will be slightly jiggly but set, resembling soft gelatin.

Refrigerate the tofu until chilled. (It will keep in the fridge for up to 3 days, but it is best served the day it's made.)

To make the perilla soy sauce, put the sake in a medium saucepan set over high heat and bring to a boil. Carefully light the sake with a lighter or a long match, then let the flames die out,

1 to 2 minutes. (If you would rather not light the sake, let it boil for 3 minutes to burn off the alcohol.) It is important to remove the alcohol from the sake, or the flavor will be very different. Remove from the heat and let cool to room temperature.

Transfer the sake to a medium bowl and add the soy sauce and vinegar. Whisk to blend. Use a spoon to stir in the garlic and perilla leaves.

To serve, scoop the tofu into four individual bowls, dividing it evenly. Sprinkle a pinch of the toasted sesame seeds on top of each serving. Scatter some scallions over the top if you like. Pour the sauce over the tofu, or serve it on the side in individual dipping bowls and let your guests use spoons to dip the tofu into the sauce.

FRIED TOFU WITH PAJEON SAUCE

Serves 2

About 4 cups canola oil for deep-frying
1 red Korean chili pepper or other long hot
    chili

Crispy Tempura Flakes (optional; alternatively,
    you can buy premade flakes)
½ cup cold water
1 teaspoon lightly beaten egg yolk
1 tablespoon tempura flour

1 cup potato starch
⅓ pound silken tofu, store-bought or
    homemade (page 67)
About 2 tablespoons Pajeon Sauce (page 59)
Toasted sesame oil for drizzling
½ bunch scallions, thinly sliced, rinsed, and
    dried as directed on page 45

This dish, which was inspired by fried mozzarella sticks, is a bestseller at Danji. Even people who think they don't like tofu love it: delectable rectangles of tofu coated in potato starch and fried until the outsides are delicately crunchy. A little bit of magic happens in the layer just below the crust, where the potato starch mixes with water released from the tofu, resulting in a gooey mochi-like texture. The tofu itself becomes extremely soft and the whole thing resembles a mozzarella stick in texture. You can use store-bought silken or soft tofu here if you don't have time to make your own.

Since you have the fryer going, you can also make little crunchy tempura flakes to garnish the dish. I use them along with sliced scallions to add a crunchy texture and bright flavor. If you don't want to make them, you can buy premade tempura flakes in most Asian supermarkets.

Spoon the dressing over the hot fried tofu, add the garnishes, and you have a dish that hits all of your taste buds. Flavorful and comforting, this will change the way you think about tofu. Timing is crucial here, as the fried tofu will become soggy in a matter of minutes. At Danji, we try to have this dish on the diner's table less than 3 minutes after it comes out of the fryer. Instead of a traditional banchan that can be left on the table for some time, this works more as an appetizer to serve once the other banchan have been laid out.

Pour the oil into a deep-fat fryer and heat to 360°F. Or pour 3 inches of oil into a large pot and heat to 360°F over medium-high heat.

Meanwhile, slice the chili pepper crosswise as thin as possible (use a mandoline if you have one). Set aside for garnish.

(recipe continues)

To make the optional tempura flakes, put the water and egg yolk in a medium bowl and whisk to blend. Add the tempura flour and whisk together. Transfer the batter to a measuring cup with a spout or a small pitcher.

Hold the measuring cup 1 to 1½ feet above the hot oil and slowly and carefully drizzle the batter into the oil. Fry for 30 seconds, or until small irregular tempura flakes form. Use a slotted spoon to transfer them to a plate lined with paper towels to drain and cool.

Set a rack on a sheet pan to drain the tofu after frying. Put the potato starch in a medium bowl. Place the tofu on a cutting board and cut it into 6 equal rectangles, approximately 2 by 1 by 1 inch. Use your fingers to gently roll 3 of the rectangles in the potato starch, coating each piece completely. Leave the tofu in the potato starch for about 30 seconds so it can absorb it, then shake off the excess starch from each piece, add them to the hot oil, and fry for 1½ to 2 minutes; they will start floating to the top when they are done and will be a light golden color. Transfer them to the prepared rack and let drain for 15 seconds.

Plate the first batch by arranging the 3 pieces of tofu on a serving plate. Spoon about a teaspoon of the Pajeon Sauce over each tofu rectangle. Drizzle a few drops of sesame oil over each as well and sprinkle about 2 tablespoons of the fried tempura bits over the entire dish, followed by half the scallions. Garnish each piece of tofu with a slice of red pepper. Serve immediately.

Repeat the procedure with the second batch of tofu and serve hot.

STEWED SWEET BLACK BEANS
콩자반 (Kong Jaban)

Makes 3 cups

1¼ cups dried black beans, rinsed and picked over

2 quarts Dashi (page 189) or water, plus more if needed

1 cup soy sauce

¾ cup sugar

2 tablespoons toasted sesame oil

1 tablespoon toasted sesame seeds

This is a sweet and savory banchan that I consider a *bap-dodok*, or "rice-robber," meaning it is so delicious that your rice will be gone in no time. It was a favorite of mine as a child, because it is both irresistibly sweet and fun to chew. The beans are cooked with soy sauce and dashi (or water) until they are quite soft, then sweetened with sugar. Canned beans will not work in this dish, because they will overcook and turn to mush. The sesame oil and sesame seeds add a nuttiness that ties the inherent flavor of the beans to the other ingredients. Even when I don't have much of an appetite, this banchan always tempts me into finishing a large bowl of hot rice.

Soak the beans in enough water to cover them by 3 inches in a covered container in the refrigerator for 8 to 12 hours.

Drain the beans, put them in a pot, and add the dashi or water and soy sauce. Set over medium-high heat and bring the liquid to a simmer. Adjust the heat to maintain a gentle simmer and cook for 1 hour, stirring the beans on a regular basis. The level of liquid will reduce as the beans cook; once it gets to the point where it does not completely cover the beans, you will need to stir more often to ensure that the beans cook evenly. After an hour, the beans should be tender but still retain a little bite. If they are still hard, add more dashi or water and cook for 15 to 20 minutes longer, until the beans are tender with a little bite.

Add the sugar, sesame oil, and sesame seeds to the pot and mix well. (It's important to wait to add the sugar until the beans are tender, as adding it in the beginning will cause the beans to harden when refrigerated.) Let the beans cool slightly, then transfer to an airtight container and refrigerate until chilled. (The beans will keep for up to 2 weeks in the refrigerator.)

Serve the beans cold with hot rice.

(photo on next page)

Stewed Sweet Black Beans, page 73 (top); Soy-Marinated Perilla Leaves (bottom)

SOY-MARINATED PERILLA LEAVES
깻잎장아찌 (Kkaennip Jangachi)

Serves 4

40 perilla leaves

Marinade
1 red Korean chili pepper or other long hot chili, thinly sliced
2 tablespoons soy sauce
2 tablespoons water
2 scallions, thinly sliced
1½ teaspoons minced garlic
1½ tablespoons gochugaru (Korean red chili flakes)
1 teaspoon Korean anchovy sauce or 2 teaspoons fish sauce
2 teaspoons sugar
1 tablespoon toasted sesame seeds
1 tablespoon toasted sesame oil

This banchan has a strong, bold flavor from the perilla leaf and the marinade. The fragrant green perilla leaves turn dark brown because of the black soy sauce, and their flavor is as aggressive as they look. But the dish is absolutely delicious, highlighting the herb's pungent aroma and earthy taste.

Perilla leaves are at their peak in the summer. Perilla is very easy to grow, and many Koreans grow it at home if they have a backyard or a sunny terrace. It's wonderful to have a fresh supply on hand whenever you want to enjoy it. This banchan pairs perfectly with fatty meat dishes, but if you like it as much as I do, all you really need is a bowl of hot rice.

Wash the perilla leaves in cold water. If they are store-bought, be sure to wash them several times, or use a baking-soda soak (see page 45). Due to its aromatic fragrance, perilla attracts many insects and so is heavily sprayed with pesticides. Once the leaves are thoroughly washed, pat them dry with paper towels.

Prepare a stovetop steamer and line a sheet pan with paper towels. Working in batches, steam the perilla leaves in a single layer for 2 minutes, then transfer to the prepared sheet pan to cool.

To make the marinade, combine all the ingredients in a medium bowl and mix to blend. Pour the marinade into a lidded container large enough so that the marinade only fills it halfway. Add the leaves to the marinade one by one, so that each leaf comes into full contact with the liquid. Cover and refrigerate for 18 to 24 hours before serving. The marinated perilla leaves can be kept in the fridge for up to 2 weeks.

(Counterclockwise from top right): Spicy Bean Sprouts, page 126; Sweet Crispy Baby Anchovies, page 79; Simmered Fish Cakes, page 77; Steamed Rice, page 212

SIMMERED FISH CAKES
어묵 볶음 (Eomuk Bokkeum)

Serves 4

½ pound frozen fish cakes (I prefer the flat rectangular cakes), cut into bite-sized pieces

2 tablespoons grape seed or canola oil

2 medium onions, thinly sliced

1 medium green bell pepper, cored, seeded, and cut into matchsticks

1 tablespoon minced garlic

¼ cup mirin

½ cup soy sauce

2 tablespoons sugar

1 cup Dashi (page 189)

2 tablespoons toasted sesame oil

Fish cakes are wildly popular in East Asia—so popular that both Korea and Japan have restaurants that specialize in fish cakes alone. Called *uh-mook* in Korean and *oden* in Japanese, they have a light, sweet flavor and a firm, springy texture similar to that of a poached French mousseline (though they aren't shaped into quenelles). The Chinese fish balls served in wonton noodle soup have a similarly soft, spongy texture.

You will find delicious commercially made fish cakes in the frozen section of most Asian supermarkets. I like the Korean brand Daelim. There are many equally tasty Japanese brands, such as Shirakiku, if you don't live near a Korean market. However, most commercial brands contain quite a bit of MSG. If you're sensitive to it, as I am, an easy way to get rid of some of the MSG is to blanch the fish cakes in boiling water for about 2 minutes. Unfortunately, though, along with most of the MSG, you will lose some of the seasoning and flavor of the fish cakes. At Hanjan, we used to make fish cakes from scratch with tilefish, which was a very labor-intensive process; ultimately it became so costly and time consuming that we ultimately decided to stop serving them. But I still make this banchan at home using store-bought fish cakes. It's just that good.

Fill a pot with 2 quarts water and bring it to a boil. Drop in the fish cakes and let boil for 2 minutes, then transfer to a plate lined with paper towels and pat dry. Set aside.

Set a large sauté pan over medium heat and add the oil. Once it begins to shimmer, add the onions and peppers and cook, stirring constantly, for 3 minutes, or until the vegetables have softened but not yet begun to brown. Add the garlic and cook for 2 more minutes, stirring, until it becomes soft and fragrant. Add

(recipe continues)

the mirin, soy sauce, sugar, fish cakes, dashi, and sesame oil. Bring the mixture to a simmer and cook until most of the liquid has evaporated, 5 to 7 minutes. You should see only oil remaining in the pan with the vegetables and the fish cakes.

Serve hot, in small bowls or family-style, alongside steamed rice. In the summertime, you may choose to serve the fish cakes chilled, with warm rice. Leftover cooked fish cakes can be kept in the refrigerator, covered, for up to 5 days; to reheat, cover and microwave for 45 to 60 seconds.

SWEET CRISPY BABY ANCHOVIES
멸치 볶음 (Myulchi Bokkeum)

Serves 4

2 tablespoons grape seed or canola oil

½ pound dried baby anchovies, ½ inch to
  1 inch long

1 cup walnuts, cut lengthwise in half

3 shishito peppers, cut into ½-inch pieces

Sauce

2 tablespoons grape seed or canola oil

1 tablespoon minced garlic

1 cup mirin

3 tablespoons soy sauce

¼ cup sugar

1 tablespoon toasted sesame oil

This banchan is my ten-year-old son's favorite. It may surprise you that a young child loves tiny fish with the heads intact, but the sweet gooey sauce and the crunchy texture remind me a little of a Rice Krispie treat. Once you taste this, you'll find it incredibly addictive. I add walnuts and shishito peppers to the anchovies for a more rounded flavor. The nuts give it more depth and bite, while the shishito peppers add a bright freshness.

This is a great banchan to serve alongside a spicy main dish such as Mae-un Tang (Spicy Fish Bone Stew, page 201) or Kimchi Jjigae (Aged-Kimchi Stew, page 198) because the sweetness helps to balance the sharp heat from the gochugaru. It is also an easy way to get kids to eat more fish, because it doesn't have the strong fishy aroma that kids dislike—and it is very nutritious. Paired with some rice and gim, these anchovies are all you need for a light lunch or an afternoon snack.

Set a large skillet over medium heat and add the oil. When the oil is hot, add the anchovies, walnuts, and shishito peppers and cook, stirring, for 5 minutes, or until the anchovies are slightly crispy, the walnuts golden, and the peppers softened. (Cooking the anchovies eliminates some of the fishy smell.) Transfer to a colander set over a plate (set the pan aside) and toss well to remove any loose bits from the anchovies. Transfer to a plate lined with paper towels to cool and drain.

To make the sauce, return the pan to low heat and add the oil. Once the oil is just smoking, add the garlic and cook for 1 minute, stirring constantly so it doesn't burn. Add the mirin and cook for 3 minutes, or until most of the alcohol has evaporated. Add the soy sauce and sugar and increase the heat to medium-high. Bring the sauce to a simmer, stirring occasionally to dissolve the

(recipe continues)

sugar, and simmer for about 5 minutes, until the sauce reduces to two-thirds its original volume. It should be thick enough to lightly coat the back of a spoon. It is very important to get the texture right: If the sauce is too thin, it won't stick to the anchovies and they will taste bland; if it's too thick, it will clump and there will be a very uneven level of seasoning on the anchovies. If the sauce seems too thin, turn the heat to high for a few minutes to evaporate more of the liquid. If the sauce is too thick, add 2 tablespoons water and stir well to loosen the sauce.

Reduce the heat to low, add the anchovy/walnut/pepper blend, and mix well, making sure the sauce coats the anchovies. After everything is mixed together, the anchovies, walnuts, and peppers will have a slight sticky texture but won't clump up. Turn off the heat, and then add the sesame oil. As the mixture cools, it will get stickier and clumpier, but that is fine, as long as it's still easy to break apart the fish using your chopsticks or fork. Refrigerate until chilled. (The cooked anchovies can be kept covered, in the refrigerator, for up to 5 days.)

Serve the anchovies cold in small bowls, with steamed rice.

SPICY RAW BLUE CRABS

양념게장 (Yangnyeom Gejang)

Serves 4

8 live, active blue crabs

Marinade
2 cups sake
1 tablespoon sugar
2 cups soy sauce
1 onion, thinly sliced
3 tablespoons roughly chopped garlic
1 tablespoon roughly chopped ginger
1 bunch scallions, thinly sliced
2 cups gochugaru (Korean red chili flakes)
¼ cup toasted sesame oil
1 tablespoon toasted sesame seeds

Marinated raw blue crabs are considered a delicacy in Korea. There are two classic versions, this one and Ganjang Gejang (Soy-Marinated Raw Blue Crabs, page 84). The spicy crab is considered the "starter" version for people who are a little wary of trying raw crab. The intense flavors of the peppery, garlicky marinade help cover any fishy flavor without overwhelming the natural sweetness of the crab. The crabs must be marinated for a minimum of 12 hours, so you will need to plan ahead. The time spent in the marinade will firm up the crabmeat a bit, giving it a succulent, gelatinous texture. The first time I tasted this dish, I fell in love. It's spicy, salty, and sweet, and when it is served with a bowl of warm rice, you won't be able to stop eating it until everything is gone.

The greatest challenge of this recipe is working with the crabs. Freshness is so important to this dish that you must bring home live crabs. Choose lively specimens that stretch out their legs like Superman when lifted with tongs in the store. It might seem easier to go for the more sluggish looking crustaceans, but the feisty ones have more flavor. At home, freeze the crabs briefly to make them easier to work with. Soft-shell crabs, which are available on the East Coast in late spring and early summer, are also good prepared this way.

Put the crabs in a large roasting pan and put it in the freezer for 40 to 60 minutes. They should stop moving, but you don't want to freeze them until they are completely hard.

Meanwhile, make the marinade: Put the sake in a medium saucepan set over medium-high heat. When it starts to boil, carefully light it with a lighter or a long match, then let the flames die out, 1 to 2 minutes. (If you would rather not light

(recipe continues)

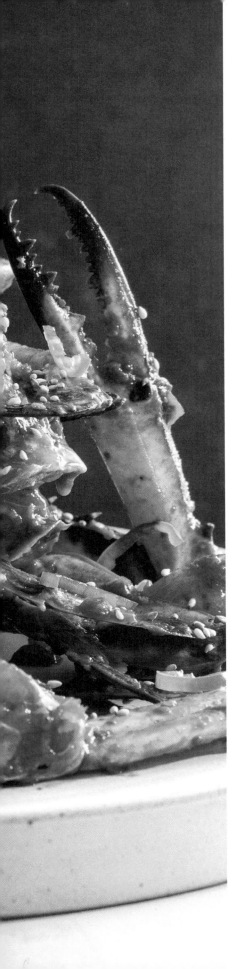

the sake, let it boil for 3 minutes to burn off the alcohol.) Add the sugar and stir to dissolve. Add the soy sauce, onion, garlic, and ginger, reduce the heat, and simmer for 20 minutes, or until vegetables are soft and translucent. Remove from the heat and let cool to room temperature.

Transfer the sauce mixture to a blender or food processor and blend until the vegetables are finely minced. Transfer to a large bowl, add the scallions, gochugaru, sesame oil, and sesame seed, and mix well.

Take the crabs out of the freezer and use kitchen scissors or a sharp chef's knife to cut off the eyes, then cut off the sharp tips of the claws and legs. Flip the crabs over and cut off the aprons at their root. Peel off the top shells and discard them. Use your fingers to remove the gills and discard them too. Cut each crab in half from head to tail and then cut each half in half or into thirds, depending on the size of the crabs, so the pieces are bite-sized. Put the crab in the marinade and mix well. Then transfer to a covered container and refrigerate for at least 12 hours, and up to 72 hours.

Serve the crabs family-style on a platter with hot steamed rice. The best way to eat them is to pick up a piece of crab with your chopsticks, put it in your mouth, and bite the partially shelled body to squeeze out all the meat. Leg meat will be difficult to get at unless you have really large crabs.

SOY-MARINATED RAW BLUE CRABS
간장게장 (Ganjang Gejang)

Serves 4

8 large live, active female Korean blue crabs (or
   local blue crabs), preferably with roe

Marinade
4 cups sake
4 cups soy sauce
6 cups still spring water, preferably Evian (see
   headnote)
One 3-inch square of dried dashima
1 head garlic, separated into cloves, smashed,
   and peeled
One 3-inch piece ginger, peeled and sliced
2 medium onions, thinly sliced
2 large Korean or Asian pears or Fuji apples,
   peeled, cored, and cut into bite-sized pieces
4 red Korean chili peppers or other long hot
   chilies, halved lengthwise
1 bunch scallions, trimmed
2½ cups sugar

Soft-Boiled Eggs
4 large eggs
1 tablespoon salt
1 teaspoon baking soda
1 tablespoon vinegar (any kind will do)

Garnish
1 teaspoon toasted sesame seeds
1 green Korean chili pepper or other long hot
   chili, thinly sliced

If Yangnyeom Gejang (page 81) is the beginner's intro-
duction to marinated raw crab, this version is the crab
connoisseur's dish, because the subtlety of the marinade
allows the natural flavor of the crab to shine. Only the
freshest female crabs are suitable for this dish. At Hanjan,
I serve this from June to September with crabs flown in
from Korea. Korean blue crabs are much bigger and meat-
ier than local ones, which makes the dish especially good.

As the more traditional version of Korean marinated raw
crab, this recipe uses a cooked soy sauce marinade. This
is one of the few times where I ask that you use spring
water rather than tap water, because the flavor of the crab
is so delicate. The soft texture and high PH level of Evian
water makes a big difference in the mouthfeel of the marinade, making it feel smoother and richer. The marinade
is boiled and cooled before the crabs are added to it. This
process is repeated daily for three days to intensify the
flavors and eliminate any harmful bacteria, so the dish
takes 4 days to make, and it *must* be eaten on the fourth
day. By the fifth day, the texture of the crab meat will have
become mushy and unpleasant.

We cut up the marinated crabs and serve them with some
of the marinade and fresh hot rice. The crabmeat is succulent and takes on a slightly fermented, deeply robust
flavor from the sauce, with a touch of heat imbued with
the aroma of the sea. Like kimchi, this dish is an acquired
taste that quickly turns into an addiction. We garnish the
dish with soft-boiled eggs that have been marinated overnight with the crabs, toasted white sesame seeds, and
sliced green Korean chili peppers.

Put the crabs in a roasting pan and put it in the freezer for 30 to 60 minutes. They should stop moving, but don't freeze them until they are completely hard.

Meanwhile, put the sake in a large pot over medium-high heat. When it starts to boil, carefully light it with a lighter or a long match, then let the flames die out, 1 to 2 minutes. (If you would rather not light the sake, let it boil for 3 minutes to burn off the alcohol.) Add the soy sauce, 4 cups of the spring water, the dashima, garlic, ginger, onion, pears, chili peppers, scallions, and sugar and bring to a simmer. Adjust the heat to maintain a slow simmer and cook the mixture for 30 minutes. Transfer the marinade to a stainless steel bowl set in an ice bath and let cool completely, 20 to 30 minutes.

Remove the crabs from the freezer. Use kitchen scissors or a sharp chef's knife to cut off the eyes and the sharp tips of the claws and legs. Flip the crabs over and cut off the aprons at their root. If the females are filled with roe, you will be able to see a bit of the orange roe oozing out from under the apron. Submerge the cleaned crabs in the cooled marinade, cover, and refrigerate overnight.

The next day, remove the crabs from the marinade and reserve them in a bowl in the refrigerator. Transfer the marinade to a medium pot. Add 1 cup of the spring water and set over medium-high heat. Bring to a boil and boil for 10 minutes. Strain the marinade through a fine-mesh sieve into a container large enough to hold it and the crabs. Set the container in an ice bath and let cool completely, stirring occasionally, 15 to 20 minutes.

Put the crabs back in the marinade, cover, and refrigerate overnight.

The next day, make the soft-boiled eggs: Pour 2 quarts water, or enough to submerge the 4 eggs, into a small pot and bring to a boil over high heat. When it comes to a fast boil, add the salt, baking soda, and vinegar. (The baking soda makes it easier to peel the soft-boiled eggs, and the vinegar will help center the

(recipe continues)

yolks.) Bring the water back to a boil and add the eggs. When the water comes back to a boil, set a timer for 6 minutes. Prepare an ice bath. When the timer goes off, transfer the eggs to the ice bath and let them cool for 5 minutes, then drain the eggs and peel right away; reserve.

Then repeat the marinating process, removing the crabs, adding the remaining 1 cup spring water to the marinade, and reboiling and cooling it. This time, add the peeled soft-boiled eggs to the cooled marinade along with the crabs. The eggs will absorb flavors from both the marinade and crab. Cover and refrigerate overnight.

On day 4, to serve, pull the crabs out of the marinade. Peel off the top shells and reserve for later. There should be some roe and innards stuck inside the shell, which you will leave intact. Use your fingers to remove the gills and discard them. Using a sharp chef's knife, cut each crab in half from head to tail and then cut each piece in half or into thirds, depending on the size of the crab. If there is any roe, leave it on the crabmeat.

Arrange all the crab pieces on a large serving plate, along with the reserved top shells. Garnish with the halved soft-boiled eggs, toasted sesame seeds, and sliced green chili. Serve right away. You can fill the empty shells with some hot rice and a few spoonfuls of the marinade to mix and enjoy after all the crabs are eaten.

SEAWEED SASHIMI
미역 (Miyeok)

Serves 4

2½ ounces (150 grams) dried miyeok (wakame)
2 tablespoons Chojang (page 58)
Toasted sesame seeds for garnish

I think of this dish as poor man's sashimi because even though it doesn't contain any fish, you can still taste the mild flavor of the sea. The seaweed is served with chojang, the traditional Korean condiment for hwe—Korean raw fish (see page 161). This seaweed, known as miyeok in Korean, has a very silky texture and a soft, smooth mouthfeel. The chojang gives it a good kick of flavor. This dish is best served at the beginning of a meal because the tangy, sweet flavor of the chojang will whet everyone's appetite. It's a great choice for any vegetarian who still craves the flavors of the sea.

Soak the seaweed in enough water to cover for 1 hour to rehydrate it.

Drain the hydrated seaweed and rinse thoroughly in cold water. (The hydrated miyeok can be kept in the fridge for up to 3 days, but a quick rinse before serving is recommended to rehydrate the seaweed again and to wash away any slimy film that may appear.) Cut into 2-inch-long strips.

Spoon some miyeok onto each plate to form a pile and drizzle some chojang on top, as you would dress a salad. Sprinkle with toasted sesame seeds and serve.

SAUTÉED GRAY SQUASH AND ONION
호박 볶음 (Hobak Bokkeum)

Serves 4

1 tablespoon grape seed or canola oil

1 tablespoon toasted sesame oil

1 medium onion, cut into 1-inch dice

2 garlic cloves, minced

Salt

2 pounds gray squash or green zucchini, or a
   combination, cut into ¼-inch-thick rounds

Freshly ground black pepper

1 teaspoon soy sauce

This banchan highlights the deliciousness of gray squash and gives an unassuming vegetable the center stage it deserves. Any Asian markets should carry gray squash (sometimes called Mexican gray squash), as will some large supermarkets, but you can replace it with green zucchini if it is difficult to find. Gray squash are a little fatter and shorter than zucchini. Because their flavors are similar, I sometimes use both zucchini and gray squash when making this banchan. Hobak bokkeum is best served in summer, when both squash are at their peak. This banchan works as a balance to spicier main dishes because of the natural sweetness of the squash and onion.

Set a 12-inch sauté pan over medium heat and add the grape seed or canola oil and sesame oil. Once the oil begins to shimmer, add the onion and garlic to the pan, along with a small pinch of salt, and cook for 3 minutes, stirring often so they do not color. Add the squash and 2 pinches each of salt and pepper and cook for 3 more minutes, stirring constantly. Add soy sauce and cook until the squash is tender, 3 to 5 minutes. Transfer to a medium bowl or container and let cool completely.

Cover the squash and refrigerate for at least 2 hours to let the flavors bloom. (The squash will keep in the refrigerator for up to 3 days.)

Serve the squash cold with hot steamed rice.

STEAMED EGG CUSTARD WITH SALTED SHRIMP

계란찜 (Gyeran Jjim)

Serves 2

4 large eggs

1 cup Dashi (page 189)

1 teaspoon pureed salted shrimp, or

   1 teaspoon Korean anchovy sauce or

   2 teaspoons fish sauce

1 tablespoon mirin

Pinch of freshly ground black pepper

3 medium (U24–30) shrimp, peeled, deveined, and cut into bite-sized pieces

---

Note: Alternatively, you can microwave the custard for 90 seconds. It will puff up in the bowl like a soufflé and should just cook through. Unwrap and serve immediately. The texture will change as it cools, collapsing into a denser custard with more chew to it. Although the microwave technique will yield a firmer texture and the result is not as good as the steaming method, the flavor is the same and the technique can be useful when you're in a rush.

Gyeran jjim is ubiquitous in Korean barbecue restaurants, but it is one of those dishes that almost always tastes better when made at home. This is especially true if you use homemade dashi. For more flavor and depth, I like to add a spoonful of pureed salted shrimp to season the eggs; if you can't find salted shrimp, Korean anchovy sauce or Asian fish sauce will also work. If you don't enjoy strong fishy flavors, though, you can use three pinches of salt in place of either of these. Sometimes I use a different kind of stock instead of dashi. If I have extremely fresh clams, for example, I will use clam juice and clams instead of the shrimp. Or, if I have a rich lobster stock, I will use that with bits of cooked lobster meat. You could also use chicken broth and small cubes of chicken if you have that. It's a very adaptable recipe.

This is a quick and comforting banchan to complement a fiery, spicy main dish in the colder months. It is often served alongside Kimchi Jjigae (Aged-Kimchi Stew, page 198), as the custard balances the spiciness and acidity of the kimchi. If you're an egg fan, like me, every meal can use an egg dish, and this is a delicious one.

Prepare a stovetop steamer or fill a large stockpot with 2 inches of water. Place a round rack in the pot and bring the water to a rapid boil.

Meanwhile, put the eggs in a medium bowl and whisk them to break up the yolks. Add the dashi, pureed salted shrimp, mirin, and pepper and whisk well to blend. Divide the shrimp between two heatproof 6-cup bowls and strain half of the egg mixture into each bowl, not going above the halfway mark. Cover each bowl with plastic wrap.

(recipe continues)

Set the bowls of custard on the rack in the pot and steam the custard for 15 minutes. Turn off the heat and leave the bowls in the steamer for 5 minutes more. The custard should be smooth and shiny and just set; it should jiggle slightly if the bowls are gently shaken. If you see waves instead of a jiggle, the custard is undercooked and needs another 5 minutes or so of steaming. The final texture will be similar to that of Japanese *chawan-mushi*, the savory egg custard.

Serve the custard hot or warm. I do not recommend saving any leftovers, because the texture changes drastically once the custard gets cold.

KIMCHI

Kimchi is the one dish most closely associated with Korean food. It used to be that its funky aroma of fermented vegetables turned many people off. Now that Korean cuisine is becoming more popular, however, kimchi has become mainstream. You can find it at Whole Foods, Trader Joe's, and large supermarkets in major US cities.

Kimchi is made by fermenting cabbage or another vegetable with lactic acid bacteria, a probiotic that is found in our digestive tracts and is associated with improved digestion, increased nutrient absorption, lower cholesterol, and better overall health. During fermentation, the lactic acid lowers the pH of the vegetable, giving the kimchi its distinct sour flavor. You can use seafood such as salted shrimp or raw oysters to jump-start the fermentation process, helping the lactic acid bacteria metabolize more quickly. Adding seafood also gives the kimchi a funkier flavor. If you prefer to make kimchi without the seafood catalyst, the process will take a bit longer. The resulting flavor is simpler, with less character, but it is perfect for vegetarians.

Kimchi is one of those acquired tastes that easily becomes an addiction. I love kimchi in part because it works so well as a balance to many other Korean dishes. Its acidity cuts through the fatty richness of pork belly. Its spicy saltiness gives subtle soups such as Galbi Tang (Beef Short Rib Soup, page 196) and Tteok Guk (Rice Cake Soup, page 193) their Korean accent. I don't think any Korean meal is complete without a bowl of kimchi—or several different kimchis—on the table for everyone to enjoy.

Kimchi is unique in that you can eat it at any stage in the fermentation process as its flavor profile matures and develops. Everyone has their own opinion as to when kimchi is best, but it always tastes great. When cabbage kimchi is only a week old, the cabbage is crunchy and sweet, with a fresh texture that can be paired with almost any dish. The seasoning marinade hasn't yet penetrated the cabbage leaves and acts more like a salad dressing. As the kimchi ages, the sweetness starts to give way to tanginess and the flavors deepen. The cabbage softens, but it still retains some crunch, like a pickle. Some kimchis are aged for many years, and older versions of aged kimchi, called *mukeunji*, are prized for their complex flavors. Mukeunji is very sour and its intense flavor is best showcased when it is cooked in a stew or sautéed with fatty pork belly, to soften the taste somewhat.

Each batch of kimchi will ripen at a different time. Some ripen slowly and others ripen more quickly, depending on the environment. Proper temperatures and the absence of light and oxygen are key factors in the quality of the fermentation. If your kimchi is not to your liking when you first taste it, you might want to keep it in the fridge for a while longer and see how the flavors change. I have made what I thought were bad batches, only to discover weeks later that they had become absolutely delicious.

Most Koreans would never use regular table salt or kosher salt to make kimchi, because they believe it will render the kimchi bitter after it ferments. Koreans have traditionally used a sea salt called *chun il yeom*, which is derived from seawater from the oceans surrounding Korea, evaporated by sunlight and wind. Due to the increasing pollution of our oceans, this salt is no longer the best one to use. I now use salt from the Andes or Himalayas, which is purer (although more expensive).

I also add salted shrimp as a catalyst for the fermentation. I puree it into a paste so that it mixes more evenly into the marinade. In Korea, families may use various kinds of salted and fermented seafood, such as anchovies, squid, oysters, or fish, which results in different flavors of kimchi.

Most Koreans consider kimchi a banchan, and so do I. However, I have dedicated a separate chapter to it because it is made using fermentation and there are several different types. The recipes I provide here are for classic kimchi using vegetables that are indigenous to Korea. When making kimchi in the United States, you can use your own local vegetables, as long as you apply the technique correctly. Turnips, beets, rutabagas, and celery root all make good kimchi. The general rule of thumb is to select a thick, dense vegetable with a high water content and a mild flavor.

When you make kimchi, try to find organically grown vegetables that are not contaminated by pesticides or other chemicals. Koreans believe that such chemicals hinder fermentation and slow the growth of the probiotic bacteria. I also recommend using spring water instead of tap water and, as mentioned above, salt from the Andes or Himalayas. These mountain salts have less contamination from man-made chemicals. It is almost impossible to make 100-percent organic kimchi, but the cleaner your ingredients, the better your end product.

Koreans have always believed that food is medicine. What we put in our bodies directly affects our health, especially over the long term. You are what you eat has never rung truer than with Korean cuisine. As a fermented food, kimchi is full of probiotics to help with digestion, and Koreans believe that the fermentation process negates any harmful effects from salt and sugar. In short, kimchi is thought to be both delicious and very good for your body.

MAKING AND STORING KIMCHI

The prime fermentation conditions for kimchi are a constant temperature of 32° to 36°F, no direct sunlight, and as little oxygen as possible. This constant temperature is the key to regulating the fermentation process, because it prevents the kimchi from getting too acidic too quickly.

Traditionally, Koreans buried kimchi three feet underground in clay jars to ensure those important conditions. Today almost every Korean household has a kimchi refrigerator. Kimchi refrigerators are slightly pricier than normal refrigerators, because they have powerful motors that keep the interior temperature constant at all times. They feature multiple compartments for storing different batches of kimchi, with separate doors and drawers, so that opening one compartment won't affect the temperatures of the other compartments. This keeps the temperature of each compartment stable.

Kimchi refrigerators are considered everyday appliances in Korea and are often given to newlyweds. If you are interested in purchasing a kimchi refrigerator, you can find ones here made by Samsung and LG. My favorite brand is Dimchae. While Samsung and LG are famous for all kinds of electronics, Dimchae is known only for its kimchi refrigerators. If you're storing your kimchi in a regular refrigerator, it's best to keep it on the bottom shelf and deep in the back corner.

NAPA CABBAGE KIMCHI
배추 김치 (Baechu Kimchi)

Makes about 2 quarts

3 pounds Napa cabbage (1 large head or 2
smaller ones)
2 cups medium-coarse salt, preferably from the
Andes or Himalayas, plus more if needed
About 8 cups spring water or filtered water

Marinade
6 cups coarse gochugaru (Korean red chili
flakes)
2 cups Dashi (page 189)
2 cups spring water or filtered water
½ cup sweet glutinous rice flour
½ cup pureed salted shrimp, pureed in a
blender
1 cup pureed onion
3 cups pureed Fuji apples (about 3 apples)
¼ cup Korean anchovy sauce or ½ cup fish
sauce
2 heads garlic, separated into cloves, peeled,
and minced
1 tablespoon minced ginger
½ medium Korean radish or daikon radish,
peeled and cut into matchsticks (use a
mandoline if you have one)
2 bunches scallions, cut into 1-inch batons

Baechu kimchi is the most widely eaten kimchi in Korea. When people say *kimchi*, they are generally referring to baechu kimchi. This base version is versatile in its flavoring and aging. I like it best because unlike most kimchi, which are only served as banchan, it can be used to create many other extraordinary dishes, such as Kimchi Jjigae (Aged-Kimchi Stew, page 198), Dubu Kimchi (Warm Tofu with Kimchi and Pork Belly Stir-Fry, page 278), and Bacon Chorizo Kimchi Paella (page 230).

Remove any wilted or brown outer leaves from the cabbage and discard. Cut the head(s) lengthwise in half, leaving the cores attached to hold the leaves together. Use 3 tablespoons salt for each large cabbage half (if you are using 2 smaller cabbages, use 1½ tablespoons for each half and adjust the quantities accordingly). Massage 2 tablespoons salt into the core and the bottom one-third of the cabbage. Sprinkle another tablespoon of salt over the rest of the cabbage half, spreading the leaves to salt them as evenly as possible. Repeat with the remaining cabbage.

Put the cabbage in a large nonreactive container and add just enough of the water to cover it halfway. Add the rest of the salt to the water. Cover the container with plastic wrap and set aside for 2 to 3 hours, until the cabbage is completely submerged in liquid brine. If it is not completely immersed after 3 hours, reposition the cabbage in the container so that the top layer becomes the bottom layer. Then leave the cabbage to brine at room temperature for a total of 10 to 12 hours.

While the cabbage is brining, make the marinade, so the flavors have time to meld: Mix the gochugaru with the dashi in a large nonreactive bowl and let the chili flakes hydrate at room temperature for 2 hours. The mixture will become paste-like in texture and will retain its bright color.

Once the gochugaru has hydrated, mix the spring water and rice flour together in a small saucepan set over low heat, bring to a simmer, and simmer for about 10 minutes; whisk occasionally so the flour doesn't burn at the bottom of the pan. When the mixture becomes thick and begins to look like Elmer's Glue, remove from the heat and whisk well to blend.

Once it cools down, add the rice flour mixture to the hydrated gochugaru paste, the shrimp puree, onion puree, apple puree, anchovy or fish sauce, garlic, ginger, radish, and scallions and mix well. Cover and refrigerate for at least 4 hours before using. (The marinade can be refrigerated for up to 1 day.)

At the end of the brining period, the cabbage leaves should be pliable enough that you can bend the leaves in half across the stem at a 90-degree angle without breaking them. Drain the cabbage in a colander set in the sink, then rinse off the salt with cold spring or filtered water and wring the leaves out. Taste the cabbage to make sure it is well seasoned but not overly salty. If it is bland, sprinkle on a bit more salt and put it back in container for another hour, then wring the leaves out without rinsing. If it is too salty, put the cabbage in a large bowl of spring or filtered water and let stand for an hour so some of the salt can escape into the water, then rinse well again and wring the leaves out. Put the brined cabbage in a large nonreactive bowl.

Wearing latex gloves, grab a handful or so of the marinade and rub it generously onto every leaf of the cabbage. The cabbage halves should be completely covered in marinade, both inside and out. Pack them into a large lidded jar or other nonreactive container, or two smaller ones; I use large Mason jars. Pour the remaining marinade over the top and cover the jar(s). Wrap the jar(s) in several layers of foil to protect the kimchi from light and refrigerate on the lowest shelf of the refrigerator, in the back corner, until the cabbage ferments into kimchi; this usually takes 2 to 3 weeks. (Many recipes tell you to leave the kimchi out overnight at room temperature before refrigerating to quicken the pace of fermentation. I find that although the kimchi will ferment faster this way, the flavor is not always as

(recipe continues)

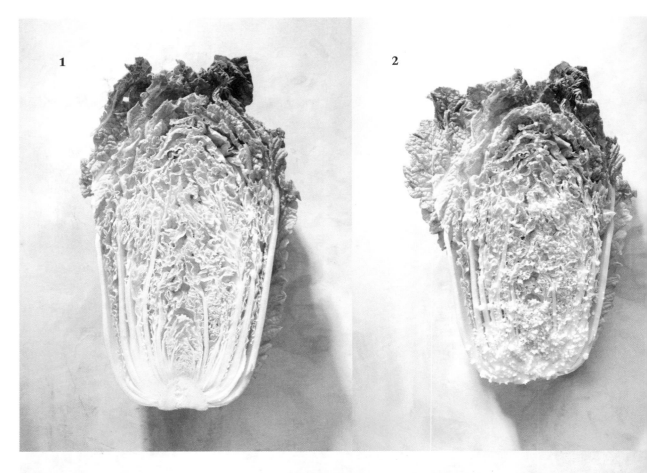

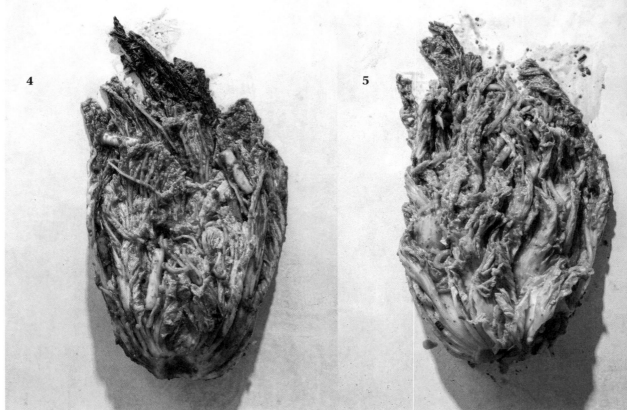

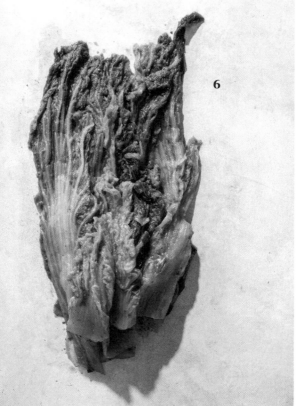

good. Too often the sour flavor achieved by fermentation overwhelms the intense flavor of the kimchi itself and the balance is off.)

Although kimchi is best left undisturbed, I do recommend that you open the jar(s) and taste the kimchi every 3 or 4 days to learn the effects of fermentation on the cabbage. The first signs of fermentation will probably appear in 7 to 9 days, when you will see small bubbles in the marinade and the leaves will have become slightly carbonated. The texture of the thick white ribs of the cabbage will still be crisp, and the sweetness of the cabbage will be more noticeable than the sour acidity of the lactic acid. The garlic will still taste a bit raw. After 2 to 3 weeks, all those ingredients will have melded into a harmonious single flavor that balances sweet, sour, salty, and spicy. This is the stage when I like my cabbage kimchi the best. It still tastes fresh, and the texture is a little crunchy, but you can definitely taste the fermentation. Once you are happy with your batch of kimchi, it should be consumed within 8 months (although some kimchis have been known to keep for up to 10 years). The texture will continue to change over time. Once the kimchi starts to get mushy, the fermentation process has ended and the kimchi will begin to go bad.

Stages of Making Kimchi: (1) Napa cabbage halved; **(2)** salted; **(3)** brined 12 hours and squeezed; **(4)** freshly marinated; **(5)** fermented 3 months; **(6)** fermented 12 months.

AGED BAECHU KIMCHI

I've included three recipes that call for aged kimchi: Kimchi Jjigae (Aged-Kimchi Stew, page 198), Budae Jjigae (Spicy DMZ Stew, page 273), and Dubu Kimchi (Warm Tofu with Kimchi and Pork Belly Stir-Fry, page 278). Aging gives the kimchi deeper flavor and more acidity. I consider any kimchi older than 3 months to be aged kimchi. But the only aged kimchi I have seen is baechu kimchi. Other kimchis are normally eaten within 3 months.

You can make your own aged kimchi by keeping a jar of kimchi in your refrigerator for up to 8 months. I do not recommend aging kimchi for longer than that unless you own a kimchi refrigerator. When aging kimchi at home, there are certain factors that you need to consider. The biggest concern is a refrigerator that fluctuates too much in temperature. If the temperature of the kimchi often goes up and down, fermentation won't occur steadily and the acidic flavor will overwhelm the kimchi.

So make sure your refrigerator is cold enough, ideally between 32° and 36°F. It helps to wrap the kimchi jar in several layers of aluminum foil to keep its temperature constant and to protect it from light.

After 3 months of proper aging, the flavor of your kimchi will be sharper and more sour. You should be able to discern a greater depth and a longer finish. As soon as you start to taste these flavors, you can start using the aged kimchi in recipes that call for it.

Finally, if you plan to age your kimchi, it is even more important to use high-quality ingredients. Kimchi that is not aged can taste good even if you don't go out of your way to find the best ingredients. However, with aged kimchi, the ingredients have a longer time to affect the flavor. You will create a deeper, more intense aged kimchi if you use top-quality ingredients.

I know a family in Korea who travels to the Korean city of Muju every fall to prepare their kimchi. They make this yearly pilgrimage because they want to ferment their kimchi with the most pristine ingredients possible. The mountainous region of Muju is known as one of the cleanest regions in South Korea and is famous for the quality of its spring water. The best Napa cabbages are deemed to be the ones that have been grown in regions like Muju, at higher elevations and in cooler areas. While we cannot all travel to Muju to procure ingredients for our kimchi, we can definitely use the best ingredients we have at our disposal and within our budget.

Be patient if the fermentation doesn't happen as quickly as you expect it to. I've had kimchi that didn't start to ferment for more than 3 weeks and was only ready after 6 weeks. Let nature take its time to create a magical process with awesome results.

WHITE NAPA CABBAGE KIMCHI
백 김치 (Baek Kimchi)

Makes about 2 quarts

3 pounds Napa cabbage (1 large head or 2 smaller heads)

2 cups medium-coarse salt, preferably from the Andes or Himalayas

About 8 cups spring water or filtered water

Marinade

4 cups Dashi (page 189)

½ cup coarse salt

1 Fuji apple, peeled, quartered, and cored

½ medium onion

6 garlic cloves

One 3-inch piece ginger, peeled and roughly chopped

3 tablespoons salted shrimp, pureed in a blender

1 small Korean radish (mu) or daikon radish, peeled and cut into matchsticks

1 bunch chives, cut into 1-inch batons

2 red Korean chili peppers or other long hot chilies, halved, seeds and ribs removed, and cut into slivers

This kimchi and the White Water-Radish Kimchi on page 108 are called white kimchi because they do not contain gochugaru; their flavor is refreshing and distinct. While it does contain some fresh chilies, Baek Kimchi is perfect for people who don't like overly spicy food but still want to enjoy the flavor and health benefits of Korean fermented vegetables. If you are very sensitive to spice, you can omit the chilies entirely. This kimchi complements rich dishes and should always be served cold.

Remove any wilted or brown outer leaves from the cabbage and discard. Cut the head(s) lengthwise in half, leaving the cores attached to hold the leaves together. Use 3 tablespoons salt for each large cabbage half (if you are using 2 smaller cabbages, use 1½ tablespoons for each half and adjust the quantities accordingly). Massage 2 tablespoons salt into the core and the bottom third of the cabbage. Sprinkle another tablespoon of salt over the rest of the cabbage half, separating the leaves to salt them as evenly as possible. Repeat with the remaining cabbage.

Put the cabbage in a large nonreactive container and add just enough of the water to cover it halfway. Add the rest of the salt. Cover the container with plastic wrap and set aside for 2 to 3 hours, until the cabbage is completely immersed in liquid brine. If it is not completely immersed after 3 hours, reposition the cabbage so that the top layer becomes the bottom layer. Then leave the cabbage to brine at room temperature for a total of 10 to 12 hours.

At the end of the brining period, the cabbage leaves should be pliable enough that you can bend the leaves in half across the stem at a 90-degree angle without breaking them. Drain the cabbage in a colander set in the sink, then rinse off the salt with cold spring or filtered water and wring the leaves out. Taste the

(recipe continues)

cabbage to make sure it is well seasoned but not overly salty. If it is bland, sprinkle on a bit more salt and put it back in the container for another hour, then wring the leaves out without rinsing. If it is too salty, put the cabbage in a large bowl of spring or filtered water and let stand for an hour so some of the salt can escape into the water, then rinse well again and wring the leaves out. Put the brined cabbage in a large nonreactive bowl.

To make the marinade, put the dashi, salt, apple, onion, garlic, ginger, and salted shrimp into a blender and puree until smooth. Transfer to a large bowl, add the radish, chives, and chilies, and mix well.

Wearing latex gloves, grab a handful or so of the marinade and rub it generously onto every leaf of the cabbage. The cabbage halves should be completely covered in marinade, both inside and out. Pack them into one large lidded jar or other nonreactive container, or two smaller ones; I use large Mason jars. Pour the remaining marinade over the top and cover the jar(s). Wrap the jar(s) in several layers of foil to protect the kimchi from light, place on the bottom shelf in the back corner of the fridge, and let ferment for 10 days.

Taste the kimchi after 10 days. It should have a balanced sweet, salty, and sour flavor and be slightly fizzy. The kimchi can be kept in the refrigerator for many months; the flavors will continue to evolve as it ages.

KOREAN RADISH KIMCHI
총각 김치 & 깍두기 (Chongak Kimchi or Kkak Dugi Kimchi)

Makes about 2 quarts

3 pounds 4- to 5-inch-long ponytail radishes
(chongak) or Korean radishes (mu)

2 cups medium-coarse salt, preferably from the
Andes or Himalayas

Marinade

4 cups gochugaru (Korean red chili flakes)

½ cup Dashi (page 189)

½ cup sweet glutinous rice flour

2 cups spring water

½ cup salted shrimp, pureed in a blender

1 cup pureed onion

3 cups pureed Fuji apple (about 3 apples)

2 heads garlic, separated into cloves, peeled,
and minced

2 teaspoons minced ginger

¼ cup Korean anchovy sauce or ½ cup fish
sauce

Cold spring water or filtered water for rinsing
the radishes

You can make this kimchi with either of two radishes. When using ponytail radishes, the kimchi is called *chongak kimchi*; when using the large Korean radishes called *mu*, it becomes *kkak dugi kimchi*. The shape of the ponytail radish used in chongak kimchi is somewhat phallic; hence the name of the kimchi, which translates as "bachelor kimchi." These radishes are about 3 to 5 inches long and thicker at the bottom. Both radishes are quite easy to find year-round in Korean markets, though they taste the best in the winter. If you cannot find them, you can substitute an equal weight of Japanese daikon, Cherry Bell radishes, French breakfast radishes, or regular red radishes.

You should always peel Korean mu radishes before brining them. Make sure to peel them deeply, because they have a thick, fibrous layer beneath the skin that has an undesirable chewy texture. This layer is ⅛ to ¼ inch thick and will be visible to the eye when you look at a slice of the radish.

The brining takes a bit longer for radishes than cabbage because the vegetables are thicker. Fermentation takes much longer too. I like my radish kimchi to be very fermented. The radishes retain their crispness for much longer than cabbage and their inherent spiciness gives the finished kimchi more character than the sweetness of Napa cabbage.

If using ponytail radishes, peel them, trim the leafy stems so they are twice the length of the radishes themselves, and cut the radishes lengthwise in half. If using mu radishes, peel them deeply and cut into bite-sized cubes. Put the salt in a small bowl. Rub the radishes in the salt to coat, transfer them to a covered nonreactive container, and set aside at room temperature for 12 hours. The radishes will release their liquid, forming a brine.

(recipe continues)

Meanwhile, make the marinade, so the flavors have time to meld: Combine the gochugaru and dashi in a large nonreactive bowl and stir well. Cover and let the chili flakes hydrate at room temperature for 2 hours. The mixture will become paste-like in texture.

When the gochugaru paste is ready, combine the spring water and rice flour in a small saucepan set over low heat, bring to a simmer, and simmer for 10 minutes; whisk occasionally so the flour doesn't burn at the bottom of the pot. Once the mixture becomes thick and begins to look like Elmer's Glue, remove from heat and whisk well to blend.

Add the rice flour mixture to the gochugaru paste, then add the salted shrimp puree, onion puree, apple puree, garlic, ginger, and anchovy or fish sauce and whisk well to combine. Cover the marinade and refrigerate until the radishes are ready.

After 12 hours, mix the radishes well in their brine again and set aside at room temperature. Let ponytail radishes brine for 48 hours longer, or cubed Korean radishes for 24 more hours.

When the radishes have been sufficiently brined, as described above, drain the radishes in a colander, rinse with cold spring or filtered water, and drain for 20 minutes.

Put the radishes in a large bowl, add the marinade, and mix well. Transfer to one or two airtight nonreactive containers (I use large Mason jars), wrap each jar in several layers of aluminum foil to block out light and keep the temperature more constant, and refrigerate to ferment the kimchi.

Taste the kimchi after 10 days. It should be full-flavored but not taste fermented at this point. The garlic and onion will still taste raw. Try the kimchi again after 20 days. Fermentation should have begun, and salty, spicy, and slightly sour flavors should be present and balanced, with a longer finish and a deeper taste. The radishes will still have their original spicy taste, but on top of that, the combination of the fermentation and the marinade gives this kimchi a multidimensional, dynamic flavor unlike any pickle I have ever tried. If the radishes are not quite ready, give them a little more time. I've had batches take up to 30 days to reach their peak. The only way to know for sure is to taste the kimchi.

You can enjoy the kimchi for up to 3 months after its maturation, but make sure you store it on the bottom shelf and in the back corner of your refrigerator to keep its temperature constant.

WHITE WATER-RADISH KIMCHI
동치미 (Dongchimi)

Makes about 2 quarts

3 pounds large Korean radishes (mu) or 2
   medium daikon radishes
1 cup medium-coarse salt, preferably from the
   Andes or Himalayas

Marinade
2 quarts spring water or filtered water
5 tablespoons sugar
5 tablespoons medium-coarse salt, preferably
   from the Andes or Himalayas
1 head garlic, separated into cloves and peeled
One 6-inch piece ginger, cut into 8 pieces
1 Fuji apple, peeled, quartered, and cored
1 medium onion, quartered
1 bunch chives, cut into 1-inch batons
4 red Korean chili peppers or other long hot
   chilies, cut into ½-inch slices

Spring water or filtered water for rinsing the
   radishes

Traditionally dongchimi was made and eaten in the winter. I actually like its sweet and sour flavors more in the warm summer months, when I feel like eating lighter fare. The recipe is very similar to the Baek Kimchi (page 101), except that it doesn't use salted shrimp and the radishes are fermented in more liquid. In fact, my favorite part of this dish is the savory, refreshing liquid. You can use shots of the liquid to chase shots of soju, kind of like a Korean pickle-back. This kimchi is always served cold, along with its liquid.

Peel the radishes deeply to remove the fibrous exterior, cutting off about ¼ inch of the outer layer. Cut the radishes into 2-by-½-by-½-inch batons. Transfer to a nonreactive bowl, add the coarse salt, and mix well. Cover and let stand at room temperature for 24 hours.

The next day, make the marinade: Combine the water, sugar, and salt in a large pot and heat, stirring, until sugar and salt dissolve. Transfer to a large bowl and cool to room temperature. Wrap the garlic, ginger, apple, and onion in a square of cheesecloth and add to the bowl. Then add the chives and chili peppers. Put the radishes in a colander and rinse with cold spring or filtered water, washing off all the salt. Drain in the colander for 20 minutes. Add the drained radishes to the marinade. Cover and let stand at room temperature for 48 hours, then refrigerate.

Once again, it can be tricky to know when the kimchi will be ready to eat. I've made some that were ready after 2 weeks and some that were not ready until they'd fermented for 2 months. The only way to tell for sure is to keep tasting the kimchi. It's ready to eat when a deep sourness starts to balance the sweetness and saltiness. There should also be a fizziness to the marinade. I would advise you to be very patient waiting for the fermentation to commence and then start tasting it after 2 weeks, and thereafter every 3 or 4 days. Serve the kimchi chilled, with the fermenting liquid.

RAMP KIMCHI
달래 김치 (Dallae Kimchi)

Makes 5 cups

2 pounds ramps
1 cup medium-coarse salt, preferably from the
    Himalayas or Andes

Marinade
2 cups gochugaru (Korean red chili flakes)
2 cups Dashi (page 189)
¼ cup Korean anchovy sauce or ½ cup fish
    sauce
1 teaspoon salted shrimp, pureed in a blender
¼ cup sugar
1 tablespoon minced garlic

Note: After 2 weeks the texture of the ramps will become softer and the flavor will become a little overpowering. The freshness of the ramps will be gone. This is a good time to throw the remaining kimchi into fried rice to finish it off.

Dallae is a wild spring Korean vegetable that resembles ramps or spring garlic. You cannot find dallae here in the US, so I use ramps instead. Ramps are one of the few truly wild vegetables we eat here in the States. They first appear in early spring and remain in season for around six weeks. They have small white bulbs, sometimes streaked with red, and soft, flat green leaves. They taste garlicky and oniony and are more aromatic than scallions or leeks. Both dallae and ramp kimchi have a wonderful strong, pungent aroma and flavor. Because of that and the short shelf life of this kimchi, I recommend making only a small portion at a time. As strong as they smell, both ramp and dallae kimchis are surprisingly refreshing and balanced on the palate.

Trim the roots from the bottoms of the ramps and peel off any wilted outer layers from the bulb. Remove any yellowing or browning leaves. Cut the ramps in half, separating the greens from the white/red stems and bulbs. Save the greens for another use, such as sautéing them in brown butter or simply grilling them. Cut the white parts lengthwise in half and place in a large nonreactive bowl. Add the salt and mix well. Let stand, uncovered, at room temperature for 1 hour.

Rinse the ramps thoroughly with cold water and dry in a salad spinner, or pat dry with a kitchen towel, then place in a large nonreactive bowl.

To make the marinade, combine the gochugaru, dashi, anchovy or fish sauce, salted shrimp, sugar, and garlic in a bowl and mix well using gloved hands. Add the marinade to the ramps, making sure all of the ramps are smothered in it.

Pack the ramps into a tightly covered nonreactive container (I use a large Mason jar) and refrigerate. This kimchi will be ready in 2 or 3 days and can be kept in the refrigerator for 2 to 3 weeks. Serve in a small bowl to be shared.

MUCHIM

Muchim dishes are also considered banchan, but they are quick-pickled (or "quick-marinated") vegetables that are served shortly after they are made. Muchim are more convenient than kimchi because you do not have to wait for them to ferment—they can be eaten the same day they are prepared. However, some muchim have a similar flavor profile to kimchi, in that they are spicy, salty, and sour, though they lack the depth that comes with time. These three flavors are very important to Koreans to balance heavier meat dishes and counteract the fattiness of these proteins. In contrast to kimchi, where it is the fermentation that creates the sour flavor, the acidity of the muchim derives from vinegar.

Muchim recipes were first developed as an alternative to kimchi. Kimchi is traditionally made in the late fall and early winter, when Napa cabbage and Korean radishes are at their best. Since kimchi was only prepared once a year, Koreans would usually run out of it by late spring or summer. They then used seasonal spring and summer vegetables such as cucumbers, chives, and lettuce to make equally piquant and sour side dishes. As I'm sure you can guess, you will find more muchim on a Korean summer dining table than in the winter.

MARINATED SPICY CUCUMBERS
오이 무침 (Oee Muchim)

Makes 2 cups

3 English cucumbers or 8 Korean, Persian,
  Japanese, or Kirby cucumbers, sliced into
  ¼-inch-thick rounds
2 tablespoons medium-coarse salt, preferably
  from the Andes or Himalayas
½ cup rice vinegar
¼ cup gochugaru (Korean red chili flakes)
3 tablespoons sugar
1 teaspoon minced garlic
1 teaspoon Korean anchovy sauce or 2
  teaspoons fish sauce

This is my favorite summer muchim. It has a lighter, sweeter flavor than the traditional cabbage kimchi that is always part of the Korean table for most of the year. The cucumbers are brined and seasoned with vinegar, salt, and sugar. I like to use English (hothouse) cucumbers because they have a nice firm texture and are deliciously sweet. You can also use smaller Korean, Persian, Japanese, or Kirby cucumbers. I usually prepare this muchim the day before I serve it, letting the flavors mellow overnight, but I've tasted it just after 3 hours and it was good enough for most.

Serve this pickle with the Beef Brisket Bulgogi Sliders (page 142) or on any burger. They are also great as a ban-chan with Yangnyeom Galbi (Soy-Marinated BBQ Beef Short Ribs, page 133) or the Fried Chicken Wings with Two Sauces (page 296). Or anytime you feel like a pickle with a Korean kick.

Put the cucumbers in a bowl, add the salt, and mix well. Transfer to a colander set in a bowl and let the cucumbers sit at room temperature for 20 minutes to drain.

Rinse all of the salt off the cucumbers with cold water, strain well, and put them in a large bowl. Add the rice vinegar, gochugaru, sugar, garlic, and anchovy or fish sauce and mix well to combine. Transfer the cucumbers to a covered nonreactive container and refrigerate. The pickles can be eaten as soon as 3 hours after they're made, but they taste better after 12 hours. The cucumbers will be slightly crisp, sweet, spicy, and sour. (They can be stored in the refrigerator for 2 to 3 days, as long as they remain firm and crunchy.)

When ready to serve, mix all the ingredients well again, because the garlic and gochugaru will have settled at the bottom.

SPICY DEHYDRATED KOREAN RADISHES
무 말랭이 무침 (Mu Mallengi Muchim)

Makes 4 cups

One 3-ounce package dehydrated Korean
 radishes (mu)

1 cup Dashi (page 189) or water, plus more if
 needed

1 cup gochugaru (Korean red chili flakes)

2 tablespoons sugar

1 tablespoon medium-coarse salt, preferably
 from the Andes or Himalayas

1½ teaspoons Korean anchovy sauce or
 1 tablespoon fish sauce

4 garlic cloves, minced

1 bunch scallions, cut into 1-inch batons

At Danji, we serve this as a side for our pork belly bossam (page 145), a braised dish. The spiciness and strong, earthy aroma of the radishes balance out the rich meat very well. This banchan is also perfect for adding a bold, spicy accent to dishes such as Tteok Guk (Rice Cake Soup, page 193) and Galbi Tang (Beef Short Rib Soup, page 196).

Although mu, Korean radish, is a winter vegetable, dehydrated mu is often used for a muchim in the summer. Koreans used to dry any leftover mu after making radish kimchi in the fall to ensure that they would have delicious dried radishes until the next autumn. Nowadays most Koreans buy the dried Korean radishes because it takes a bright sun, strong wind, and a lot of time and patience to dry them at home. Dried radishes can be found in Korean markets and online. They should be light tan in color—avoid darker specimens. The dehydration intensifies the flavor of the watery radishes and makes for a spicy, bold, funky taste. Keep an eye on the radishes during the rehydration process, because you don't want to rehydrate them all the way, just enough so that they are easy to chew but still retain a little bite (think of "al dente").

Wash the dehydrated radishes well in cold water. Drain in a colander, then transfer to a bowl and add the 1 cup dashi or water, gochugaru, sugar, salt, anchovy or fish sauce, garlic, and scallions. Mix well. Cover with plastic wrap and leave the radishes at room temperature for 2 hours, stirring every 15 minutes so they rehydrate evenly.

(recipe continues)

When all the liquid has been absorbed by the radishes, check the texture by biting into one. If it is still dry in the middle or difficult to chew, add another ½ cup of dashi or water, mix well, and let stand, stirring occasionally, until the desired texture is achieved. The radishes should be crunchy but not hard to chew, and the marinade should be pasty.

Transfer the radishes to a covered nonreactive container and refrigerate for 6 hours before serving. The radishes will still be a bit crunchy and very slightly chewy. They can be kept in the refrigerator for up to 4 weeks.

SPICY GARLIC CHIVES
부추 무침 (Buchu Muchim)

Makes 4 to 6 cups

2 bunches garlic chives (you should be able to
wrap your thumb and middle finger around
the fattest part of the bunch) or 3 bunches
scallions, ramps, or 2 pounds baby bok choy

Marinade
¼ cup gochugaru (Korean red chili flakes)
2 tablespoons water
2 tablespoons salted shrimp, pureed in a
blender
2 tablespoons sugar
¼ cup soy sauce
2 tablespoons rice vinegar
4 garlic cloves, minced
2 tablespoons toasted sesame oil
1 tablespoon toasted sesame seeds

Garlic chives are called *buchu* in Korean. They are long, grassy-looking plants that are thinner than scallions but thicker and longer than regular chives. Buchu have an intensely garlicky profile and an amazingly fresh, pungent, savory flavor. The garlic chives found in the US are a bit thicker than buchu but work just as well in this recipe. You can also substitute scallions, ramps, or baby bok choy for the garlic chives for different yet equally delicious results. This muchim is traditionally paired with fattier Korean dishes such as Galbi Jjim (Braised Beef Short Ribs, page 135) and Yangnyeom Galbi (Soy-Marinated BBQ Beef Short Ribs, page 133). But my favorite approach is simply sautéing the thinly sliced fattier end of a beef brisket and serving this muchim alongside it.

Buchu muchim is a dish you should serve right away because the garlic chives wilt easily. Most often, after I wash and dry the garlic chives, I reserve the amount I want to use for that meal and then wrap the rest in a paper towel and store it in a sealed container in the refrigerator, where they will keep well for 3 to 4 days. I dress the garlic chives with the premade marinade just before serving. If you are using scallions, ramps, or baby bok choy they will hold up for a few days longer, so you can go ahead and make a whole batch.

If using garlic chives, wash them and cut into 2-inch batons. If using scallions or ramps, trim and cut into 1-inch batons. Or, if using baby bok choy, remove any roots, trim the bottoms, and separate the leaves. Using a salad spinner, dry the vegetables and then pat thoroughly dry with paper towels. Put the garlic chives or other greens in a large ceramic or glass bowl and set aside while you make the marinade.

(recipe continues)

Combine the gochugaru, water, salted shrimp, sugar, soy sauce, rice vinegar, garlic, sesame oil, and seeds in a bowl and mix well. (The marinade will keep in a covered container in the refrigerator for up to 4 weeks.)

To serve, dress the garlic chives (or other greens) with the marinade. Serve immediately.

SPICY LETTUCE SALAD
겉저리 (Geot-jeori)

Serves 4

1 head green leaf lettuce
1 head red leaf lettuce
1 head romaine lettuce
1 medium red onion
1 bunch chives, cut into 2-inch batons

Dressing
¼ cup gochugaru (Korean red chili flakes)
¼ cup water
1 tablespoon Korean anchovy sauce or 2
  tablespoons fish sauce
¼ cup rice vinegar
1 tablespoon sugar
4 garlic cloves, minced

Toasted sesame oil for serving
Toasted sesame seeds for garnish

Geot-jeori works as a nice light, spicy complement to a rich meat dish in the hot summer months, such as Korean-style barbecue or even just grilled steaks or chops. My wife always eats this with fried chicken. Traditionally this was made with summer cabbage, but I prefer to use lettuce, because it is more delicate and more refreshing, with a sweeter flavor and a crisp, tender texture. I have also added chives and red onion. Feel free to add your favorite spring/summer vegetables, such as blanched green beans, asparagus, or even corn.

Wash the lettuce and drain well. Cut off the stems of the red and green leaf lettuce. Trim off the core of the romaine lettuce. Chop the lettuce into bite-sized pieces as you would for a Caesar salad and set aside in a colander so it can continue to drain.

Slice the onion very thin, rinse with cold water to remove some of the sharp bite, and dry with paper towels. Transfer the lettuce to a large bowl, add the onion and chives, and gently toss together. (You can prepare the vegetables ahead and refrigerate until ready to serve.)

To make the dressing, combine the gochugaru, water, anchovy or fish sauce, rice vinegar, sugar, and garlic in a small bowl and mix well. (If you are making a smaller salad, the extra dressing will keep for a couple of weeks in a covered container in the refrigerator.)

Transfer half the greens to a large bowl and add half the dressing, tossing gently and mixing well. Transfer to a large plate. Repeat with the remaining greens and dressing and add to the plate. Drizzle with toasted sesame oil, sprinkle with sesame seeds, and serve immediately, as the greens will lose their texture very quickly.

SPICY BRUSSELS SPROUTS
싹양배추 무침 (Ssak Yang Bechu Muchim)

Makes about 4 cups

1 pound Brussels sprouts
6 tablespoons kosher salt

Marinade
1 cup gochugaru (Korean red chili flakes)
1 cup Dashi (page 189) or water
4 garlic cloves, minced
2 tablespoons Korean anchovy sauce or ¼ cup
    fish sauce
2 tablespoons sugar
2 tablespoons apple cider vinegar or rice
    vinegar

2 tablespoons toasted sesame oil
1 tablespoon toasted sesame seeds

This recipe is an example of fusion cuisine at its best, combining seasonal local produce with classic Korean flavors. The result is an East-meets-West dish that will have you craving seconds. Brussels sprouts are not indigenous to Korea, but their flavor pairs wonderfully with this traditional dressing. The pungent, earthy Brussels sprouts are transformed into a bright, spicy, acidic dish that is refreshing to the palate. The soft but still chewy Brussels sprout leaves give the muchim a unique texture. This particular muchim can sit in the fridge for a few days, as it only gets better as the flavors harmonize. We serve this at both of my restaurants.

To prepare the Brussels sprouts, trim the bottoms and gradually peel off the leaves; you may need to continue to trim the bottoms as you go to release the leaves.

Pour 1 gallon water into a stockpot or other large pot, add the salt, and bring to boil over high heat. Meanwhile, prepare an ice bath. Once the water reaches a hard boil, add the Brussels sprout leaves and blanch for 1 minute, or until they turn bright green. Transfer to the ice bath to cool, about 30 seconds. Drain and pat dry with a kitchen towel.

To make the marinade, put the gochugaru, dashi, garlic, anchovy or fish sauce, sugar, and vinegar in a bowl and mix well. Add the Brussels sprouts and mix thoroughly to coat them with the marinade, then transfer to a covered container and refrigerate for 6 hours before serving. The leaves will turn a slightly darker green in the marinade but should still have a firm texture; they will retain their flavor and be infused with the tangy seasoning. (This will keep in the refrigerator for 2 to 3 days, until the Brussels sprout leaves start turning dark brown.)

To serve, put the sprouts in a serving bowl, drizzle with the sesame oil, and sprinkle the sesame seeds on top.

STEAMED EGGPLANT
가지 무침 (Gaji Muchim)

Serves 4

4 Japanese or Korean eggplants (about 1
  pound)
2 red Korean chili peppers or other long hot
  chilies, thinly sliced
½ bunch scallions, thinly sliced
3 medium garlic cloves, minced
1¼ cup soy sauce
1 teaspoon salt
2 teaspoons toasted sesame oil
1 tablespoon rice vinegar
1 teaspoon toasted sesame seeds

I love the soft, delicate texture of eggplants and their sweet, earthy flavor. The texture becomes even more velvety when they are steamed. Here it contrasts beautifully with the sharp spice of the seasoning. It is important to use small Korean or Japanese eggplants, available in Korean and Asian markets and some supermarkets, instead of a larger American variety, because their skins are very thin and delicate, and not at all bitter. Korean/Japanese eggplants are slim and bright purple and they range from 3 to 8 inches in length.

Cut the eggplants lengthwise in half and put them in a large bowl of cold water. Let them soak for 30 minutes; this draws the bitterness out of the eggplant.

Meanwhile, set up a stovetop steamer and bring the water to a simmer over medium heat.

Drain the eggplant, pat dry, and score the skins in a crosshatch pattern, being careful not to cut too deeply into the flesh. Steam the eggplant until the flesh is completely soft, 10 to 15 minutes. You can check their texture with your finger or a spoon. Remove from the steamer, transfer to a rack set over a sheet pan, and let them air-dry for about 10 minutes, until they are just cool enough to handle comfortably.

Put the chili peppers, scallions, garlic, soy sauce, salt, sesame oil, and rice vinegar in a large bowl and stir gently to blend. Cut the eggplant lengthwise into long strips, approximately 2½ inches by ½ inch and add them to the bowl, tossing gently to coat with the sauce. Sprinkle the sesame seeds on top. Serve warm or at room temperature. You can also refrigerate this to serve cold within the next few days. However, don't store it for too long, or the eggplant will start to become bitter with a sharp tongue-prickling effect.

SPICY BEAN SPROUTS
콩나물 (Kong Namul)

Makes 4 cups

1½ gallons water

½ cup salt, or as needed

1½ pounds bean sprouts

1 tablespoon gochugaru (Korean red chili flakes)

1 tablespoon toasted sesame oil

1 garlic clove, minced

Note: The marinated bean sprouts will keep for 2 to 3 days in the refrigerator. Be aware, though: They can spoil very easily during hot humid months. Make sure you always smell and taste them before serving. A spoiled bean sprout will be gray in color and have absolutely no flavor.

This is a classic banchan, found on most Korean family tables and at restaurants alike. In Korea, bean sprouts are said to counteract some of the negative effects of drinking alcohol and are considered a hangover cure. This recipe is best made with very fresh bean sprouts. You can use either soy bean sprouts or mung bean sprouts. I prefer mung bean sprouts, with their slightly smaller heads; they have a softer texture than soybean sprouts. But I like soy bean sprouts, too, because the flavor is refreshing and I enjoy the contrast between the soft beans and the crunchy sprout stems. Soybean sprouts have larger yellow heads and more flavor but are a little more fibrous.

Put the water and salt in a large stockpot set over high heat and bring to a boil.

Meanwhile, wash the bean sprouts in cold water and drain them in a colander. Trim off any brown ends and discard.

Drop the bean sprouts into the boiling salted water and blanch for 1 minute. Using a spider or slotted spoon, transfer them to a clean colander to drain. Then spread them out on a large sheet pan lined with paper towels and let air-dry until they are cool, 5 to 10 minutes.

Transfer the bean sprouts to a large nonreactive bowl. Add the gochugaru, sesame oil, and garlic and mix well. Taste for seasoning, and, if you'd like, add a pinch of salt for a more aggressive flavor. Transfer the sprouts to a covered container and refrigerate for at least 4 hours to chill and marinate before serving.

Serve the marinated sprouts cold with hot steamed rice.

SPINACH WITH SESAME
시금치 나물 (Sigeumchi Namul)

Makes 2 cups

2 bunches spinach (1 pound)
1 tablespoon soy sauce
1 teaspoon sugar
2 tablespoons toasted sesame oil
5 garlic cloves, minced
1 teaspoon toasted sesame seeds

Note: Fresh spinach can be found at your local farmers' market almost all year round, except for the extremely cold winter months. Packaged prewashed spinach or baby spinach will be tasteless and should be avoided.

This recipe can also be made with watercress instead of spinach to change things up. Watercress has a bit of a spicy kick, which will give the banchan a very different flavor profile.

Here nutty sesame oil gives fresh spinach leaves a sweet, earthy flavor. This banchan tastes nothing like the spinach that is usually served in the United States. Most recipes cover up the flavor of the vegetable with a sauce, as in creamed spinach, or present raw spinach in a salad with a strong vinaigrette, where the flavor of the vegetable is muted. This dish is designed to highlight the true flavor of the greens.

Fill a large stockpot three-quarters full with water and set over high heat. While the water is heating, remove the stems from the spinach leaves. Wash the spinach thoroughly to remove any dirt or sand: The best way is to briefly soak the spinach in a large bowl of cold water and then lift the leaves out of the water with your hands, leaving any dirt in the bottom of the bowl. Rinse the spinach and repeat at least 3 times, until the water at the bottom of the bowl is clear.

Prepare an ice bath in a large bowl. When the pot of water is at a rolling boil, add half the spinach and immerse it completely using a spider or large slotted spoon. Blanch the spinach for 30 seconds, then immediately transfer it to the ice bath. Repeat with the rest of the spinach.

Once the spinach is cold, use your hands to gather some of the spinach into a ball and squeeze out as much water out as you can, then put it in a bowl. Repeat until you have squeezed out all of the spinach. Use your fingers to gently separate the leaves, so as to not rip them. Add the soy sauce, sugar, sesame oil, garlic, and seeds and mix well. Transfer the mixture to a lidded container and refrigerate for at least 2 hours. (Just like bean sprouts, spinach tends to spoil fast. It should be good for 2 or 3 days in the fridge, but check before you serve it. If it does not give off a wonderfully nutty sesame oil aroma, it should be discarded.) Serve the spinach cold.

MEAT

In this chapter, more than any other, I highlight various cooking techniques. These include quick marinades, two-day marinades, braising, panfrying, and grilling. The recipes illustrate the diverse ways in which Koreans enjoy meat. At barbecue restaurants, Koreans love to grill meat tableside and wrap it inside a fresh lettuce leaf. They add jang, garlic, kimchi, muchim, and/or another banchan to the meat before wrapping it and eating everything together. These restaurants are everywhere in Korea, as we grill pork, beef, chicken, seafood, vegetables—you name it. The easy accessibility of these (mostly) affordable restaurants means that at home, meat is generally braised or panfried. It's so much easier to visit your local barbecue restaurant to grill your meat over a charcoal flame tableside than it is to do it at home.

These recipes also showcase my best-selling dishes at Danji and Hanjan. From Yangnyeom Galbi (Soy-Marinated BBQ Beef Short Ribs, page 133) to Dak Bokkeum Tang (Spicy Braised Chicken, page 153), they are great examples of how well bold Korean flavors work with meat. They are my favorite dishes to eat whether here or in Korea.

As with other ingredients, I am very careful when sourcing meat for my restaurants or for my home. As mentioned elsewhere, Koreans have always believed that food and medicine have the same roots and that your health is a reflection of what you eat. Hence, as a Korean chef, I choose to serve only naturally raised meat that comes from animals that have not been injected with antibiotics and growth hormones. It is all part of my conscious effort to serve and eat foods that have not been contaminated by drugs, pesticides, and other chemicals. It is a decision I've made to take care of my family's and my own health and to shoulder some of the responsibility for my diners as well. Yes, these ingredients can be expensive and hard to source, but they are worth it. Nothing is more important than eating healthy, natural foods (and drinking lots of water)—it is the best form of preventive medicine.

Tabletop grilling of beef brisket
and small intestine at Pyongyang
Jip in Samgakji, Seoul.

Soy-Marinated BBQ Beef Short Ribs with lettuce ssam (wrap), scallions, and Ssamjang (page 57).

SOY-MARINATED BBQ BEEF SHORT RIBS

양념갈비 (Yangnyeom Galbi)

Serves 6 to 8

Marinade

1 cup sake

2 Korean or Asian pears, peeled, cored, and cut
   into cubes

1 head garlic, separated into cloves and peeled

A 1-ounce piece ginger, peeled and coarsely
   chopped

¾ cup soy sauce

½ cup mirin

¾ cup sugar

1 teaspoon coarsely ground black pepper

½ cup Dashi (page 189) or water

5 pounds bone-in flanken-style short ribs, ⅓ to
   ½ inch thick

2 heads garlic, separated into cloves and peeled

2 to 4 tablespoons grape seed or canola oil, or
   as needed, if pan searing the meat

1 bunch scallions, thinly sliced

½ cup Scallion Dressing (page 59)

2 heads iceberg lettuce, cored and separated
   into leaves

Ssamjang (page 57)

This short rib dish is what most Americans equate with Korean barbecue. Traditional Korean barbecue uses thinly sliced short ribs for their rich flavor and tender texture. You can substitute 3 pounds of rib-eye for a more beefy flavor, or beef tenderloin for a more tender texture, and to cut back on the fat. The marinade gives the beef a sweet, salty, complex flavor and the acid in the alcohol and the pear breaks down the muscle fibers to tenderize the meat. For that reason, it's important to marinate the meat overnight or, even better, for 48 hours.

This dish works best cooked on a grill, where the marinated meat can absorb the flavors from an open fire or coals. It will be even more savory if you add wood chips to the grill to give the meat a pronounced smoky flavor. If you don't have access to a grill, I've provided an alternative method of pan searing, but I strongly recommend that you grill the meat.

Korean barbecued beef can be served many ways. Most Koreans love to eat it wrapped in lettuce with slices of fresh or grilled garlic, scallions, and Ssamjang (page 57). A tangy kimchi or a muchim such as Geot-jeori (Spicy Lettuce Salad, page 121) or Buchu Muchim (Spicy Garlic Chives, page 119) will liven things up and balance the bold flavors of the marinated beef.

To make the marinade, put the sake, pears, garlic, ginger, soy sauce, mirin, sugar, black pepper, and dashi in a food processor or blender and process for 30 seconds, or until smooth. Set aside.

(recipe continues)

Score the short ribs lightly in a crosshatch pattern on both sides with a sharp knife. Put the beef slices in a large bowl and add the marinade, turning gently to thoroughly coat the meat. Cover and refrigerate overnight.

If grilling the meat, prepare a hot fire in a charcoal grill or preheat a gas grill, preferably with a few wood chips added for flavor. Since the slices of beef are so thin, the meat will cook fairly quickly. Grill the meat just like a hamburger patty, flipping when charred on the first side, about 2 minutes, and then cooking until the second sides are equally charred, another 2 to 3 minutes. Transfer to a serving platter(s). After you've cooked the meat, set a heatproof mesh rack on the grill and cook the garlic cloves, turning as necessary, for 3 to 4 minutes, until golden brown on all sides. Transfer to a small serving bowl.

For indoor cooking, heat a large skillet over medium-high heat until hot. Add 1 tablespoon of the oil and place the beef in the pan; make sure not to overcrowd the pan. (You will have to cook the meat in batches, adding more oil as needed; periodically wipe out the pan.) When the strips are evenly browned on the first side, about 2 minutes, flip and sear the other side, another 2 minutes or so. (Because the marinade contains sugar, you will need to be careful not to burn it.) Remove the meat from the pan and transfer to a platter. After you've cooked all the meat, reheat the skillet, add the remaining tablespoon of oil, and sauté the garlic cloves, stirring constantly, for 3 to 4 minutes, until they are golden brown on all sides. Transfer to a small serving bowl.

Toss the scallions with the dressing and put them in another small serving bowl.

Serve the beef family-style, with a platter of the iceberg lettuce leaves, the dressed scallions and the grilled garlic, and a bowl of the ssamjang.

BRAISED BEEF SHORT RIBS
갈비찜 (Galbi Jjim)

Serves 6 to 8

2 tablespoons grape seed or canola oil

12 beef short ribs cut into 2- to 2½-inch segments (about 5 pounds total)

Salt and freshly ground black pepper

2 onions, cut into ½-inch dice

2 medium carrots, peeled and cut into ½-inch dice, plus 1 pound carrots, peeled and cut into bite-sized pieces

2 medium celery stalks, cut into ½-inch dice

2 cups sake

1 cup mirin

1 cup soy sauce

2 Korean or Asian pears, peeled, cored, diced, and pureed in a food processor

3 tablespoons sugar

10 garlic cloves, minced (or pureed in a small food processor)

A 1-ounce piece ginger, peeled and minced (or pureed in a small food processor)

About 4 cups Dashi (page 189)

1 pound pearl onions, peeled

1 pound small Yukon Gold potatoes, quartered

Note: Any leftovers can be kept in the fridge and reheated the next day. Add a cup of dashi or water to the braise when you reheat it, and warm very gently over low heat, covered, on the stovetop or in a 325°F oven. The texture of the meat will firm up if you shock it with high heat while it is still cold.

This dish marries the flavors of my heritage with my experience as a French-trained chef in a way that is very special to me. I borrowed the technique for a classic French red wine braise from restaurant Daniel and added the flavors of a traditional Korean galbi jjim, braised short ribs. At Daniel, I learned that the technique of braising isn't difficult, but it is exact, especially when it comes to temperature and timing. Short ribs should always be cooked at 325°F for 2 to 2½ hours for the best texture and flavor. The perfect braise allows the meat to absorb all the flavors of the braising liquid while the muscle fibers soften to tender wisps but the beef retains some fat and all of its flavor. If you don't cook the ribs long enough or use too low a temperature, you'll end up with tough, flavorless meat, because the tough collagen fibers won't have been cooked away and the braising liquid won't have been able to sufficiently penetrate the meat. If you cook the ribs for too long or at too high a temperature, all of the fat will melt into the braising liquid and you'll end up with dry, chewy meat.

Even today, most home kitchens in Korea do not have ovens. Koreans braise on the stovetop or, more traditionally, over a wood fire, so the specific temperatures and times have never been consistent. It took a skilled mother with lots of experience to cook a delicious galbi jjim. Here in the States, most of us have ovens at home, so this dish is easy to master.

There is something very warming about the flavor and texture of braised short ribs in any cuisine. To me, Korean galbi jjim is the most special braise of them all. The strong soy sauce is balanced by the many different aromatic vegetables that give the meat an incredible depth and complexity of flavor, while the soft texture of the slow-cooked

(recipe continues)

beef makes you feel safe and comfortable. These flavors are further intensified when you serve the braise with a spicy kimchi and/or muchim such as Baechu Kimchi (Napa Cabbage Kimchi, page 96), Chongak or Kkak Dugi Kimchi (Korean Radish Kimchi, page 105), and/or Oee Muchim (Marinated Spicy Cucumbers, page 114). Serve with hot rice, of course.

Of all the recipes in this book, this is my favorite to share, teach, and cook. If you were only to make one dish from this book, I would recommend it be this one. Galbi jjim is so delicious you could serve it three nights in a row for dinner and no one would complain. Just be sure to make enough of it.

Preheat the oven to 325°F.

Set a large Dutch oven over high heat and add the oil. Season the ribs all over with salt and pepper. Add 5 or 6 of the ribs to the pot in one layer, being careful not to crowd the pot, and sear on all sides until deep brown, 5 to 8 minutes. Remove the ribs and set aside on a large plate or sheet pan. Repeat with the remaining ribs.

Add the diced onions, carrots, and celery to the pot and cook for about 3 minutes, stirring, until aromatic. Add the sake and mirin. Wait until the liquid is at a full boil, then carefully light it with a lighter or a long match and let the flames die out, 1 to 2 minutes. (If you would rather not light the sake, let the liquid boil for 3 minutes to burn off the alcohol.) Once the alcohol has cooked off, add the ribs, soy sauce, pear puree, sugar, garlic, and ginger. Add enough dashi so the ribs are fully immersed in liquid, bring the mixture to a simmer, and cover the pot.

Transfer the pot to the oven and cook the ribs for 1 hour, then skim the excess fat from the top layer of the braising liquid and put the pot back in the oven. After another hour, check the meat; if it is not really tender, braise for another 20 to 30 minutes or so.

(recipe continues)

Remove the meat from the oven and let it rest in the cooking liquid, covered, at room temperature, for at least 3 hours, or overnight in the refrigerator, to let the beef continue to absorb the braising flavors. Remove any fat on the surface of the braising liquid before reheating.

Set the Dutch oven over low heat and heat just until the braising mixture is liquefied. Remove the short ribs from the Dutch oven and transfer to a platter or sheet pan. Strain the liquid and discard the solids. Pour the liquid back into the Dutch oven, set over high heat, and bring to a boil. Add the pearl onions, the remaining carrots, and the potatoes and cook for 10 to 15 minutes, until the vegetables are tender and the braising liquid is thick enough to coat them with a light glaze. Reduce the heat to low, add the short ribs, cover, and cook for 10 minutes, or until the beef is warmed through. Serve with rice and banchan on the side.

BEEF TARTARE WITH SOY AND KOREAN PEAR
육회 (Yukhwe)

Serves 4

Marinade

1 Korean or Asian pear, peeled, cored, and cut into rough dice

½ cup soy sauce

1 tablespoon dark brown sugar

2 garlic cloves

Tartare

2 tablespoons unsalted butter

2½ ounces (about ½ cup) pine nuts

1 garlic clove, lightly crushed and peeled

1 pound beef tenderloin, preferably prime

1 teaspoon salt

1 teaspoon freshly ground black pepper

3 medium shallots, cut into fine dice, rinsed, and dried

2 medium jalapeños, cut into fine dice

½ bunch chives, finely sliced

¼ cup toasted sesame oil

To Serve

About 1 tablespoon Chojang (page 58)

4 teaspoons toasted sesame seeds

2 Korean or Asian pears, peeled, cored, and cut into matchsticks

4 quail eggs

We Koreans have our own version of French steak tartare. Unlike the French classic, though, which uses capers, olive oil, and sometimes mayo and mustard, yukhwe features pear puree, soy sauce, garlic, and sesame oil. The result is a tartare with a sweet, nutty flavor and hints of bright fruit and aromatic garlic that balance the richness of the beef.

It is very important to get high-quality meat since you will be serving it raw. I like to use tenderloin because of its texture. If you have a butcher you trust, ask for his or her recommendation for other suitable cuts, such as sirloin or top round.

Traditional Korean steak tartare recipes do not contain any shallots or jalapeños. Since beef used to be so valuable and rare, cooks didn't want to distract from its flavor in any way. However, I like how shallots and jalapeños give the tartare some crunch and add a lighter, spicier dimension to the dish. I serve a quail yolk in the center of the tartare that each diner can mix in at the table to give it a rich, creamy layer of fat, which adds to the overall flavor.

Yukhwe is traditionally served as an appetizer along with banchan before the entrées. We also serve it on top of bibimbap (see Yukhwe Bibimbap, page 222), a combination that started in Jeonju, a city in Jeolla province in southwestern Korea. The tartare must be served as soon as it is made, or the flavor of the soy sauce will start to overpower the beef and the meat will start to dry out.

(recipe continues)

To make the marinade, put the pear, soy sauce, brown sugar, and garlic in a blender and puree for 10 to 15 seconds, until completely smooth. Transfer to a bowl and set aside.

To make the tartare, put the butter in a small sauté pan set over medium heat. When the butter starts foaming, add the pine nuts and garlic, lower the heat, and cook, moving the pan constantly so the nuts don't burn, until they turn golden, about 5 minutes. Transfer the nuts to a plate lined with paper towels to cool and drain (if you leave the nuts in the pan, they will continue to brown); season them with a pinch of salt while still hot.

Once the nuts are completely cool, discard the garlic and finely chop the pine nuts. Put the nuts in a covered container and reserve at room temperature.

Trim the beef of all outer fat and silver skin. Cut into ¼-inch cubes and put in a medium bowl. Season with the salt and pepper, then add the shallots, jalapeños, and chives. Add about 1 cup of the marinade and the sesame oil and mix gently but thoroughly with a rubber spatula. Taste to make sure the flavors are balanced. If you'd prefer a little more seasoning for the beef, add another few tablespoons of the marinade.

Brush some chojang over the center of four chilled serving plates, using a paintbrush or the back of a spoon. Then scoop out a spoonful of the tartare, form into a round with a slight indentation in the center, and place on one of the plates; repeat with the remaining tartare. Sprinkle with the chopped pine nuts and sesame seeds and scatter the pear matchsticks over the top. Arrange a teaspoon of sesame seeds in a small mound on each plate alongside the beef. Use scissors to cut open the quail eggs, separate out the yolks, and place one yolk in the center of each mound of steak tartare (discard the whites). Serve immediately.

141

BEEF BRISKET BULGOGI SLIDERS
불고기

Makes 12 sliders (serves 4 – or just 2 hungry people)

Bulgogi

2 pounds thinly sliced beef brisket (about ⅛ inch thick; buy it presliced or have your butcher slice the meat)

1 cup soy sauce

½ cup natural apple juice or cider (not from concentrate)

3 tablespoons sake

2 tablespoons mirin

2 tablespoons sugar

1 tablespoon minced garlic

1 tablespoon toasted sesame oil

1 Korean or Asian pear, peeled, cored, finely chopped, and pureed in a food processor

1 small carrot, peeled and cut into matchsticks

1 medium onion, cut into matchsticks

To Serve

12 slider buns

Unsalted butter

1 cup Spicy Mayo (page 61)

1 bunch scallions, thinly sliced on the bias

¼ cup Scallion Dressing (page 59)

Salt

Marinated Spicy Cucumbers (Oee Muchim, page 114) for serving

Bulgogi is a traditional dish of thinly sliced soy-marinated beef. I use brisket in this recipe because it tastes more beefy and is cheaper than the tenderloin and sirloin traditionally used in Korea. Brisket is tougher than these cuts, but marinating overnight helps to tenderize the meat. Traditionally the dish is eaten with lettuce wraps, scallions, and kimchi or a muchim.

I wanted to re-create this traditional experience but make it more approachable, so I serve the bulgogi as sliders. The original Korean components are still there, but I simply replaced the lettuce cups with buttered and toasted brioche buns smeared with spicy mayo, and that worked brilliantly. To this day, this is the best-selling dish at Danji.

To make the bulgogi, put the brisket, soy sauce, apple juice, sake, mirin, sugar, garlic, sesame oil, pear puree, carrots, and onion in a large bowl and mix well. Cover and refrigerate overnight.

The next day, set a large sauté pan over medium-high heat. Once the pan is hot, add the beef, working in batches to avoid overcrowding the pan and leaving any liquid in the bowl. Cook, stirring occasionally and flipping the meat, until the beef is browned, 3 to 5 minutes. Transfer to a platter.

When the beef is cooked, open the slider buns, butter the interiors, and toast them until they are a light golden brown.

Toss the scallions with the dressing and season with salt to taste.

To serve, spread both cut sides of the buns with a healthy smear of spicy mayo and pile the bulgogi generously onto the bottom halves. Top with the dressed scallions and pickled cucumbers. Serve immediately.

SPICY PORK BELLY SLIDERS
제육볶음 (Jeyuk Bokkeum)

Makes 12 sliders (serves 4 – or 2 hungry people)

Marinade
1 medium onion, thinly sliced
1 cup gochujang (Korean red chili paste)
¼ cup soy sauce
¼ cup minced garlic
¼ cup sugar
3 tablespoons sake
2 tablespoons mirin
2 tablespoons toasted sesame oil
2 pounds skinless pork belly, sliced ¼ inch thick (ask the butcher to slice it) and cut into 2-inch squares

To Serve
Unsalted butter
12 slider buns
Mayonnaise
2 English cucumbers, peeled, halved lengthwise, seeded, and sliced into matchsticks

Note: The pork belly must be marinated overnight. The instructions below are for cooking the meat on the stovetop, but you can also grill the pork on an outdoor grill over a high flame. The sugars in the marinade will char and caramelize, giving you a more interesting texture and flavor, but be careful not to burn the pork.

The brisket bulgogi slider (page 142) became so popular at Danji that I decided to make another version. Jeyuk bokkeum is a popular Korean dish made with gochujang (Korean red chili paste) and pork. The fermented chili paste adds a nice kick and a deep, complex flavor. In Korea, jeyuk bokkeum is served as a main dish along with rice and banchan. Because of the gochujang, the meat burns easily when grilled, so it's not often found in tableside barbecue restaurants. Traditionally, thinly sliced pork shoulder is used, but for these sliders, I use pork belly, because it is more flavorful and has a softer texture. And the fat from the belly is easily absorbed into the bun, which adds to the deliciousness!

To make the marinade, put the onion, gochujang, soy sauce, garlic, sugar, sake, mirin and sesame oil in a bowl and mix well to combine. Add the pork and turn to coat the meat. Cover and refrigerate overnight.

The next day, set a large sauté pan over medium heat. Once it's hot, add the pork, working in batches so as not to overcrowd the pan and leaving any liquid in the bowl. Cook, stirring occasionally and flipping the meat, until lightly caramelized and golden brown on both sides, about 10 minutes. (If you overcrowd the pan, the meat will steam instead of sear.) Transfer to a platter.

When the meat is cooked, open the buns, butter the interiors, and toast them until they are a light golden brown.

To serve, spread both cut sides of each bun with a healthy smear of mayo and pile the spicy pork generously on the bottoms of the buns. Top with the sliced cucumbers. Serve immediately.

BRAISED PORK BELLY

보쌈 (Danji's Bossam)

Serves 4

Bossam

3 pounds skinless pork belly

Salt and freshly ground black pepper

5 tablespoons canola oil

2 medium carrots, peeled and cut into 1-inch
  pieces

2 medium onions, cut into ⅛-inch-thick slices

2 cups sake

2 cups mirin

2 cups water

2 cups soy sauce

10 garlic cloves, peeled and minced

A 1-ounce piece ginger, peeled and minced

¾ cup sugar

5 dried shiitake mushrooms

A 10- to 12-inch square of dashima

Cabbage

1 head Napa cabbage

½ cup sugar

½ cup salt

To Serve

1 bunch scallions, thinly sliced, rinsed, and
  dried as directed on page 45

1 cup Scallion Dressing (page 59)

Spicy Dehydrated Korean Radishes (Mu
  Mallengi Muchim, page 115)

I came up with this dish when the First Lady of Korea visited Danji in the spring of 2011. She was promoting her Korean cookbook and asked if I would use one of her recipes as an inspiration to create a dish specifically for her. I chose bossam, a dish traditionally made with boiled unseasoned pork belly wrapped in baek kimchi leaves (see White Napa Cabbage Kimchi, page 101), dipped in salted shrimp, and served with a spicy kimchi. All of these parts are served separately, and you use the cabbage leaves to wrap the components and eat them with your hands.

When I paired the flavorful meat with the traditional white cabbage kimchi, though, I quickly realized that the kimchi overwhelmed the dish. With this in mind, I decided to boil the Napa cabbage for the wraps and make them a neutral ingredient, letting the braised pork belly take center stage. I serve my Mu Mallengi Muchim (Spicy Dehydrated Korean Radishes, page 115), made with fish sauce, alongside the meat as it is strong and complex enough to cut the richness of the pork while giving it the spice it needs. I like this version better than traditional Korean bossam, and I think it works perfectly for both American and Korean palates. The First Lady loved the dish and I still enjoy telling the story when diners at Danji ask about its inspiration.

Preheat the oven to 325°F.

Cut the pork belly into 4 or 5 rectangular pieces so it will fit into a large Dutch oven. Season it generously on all sides with salt and pepper. Set the pot over high heat and add 3 tablespoons of the canola oil. When the oil begins to shimmer and just barely smoke, add the pork. (Sear it in batches if all the pieces will not fit without crowding the pot.) Cook, turning

(recipe continues)

A bossam preparation inspired by the plating at Daniel. We use the cabbage as a wrap for the 3 ingredients. (Left to right): Spicy Dehydrated Korean Radishes, page 115 (top); thin scallions with Scallion Dressing, page 59 (bottom); Braised Pork Belly, page 145; braised cabbage.

once, for 3 to 5 minutes on each side, until the pork is a deep golden brown. Transfer to a large plate or platter and set aside.

Lower the heat to medium-high, add the carrots and onions to the pot, and cook for 8 to 10 minutes, stirring, until a deep golden brown. Add the sake and mirin, increase the heat to high, and cook for 3 minutes to burn off the alcohol. Reduce the heat to maintain a simmer and let the sake/mirin mixture reduce to about ½ cup, about 10 minutes. Be sure to scrape up all the fond, or browned bits that have caramelized on the bottom of the pot; this will give more flavor to the braise.

Add the water, soy sauce, garlic, ginger, sugar, shiitakes, dashima, and pork belly to the pot. Make sure the meat is fully submerged in the liquid; if necessary, lay a round of parchment over the meat and place a plate on top of it to keep it submerged. (Or use a drop lid if you have one.) Cover the pot with a lid and bring the liquid to a boil.

Transfer the pot to the oven and braise for 1½ hours, or until the meaty part of the pork belly is tender. Remove from the oven and let the pork belly rest in its liquid.

Meanwhile, quarter the cabbage. Pour a gallon of water into a stockpot or other large pot set over high heat and bring to a boil. Add the sugar and salt and stir until they dissolve. Add the cabbage and cook for 10 minutes, until the thick center ribs of the leaves bend easily. Remove the cabbage from the pot, drain, pat dry, and let cool slightly.

Remove the core from each cabbage quarter and separate the leaves. Cut the leaves into pieces approximately 2 x 4 inches to use to wrap the meat. Arrange the cabbage on a platter and set aside.

Transfer the meat to a large heatproof container. Strain the braising liquid over the pork belly, cover, and keep the container warm over low heat or on low in the oven until you're ready to panfry the meat. (Or the pork can be braised ahead and kept covered in the refrigerator, in its liquid, for up to 3 days.)

(recipe continues)

When ready to serve, reheat the pork, if necessary: Transfer the meat and liquid to a large pot set over medium heat, bring to a bare simmer, and simmer for 15 minutes to ensure that all of the meat is hot. Remove the pork, let it drain briefly in a colander, and pat dry; discard the braising liquid.

Set a large skillet over medium heat, add the remaining 2 tablespoons of canola oil, and heat until hot. Add the pork belly and sear the pieces for about 15 seconds on each side to caramelize the soy and sugar from the braising liquid and give the pork belly a more concentrated flavor.

Slice the pork belly into bite-sized pieces and serve family-style on a large plate, with the platter of cabbage alongside. Serve with the mu mallengi muchim, sliced scallions, and the scallion dressing in a small bowl on the side. To eat, take a piece of cabbage and put some meat in the center. Finish with any or all of the toppings, wrap up the cabbage leaf into a packet, and enjoy.

HANJAN CHICKEN SKEWERS
닭 꼬치

Serves 6 to 8

1 whole chicken (3 to 4 pounds), preferably butchered the day of or purchased from a trusted farm

Marinade
¼ cup soy sauce
¼ cup sake
1 teaspoon minced garlic
½ teaspoon minced ginger

Salt and freshly ground black pepper
Olive oil for brushing the skewers

Special Equipment
6-inch bamboo skewers, soaked in water for 30 minutes
2 to 4 fireproof bricks from the hardware store

Chicken in Korea is amazingly fresh. The best chickens are found at street markets, where they have either been recently butchered or are butchered right in front of you. The chickens are never refrigerated; you cook and eat them the same day you purchase them. It's a completely different experience from eating chicken that has been frozen or refrigerated for days. The chilling process toughens the muscle fibers and mutes the natural flavor of the meat. A fresh chicken has a stronger flavor and a silkier, more tender texture.

At Hanjan, not a single part of a fresh chicken goes to waste. We skewer and grill the skin, hearts, gizzards, and wings. We bread and fry the thighs and legs. We poach the breasts. We roast all of the bones, head, and feet and put them in our ramyeon broth the next morning. It feels wonderful to be able to use every inch of a nutritious chicken that has sacrificed its life for our table.

Thoroughly rinse the bird, inside and out, and pat it dry with paper towels. Remove any innards (reserve the neck for stock or another use, or discard) and reserve in a covered container in the refrigerator. Lay the bird back side up on a cutting board. Gently lift up one of the legs and press your thumbs into the thigh joint, where it attaches to the back, applying steady pressure, until the joint comes out of the socket. Using a small sharp knife, cut through the joint, separating the leg from the body. Repeat with the second leg. Carefully pull the skin off the legs and set aside on a plate. Cut through the joint between the thighs and drumsticks. Turn each thigh over and cut down the backside to the bone, then run your knife along the bone to separate it from the meat. Put the bones in a small bowl and reserve the thigh meat. Run your knife around the bottom circumference of each drumstick to cut through the sinews that hold the

(recipe continues)

meat to the bone. Cut the meat off the bone and reserve with the thigh meat; add the bones to the bowl.

Turn the chicken over. Gently lift one of the wings and press your thumb into the joint where the drummette is attached to the breast, applying steady pressure until the joint moves out of the socket. Cut the wing from the breast at that joint. Repeat with the other wing. Pull the skin off the breast and add it to the rest of the skin. Separate the wing flats and tips from the drummettes (leave the skin on) by cutting through the joint that attaches them to each other, then separate the wing tips from the flats and add them to the bowl of bones. Reserve the wing flats and drummettes in the refrigerator.

Turn the chicken so the neck is toward you. Feel around the area between the two breasts to find the wishbone, then use your knife to trace around the perimeter of the bone and separate it from the breasts. Set it aside with the wing tips and bones. Run your knife down the center of the breast meat, separating the two halves, and then run it down along one side of the breastbone, separating the meat from bone—you should be able to trace all the way down and around the rib cage so you can separate the whole breast half, including the tender, in one piece. Repeat with the other breast half. Add the bones to the other bones and refrigerate or freeze to use for stock.

Cut the breast and thigh meat into ¾-inch cubes, keeping the white and dark meat separate. They will have different textures when cooked, so be sure to keep like with like as you load the skewers for consistency. Thread the diced meat onto bamboo skewers, 3 pieces per skewer; leave about ½ inch of the skewer clear at the tip and at least 2 inches at the bottom so you can pick up the skewers to eat them. Line a sheet pan with plastic wrap and lay the skewers out on it. Cover with another sheet of plastic wrap so the meat doesn't dry out.

One by one, spread out the pieces of skin on a cutting board and use the dull side of your knife to scrape off any excess fat clinging to the inside. Cut the skin into strips approximately 4 inches long and 1 inch wide. Thread 3 pieces of skin onto each skewer accordion-style so that the stick runs along the backside and the skin bunches out along the front; again, leave about a ½ inch clear at the tip and at least 2 inches at the bottom. Add to the sheet pan with the other skewers.

To make the marinade, put the soy sauce, sake, garlic, and ginger in a small bowl and mix well to blend. Put the wings in a small resealable bag and pour the marinade over them. Press as much air out of the bag as possible and seal it. Let the wings rest in the marinade until you are ready to cook them, at least 30 minutes but no more than an hour.

At Hanjan, we use a yakitori grill. You can set up a homemade yakitori grill by arranging bricks wrapped in aluminum foil on the grate of a charcoal grill. First prepare a hot fire in the grill, mounding the hot coals higher under the grate than usual so the skewers will be exposed to high heat even though they are not resting directly on the grate. Arrange the bricks parallel to each other, leaving 4 to 5 inches between them. When you lay the skewers on the bricks, the meat will be exposed to the heat and the bricks will protect the ends of the skewers. Season the breast meat skewers with salt and pepper and set them on the bricks. Cook for 1 minute, then use tongs to give the skewers a quarter-turn. Brush them with olive oil and continue to rotate the meat a quarter-turn every minute. After 4 minutes, they will have been exposed to the grill on all sides. The meat should be firm and opaque throughout; if it still feels a little soft in the center, give the skewers another turn to finish them. The meat will be cooked through but not charred. Brush with olive oil, transfer to a platter, and serve immediately. Repeat with dark meat skewers, cooking them for the same amount of time.

If your chicken came with the heart, gizzards, and liver, you can grill these as well. Thinly slice the heart, about ¼ inch thick. You will probably get 3 slices from one heart. Slide the slices of heart onto a skewer, season lightly with salt, and grill very gently on the coolest part of the grill for about 60 to 90 seconds on each side. Be careful not to overcook the heart, or it will become tough and chewy. The meat will just firm up and heat through, gaining a little smoky flavor from the grill. As long as your chicken is as fresh as it should be, don't be afraid to cook this the way we do at Hanjan, which is medium-rare. Serve immediately,

(recipe continues)

or eat it at the grill as a special snack for the chef. If you've never had chicken hearts, you will be surprised by the tender texture and rich, meaty taste.

The gizzard meat is a little bit chewy, so cut it into slightly thinner slices, just under ½ inch. Thread 4 to 6 slices on each skewer. Season lightly with salt and cook slowly on the cooler part of the grill for 4 to 5 minutes, giving the skewers a quarter-turn every 30 seconds or so. You want the gizzards to firm up but still be juicy and cooked to medium to medium-rare. Serve immediately.

Cut the liver into bite-sized pieces. Thread the pieces onto a skewer and season lightly with salt. Grill for 3 to 4 minutes, giving the skewers a quarter-turn every 30 seconds or so, until the livers firm up and are just pink in the center. Serve immediately.

When you're ready to cook the skin, move the bricks to the coolest part of the grill. Season the skin heavily with salt, as most of it will melt away with the fat, and set the skewers on the bricks. Slowly cook the skin, rotating the skewers a quarter-turn every minute, for 20 to 30 minutes, until the fat renders out. Then move them to the hot part of the grill and cook them for 8 to 10 minutes, giving them 8 or so full rotations, a half-turn at a time, until the skin is very crispy on the outside and still slightly chewy within. Season lightly once more and serve immediately. (These skewers are my very favorite part of the chicken. Eating them is almost like biting into freshly made chicken-fat fried potato chips.)

Lay the wings out on the cooler part of your grill to cook slowly. Turn the wings occasionally, about every 2 minutes, so the skin doesn't burn. After 8 to 10 minutes, check to see if the wings are done by either squeezing them to see if they have a firm texture or by cutting into one with a small knife to see if the juices run clear. The drummettes will take 3 to 5 minutes longer to cook than the flats. (The flat part of the wing is tastier than the drummette because the two small bones going through it give the meat more flavor and help keep it moist.) When the drummettes and flats are just about done, move them to the hot part of the grill for the last minute to crisp up the skin. Serve immediately.

SPICY BRAISED CHICKEN
닭볶음탕 (Dak Bokkeum Tang)

Serves 4 to 6

Gochugaru Sauce Base

1 cup grape seed or canola oil

1 onion, cut into fine dice

1 bunch scallions, very thinly sliced

2 cups gochugaru (Korean red chili flakes)

Chicken

¼ cup grape seed or canola oil, plus more if needed

4 whole chicken legs, separated into thighs and drumsticks

Salt and freshly ground black pepper

2 medium onions, cut into 2-inch dice

2 green bell peppers, cored, seeded, and cut into 2-inch pieces

2 cups sake

4 medium Yukon Gold potatoes, peeled and quartered

2 tablespoons minced garlic

1 tablespoon minced ginger

2 cups Dashi (page 189) or low-sodium chicken stock

2 tablespoons gochujang (Korean red chili paste)

¼ cup soy sauce

¼ cup sugar

1 bunch scallions, thinly sliced, rinsed, and dried as directed on page 45

This spicy winter dish is seasoned with gochujang, Korean red chili paste. I like to add more gochugaru, Korean red chili flakes, than traditional recipes generally call for. They give the sauce a looser texture and then the gochujang doesn't dominate the flavor of the chicken as much. This is a rustic one-pot dish that can be enjoyed for days, until it disappears. It actually tastes better on the second day, when the flavors have had more time to penetrate the chicken.

The classic version uses cut-up whole chickens. I prefer to use all dark meat, because it has a deeper flavor that stands up to the spiciness of the dish, and it keeps its juicy texture better than white meat. Yukon Gold potatoes improve the dish tremendously, because they pair so well with the chicken and help soak up all the delicious sauce. There are so many vegetables in this rich dish that no banchan are necessary to accompany it, unless you'd like to serve something to soothe your tongue from all the spice. I would suggest Gyeran Jjim (Steamed Egg Custard with Salted Shrimp, page 89) and Hobak Bokkeum (Sautéed Gray Squash and Onion, page 88) or a sweet banchan such as Myulchi Bokkeum (Sweet Crispy Baby Anchovies, page 79). I like to serve this with a chilled bottle of soju on a cold winter night. Save any leftover sauce to make delicious fried rice the next day for a lighter meal.

To make the sauce base, set a wok or medium pot over low heat and add the oil. When the wok and oil are hot, add the onions and scallions and stir for 1 minute. This will ensure the oil is not too hot—you don't want to burn the gochugaru, or it will get a bitter taste. Add the gochugaru and cook, stirring constantly, for 5 minutes, until the mixture becomes paste-like.

(recipe continues)

Make sure the bottom of the pan does not scorch. Transfer the mixture to a bowl and set aside. (Note—this makes 4 cups of sauce base, but, depending on your taste for heat, you may not use it all.)

To braise the chicken, set a large wide pot over medium-high heat and add the oil. Season the chicken with salt and pepper. Once the oil just begins to smoke, add 3 or 4 pieces of chicken to the pot and sear, turning occasionally, until golden brown on all sides, 2 to 3 minutes per side. Transfer to a platter. Repeat with the remaining chicken, adding a little more oil if necessary.

Once all of the chicken has been browned, add the onions and peppers to the pot and sauté for 3 to 5 minutes, until soft and golden brown. Add the sake, turn the heat up to high, and bring to a boil. Carefully light the sake with a lighter or a long match, then let the flames die out, 2 to 3 minutes. (If you would rather not light the sake, let it boil for 3 minutes to burn off the alcohol.) Add the potatoes, garlic, and ginger and cook for 5 minutes. Add the stock, dashi, gojuchang, 3 cups of the gochugaru sauce base, and the soy sauce. Return the chicken to the pot, nestling it into the sauce, lower the heat to maintain a gentle simmer, cover, and cook for 20 minutes.

Taste the sauce and add some or all of the remaining sauce base if you want it spicier. Continue cooking, uncovered for 20 minutes, or until the chicken is tender. Transfer to a platter, garnish with the scallions, and serve with rice or soju, or both.

SEAFOOD

One of the largest and busiest wholesale seafood markets in Korea is Jukdo Fish Market in Pohang, South Korea.

Korea is a peninsula surrounded by the Yellow Sea to the west, the East Sea to the east, and the East China Sea to the south. It's a small country, approximately the size of Maine, and over eighty percent of its border is coastline. It should come as no surprise, then, that Koreans are passionate about seafood. The sea has fed them well for centuries.

Koreans usually serve fish whole, with the head and bones still attached. With its rich flavor, the skin is considered a prize that one would never think of discarding. Oily fish such as mackerel and hairtail are especially popular because of their intense flavor of the sea. Other favorites are crabs (served raw) and squid, as well as seaweed. The most common way to prepare fish in Korea is simply to salt it and then grill, broil, or panfry it. The result, as in the recipe for Godeung-uh Gui (Grilled Salted Mackerel, page 169), is juicy meat and crisp, delicious skin. (Fish stews are also very popular in Korea; see Soups and Stews, page 185.)

Every city in Korea has a large fish market that specializes in live seafood. Koreans believe seafood should remain alive until just before eating. That is why many seafood restaurants in Korea have water tanks with live fish, crabs, abalone, squid, and more. The chef will grab the live seafood from the tank after you order it and kill it in the kitchen before preparing it. If you're close to a Korean market, check out their seafood section; many in the US sell live seafood from tanks as well.

Korean-Style Sashimi (Hwe)
with lettuce ssam (wrap)
and condiments

KOREAN-STYLE SASHIMI
회 (Hwe)

Serves 4

1 live red snapper (2 to 3 pounds; you can
   have the fishmonger prep the fish for you if
   desired; see below)
1 cup Chojang (page 58)
1 cup soy sauce
1 tablespoon grated fresh or frozen wasabi

Korean sashimi, or hwe (pronounced *hwae*) is very similar to Japanese sashimi when it comes to the techniques of filleting and slicing the fish. The difference is in the type of fish we use. Koreans tend to prefer white or silver fish. Korean hwe is not intended to melt in your mouth as Japanese sushi is. Unlike Japanese sashimi, Korean hwe is eaten as fresh as possible; in fact, it is referred to as *hwal-uh*, which means live fish. The fish is killed on the spot and served within minutes, resulting in a texture that is pleasantly chewy, bringing out an inherently sweet flavor with each bite. Many Koreans believe the best hwe can only be had on a fishing boat, where the fish is filleted as soon as it is line-caught. The texture of this very fresh fish is the reason why Koreans serve Chojang (page 58) as well as soy sauce and wasabi with hwe. The chewiness of hwe needs a condiment that will last longer on your taste buds than soy sauce, which is better suited to Japanese sashimi.

My favorite fish to eat as hwe is red snapper, because of its sweet flesh. Widely available in the US, red snapper is at its most delicious in the summertime. You can find live fish at some Korean supermarkets. The fishmonger will kill it and scale, gut, fillet, and slice it for you to take home. Or, if you're lucky enough to catch the fish yourself, you can enjoy the whole *hwal-uh* experience by following the directions below.

You can also serve the sliced raw fish with red or green leaf lettuce to use as wraps. I like to add Ssamjang (page 57) and shavings of raw local or California garlic.

(recipe continues)

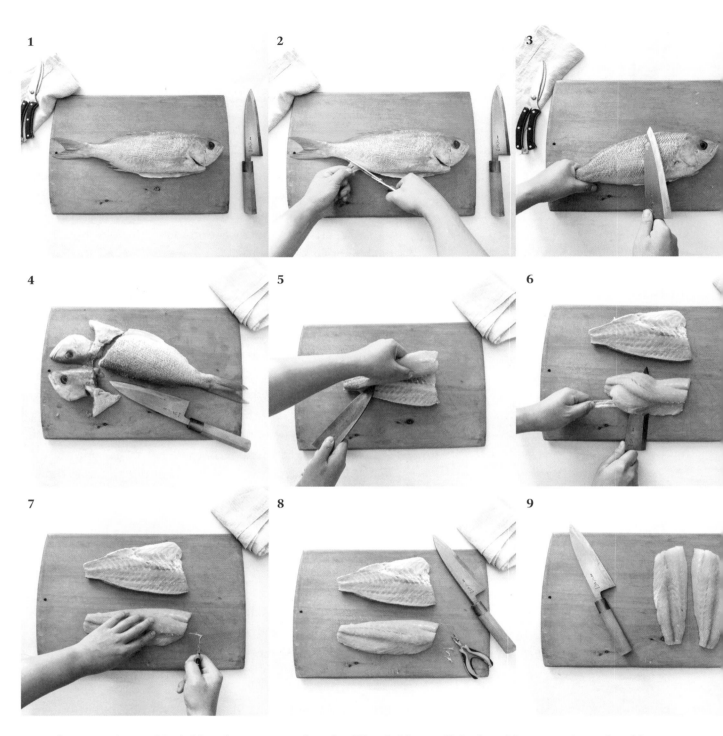

Steps for preparing sashimi: (1) Red snapper ready to be filleted; (2) cut off the fins; (3) remove the scales; (4) remove the head and collar; (5) slice off a filet; (6) remove the skin; (7, 8) remove the pin bones; (9) repeat with the other side.

The key to creating the desirable firm chewy texture of hwe is to shock the fish while killing it. (If you're not ready to kill the fish yourself, ask the fishmonger to do it for you. He can also fillet the fish; just be sure they give you the skeleton and the collar along with the fillets.) I use the back of a heavy knife to hit the head of the live fish in the kitchen sink to kill it. When the fish has stopped moving, leave it in the sink and remove all the fins using a pair of scissors. Scale the fish very well, using a fish scaler or the back of your knife, still in the sink, to catch all the scales. Rinse the fish and pat it dry with paper towels or a lint-free kitchen towel. Set the fish aside on a tray while you wash the sink well, then return the fish to the sink and remove any remaining scales.

Pat the fish dry with a paper towel and transfer to a cutting board. Use a heavy knife to cut off the head and collar behind the spot where you removed the fins on that part of the fish; refrigerate the head and collar to use for the Spicy Fish Bone Stew (Mae-un Tang, page 201). Cut through the stomach until you reach the end of the pouch that holds all the organs. Remove and discard all the innards. Rinse the stomach cavity under cold running water to wash all the blood away. Pat dry with paper towels or a lint-free kitchen towel.

Use the heavy knife to cut the tail off, about an inch from where it starts. Turn the fish around so you can run your knife along the top of the fish, slicing from the head to the tail. Once you reach the bones, run the knife along them as close as possible to remove the fillet on that side; you want to get as much of the meat as possible. When you reach the bottom of the bones, gently slice through the meat so that the boneless belly stays attached to the fillet, and remove the fillet. Repeat on the other side. You should end up with 2 beautiful fillets and a well-scraped skeleton.

Refrigerate the skeleton along with the head and collar to use for the fish stew. There will be pin bones in the middle sections of the fillets that need to be removed with a pair of tweezers. Lay each fillet skin side down on a cutting board. Run your

(recipe continues)

finger along the midline, pressing gently against the flesh so you will feel the bones you need to remove. Use the tweezers to pull them out at an angle, being as gentle as possible so you don't shred the flesh.

When all the bones have been removed, you may choose to skin the fish. I prefer my raw fish with the skin on.

If you want to skin the fish, hold onto the tail end of one fillet and make a small cut to start separating the skin from the flesh. Keeping the knife blade between the skin and the flesh and holding it flat against the cutting board, run it down the length of the fish, pulling the skin away from the flesh. It should come off fairly easily. Repeat for the other fillet. Rinse the fillets to remove any blood or scales and pat dry with paper towels or a lint-free kitchen towel.

Lay the fillets on a clean cutting board. Slice the fish diagonally, against the grain, into thin bite-sized pieces. You want to get approximately 12 to 15 pieces from each fillet. (If there is any fish left over, refrigerate it immediately and reserve for the fish stew.)

Arrange the sliced fish on a chilled platter. Serve immediately with the chojang and soy sauce on the side for dipping, along with a little bowl of the wasabi. Place a tiny bit of wasabi on your piece of fish just before dipping for a heady kick.

SALMON SASHIMI SALAD WITH CHOJANG

Serves 4

A 1-pound sashimi-grade salmon (belly or fillet)

1 tablespoon salt

½ pound mixed leafy salad greens

1 small red onion, thinly sliced

1 bunch chives, cut into 1-inch batons

2 tablespoons toasted sesame oil

3 tablespoons Chojang (page 58)

Salt and freshly ground black pepper

1 tablespoon toasted sesame seeds

Note: Any leftover fish will keep, well wrapped, in the fridge for up to 48 hours, but you should use it in a cooked preparation, rather than serving it raw.

This refreshing salad is the foundation of Hwe Deop Bap (Marinated Rice with Sashimi Salad, page 225), a traditional dish that is basically this salad served over rice. We serve both of these at Hanjan. If you're not a fan of salmon, you can substitute fluke for its lighter, sweeter flavor in the summer, or yellowtail for its luscious fatty texture in the winter.

I like to use wild Alaskan salmon, which is in season from late spring to early autumn. The flavor, nutritional value, and texture of farmed salmon cannot compare. However, in the wintertime, when wild salmon is not available, farmed salmon, which tends to be much softer than wild salmon, especially if it's been frozen and thawed, can be given a quick cure to firm up the flesh just enough to add some bite; I like to use the quick cure in any case. The combination of chojang, fresh salad, and raw fish is a great beginning to a hearty meal or light meal in itself.

To cure the salmon, sprinkle the fish on both sides with the salt. Put it on a rack set over a baking pan or a tray and refrigerate, uncovered, overnight. The fish will firm up slightly and its flavor will concentrate.

The next day, wash off the salt and pat the salmon dry. Use a sharp knife to slice it diagonally against the grain into slices no more than ¼ inch thick. Arrange the slices on a plate, cover loosely with plastic wrap, and refrigerate until you are ready to serve.

Combine the salad greens, red onion, chives, sesame oil, and chojang in a large bowl and toss well. Add salt and pepper to taste. Sprinkle the sesame seeds over the top. Divide the salad

(recipe continues)

equally among four serving bowls. You can serve the fish on the side, as we do at Hanjan, where diners wrap leaves from the salad with the fish to make individual bites, or you can toss the fish with the salad and serve it in individual bowls. Serve immediately.

Yellowtail sashimi and salad with chojang at Hanjan.

SPICY WHELK SALAD WITH SOBA NOODLES

골뱅이 무침 (Golbaengi Muchim)

Serves 4

Court Bouillon

4 quarts water

1¼ cups salt

One 24-inch stalk lemongrass

2 heads garlic, cut horizontally in half

2 medium onions, quartered

1 leek, trimmed, cleaned, and roughly chopped

2 oranges, quartered

2 tablespoons black peppercorns

20 to 25 small whelks in the shell (about the size of a golf ball)

2 bunches (150 grams) soba noodles, preferably Sukina Brand

6 tablespoons Chojang (page 58)

3 tablespoons toasted sesame oil

2 tablespoons BKO (Bacon Kimchi Onion) Sauce (page 60)

1 tablespoon soy sauce

2 bunches watercress, rinsed, dried, and thick stems removed

1 red onion, thinly sliced, rinsed under cold water, and dried

1 bunch chives, cut into 1½-inch batons

Salt

Toasted sesame seeds

Whelks are a type of sea snail that are very popular in Korea—so much so that you can easily find canned seasoned and cooked whelks that are very tasty (albeit full of MSG and preservatives). If whelks aren't in season (they are at their best from December to April), you can use canned whelks. I recommend Dongwon brand. Most restaurants in Korea use the canned ones because they are more economical than preparing fresh whelks. Canned whelks, cleaned and ready to go, are available at Korean markets; to use them for this salad, omit the cooking and cut them into pieces as described below.

The best way to experience whelks, though, is to cook fresh ones during peak season. The fresh, sweet, salty sea flavor will jump out as soon as you pop one in your mouth and their soft, juicy texture will make you feel giddy. I can almost guarantee eating one of these will put a smile on your face. These whelks are slightly larger and plumper than French escargots. When they are cooked properly, their texture is both chewy and tender at the same time, and to me, they taste a little more briny than their Gallic counterparts. I like to serve whelks with chilled soba noodles to sop up all the delicious sauce.

In Korea, ice-cold soju is the traditional pairing with golbaengi muchim. I like to pair it with very cold makgeolli (rice beer), because it balances the spiciness of the dish.

To make the court bouillon, pour the water into a large pot set over high heat, add the salt, and bring to a boil. Put the lemongrass on a cutting board and smash it 5 or 6 times with the back of a heavy knife to break it up and release the essential

(recipe continues)

oils. Cut the stalk into 4 pieces and add it to the boiling water, along with the garlic, onions, leek, oranges, and black peppercorns. Reduce the heat to medium and simmer the broth for 30 minutes.

Increase the heat to high, add the whelks, and cook for 6 minutes (if the whelks are as large as a squash ball, cook for 8 minutes). Meanwhile, prepare an ice bath. When the whelks are done, put them in the ice bath for 3 minutes, or until they have cooled; drain. Discard the broth.

Use a skewer to remove the whelks from their shells. The whelks should be quite tender and well seasoned. Cut them into bite-sized pieces: Small to medium whelks will yield 1 to 3 pieces; larger whelks will yield 4 or 5 pieces each. Set aside.

Set a large pot of water over high heat and bring to a boil. Prepare an ice bath. Add the noodles to the boiling water and cook according to the instructions on the package, usually 6 minutes; immediately transfer to the ice bath to cool.

Drain the noodles thoroughly and put them in a bowl. Add 3 tablespoons of the chojang, 1½ tablespoons of the sesame oil, the BKO, and soy sauce and mix well; reserve.

Combine the whelks, watercress, red onion, chives, and the remaining 3 tablespoons chojang and 1½ tablespoons sesame oil in a medium bowl. Season lightly with salt and mix well. Arrange the noodles and salad in separate piles on a large serving plate. Garnish by sprinkling the toasted sesame seeds over everything. This dish is best served immediately because the sauce tends to wilt the vegetables after 10 minutes or so.

GRILLED SALTED MACKEREL
고등어 구이 (Godeung-uh Gui)

Serves 4

2 whole mackerel (10 to 13 inches in length),
　　preferably from Norway
Salt
Grape seed or canola oil for brushing
Juice from ½ lemon for serving (optional)

I love the intense ocean flavor, oily skin, and meaty flesh of Atlantic mackerel from Boston or, even better, Norway. The skin does a wonderful job of keeping the flesh moist. When the fish is salted and grilled, the salty, crispy skin makes a wonderful contrast to the meaty flesh. These days mackerel from Norway are available year-round and are of consistently high quality. They tend to be hefty, about 10 to 13 inches long. You can have your fishmonger remove the heads and innards, or just remove the innards and leave the heads intact, depending on your personal preference. You can also ask him to butterfly and bone the fish for you.

You need to season the fish with salt and let them dry out on a rack in the refrigerator overnight before grilling. The salt will give the flesh a light cure and the dry skin will blister and crisp on the grill or under the broiler.

If the fishmonger did not butterfly the fish (see headnote), cut each one open along its belly, then lay the fish on its side and run a very sharp knife along the rib bones up to the backbone. Flip the fish over and repeat on the other side. Once you have separated the ribs from the flesh, turn the fish onto its back and carefully pull the fillets away from the bones. The line of rib bones will be standing up in the center of the fish. Use kitchen shears to snip the backbone at the head and the tail so that it is no longer attached. Carefully remove the back bone from the fish, using the tip of your knife to help separate it, and lift the bones away. Be careful not to cut through the skin at the top of the fish. Don't worry about any pin bones; they are extremely small in mackerel and not worth the trouble of searching them out. Liberally season the flesh with salt and place the fish skin side down on a rack set on a large plate. Let sit, uncovered, in the refrigerator for 24 hours. The salt will penetrate the flesh, acting as a quick cure.

(recipe continues)

Preheat a grill to medium heat. When it is hot, using a paper towel, brush the grill grate with oil so the skin of the mackerel will not stick to it. Brush the skin of the mackerel as well and lay it skin side down on the grill. Cook for 8 to 10 minutes, until the skin is nicely browned and crispy. Flip the fish carefully using a spatula (trying to flip the fish before the skin side is fully cooked will result in the skin ripping or sticking to the grill). Cook for 2 to 3 minutes more, until the flesh is cooked through; it should be slightly firm and gray.

Alternatively, you can cook the fish under the broiler. Position a rack in the upper part of the oven and preheat the broiler. (Make sure the broiler flame will not be too close to the fish, or it will burn the skin.) Line a sheet pan with foil and brush it with oil, then arrange the fish skin side down on the foil. Cook for 2 to 3 minutes, then flip and cook for 8 to 10 minutes.

Transfer the mackerel to a platter, skin side up, and drizzle with the lemon juice if desired; I recommend tasting the fish before adding lemon juice; salt and lemon work well together in seasoning fish, but if you have sufficiently salted your mackerel, the acid from the lemon may make it seem too salty. Serve with banchan and individual bowls of rice.

A typical Korean dinner table for four with Spicy Stir-Fried Squid, page 174; Grilled Salted Mackerel, page 169; Stewed Sweet Black Beans, page 73; Spicy Dehydrated Korean Radishes, page 115; Napa Cabbage Kimchi, page 96; Spicy Fish Bone Stew, page 201; Sweet Crispy Baby Anchovies, page 79; and Simmered Fish Cakes, page 77.

SPICY STIR-FRIED SQUID
오징어 볶음 (Ojingeo Bokkeum)

Serves 4

Sauce

¼ cup gochugaru (Korean red chili flakes)

1 tablespoon gochujang (Korean red chili paste)

1 tablespoon sake

1 tablespoon mirin

1 tablespoon soy sauce

2 tablespoons sugar

1 teaspoon minced ginger

5 garlic cloves, minced

1 tablespoon toasted sesame oil

3 pounds fresh squid, cleaned

Salt and freshly ground black pepper

¼ cup grape seed or canola oil

2 medium onions, thinly sliced

1 green Korean chili pepper or other long hot chili, thinly sliced

½ bunch scallions, cut into 1-inch batons

Toasted sesame oil for drizzling

Toasted sesame seeds

Hot rice or somyeon noodles for serving

This dish is a great example of the way Koreans use the nutty, comforting properties of sesame oil to balance a spicy dish. The natural sweetness of the squid and the vegetables complete the dynamic flavors of the stir-fry. You can serve this dish on its own with a bowl of rice or somyeon noodles on the side, or over the rice or noodles, *deop-bap* style, for an easy lunch.

It's important to use very fresh squid so its natural flavors won't be drowned out by the strong spice and aromatics. Most squid is flash-frozen on the boat when it is caught, so don't worry if the squid is still frozen at your local fish market. I would, however, urge you not to make this dish with packaged calamari from your supermarket, because they may be older and not handled as well, and you may miss out on the firm flesh and natural sweetness of fresh squid. I like to make this dish extremely spicy, particularly since the other ingredients help to sweeten and neutralize the burn of the spice. This preparation also works well with octopus.

To make the sauce, combine the gochugaru, gochujang, sake, mirin, soy sauce, sugar, ginger, garlic, and sesame oil in a bowl and mix well to blend. Set aside.

Set a large skillet over medium-high heat—a heavy stainless steel pan works best here—and heat for 5 minutes, or until it is smoking. Season the squid with salt and pepper. Add 2 tablespoons of the oil to the hot pan, then add half the squid, being sure not to overcrowd your pan, and cook, stirring constantly with a wooden spoon, for 2 minutes, or until the squid is just cooked through. Remove from the pan and transfer to a plate. Repeat with the next batch, and add it to the first.

(recipe continues)

Wipe out the pan and set it over medium-high heat. When it's hot, add the remaining 2 tablespoons oil, the onions, peppers, scallions, and salt to taste and stir for about 2 minutes, until the vegetables begin to soften. Add the sauce and cook, stirring constantly, for 1 minute. Add the reserved squid and cook, stirring constantly, for 1 minute more, or until everything is hot and well combined.

Transfer the stir-fry to a large platter. Add a drizzle of sesame oil and sprinkle the toasted sesame seeds over the top. Serve with hot rice or somyeon noodles (see headnote).

SOY-POACHED BLACK COD WITH DAIKON
은대구 조림 (Eun-dae-gu Jorim)

Serves 4

1 pound daikon radishes

1 pound yu choy or bok choy, cut into bite-sized pieces

One 2-inch piece ginger, peeled

Sauce

2 cups sake

1 cup mirin

1 cup soy sauce

¾ cup sugar

6 garlic cloves, minced

1 teaspoon minced ginger

½ medium onion, minced

3 tablespoons gochugaru (Korean red chili flakes)

1½ pounds pounds black cod fillet, skinless, cut into eight 3-ounce pieces (you can ask the fishmonger to do this)

Also known as sablefish, black cod is a black-skinned fish with small scales and creamy white flesh. It may be as short as 24 inches and as long as 48 inches. When it's cooked, the texture becomes silky and plush. It has a decadent taste due to the high fat content. This is my young son's favorite fish dish—minus the gochugaru. It's not a super spicy dish per se, but you can omit the gochugaru to make a milder version. It'll be almost as good!

Black cod is very expensive and there is no real equivalent to its flavor and texture. Chilean sea bass would be a close substitute, but it is overfished and endangered. Halibut and other white fish aren't as fatty as black cod and can easily overcook. Farmed salmon, with its rich fat content, could be substituted, though the texture will be different. But truly, it's worth searching for black cod to make this dish because it will make for an unforgettable experience—especially for anyone who has never tasted the fish.

For a vegetarian version of this dish, you can substitute an equal amount of peeled daikon, cut into 3-inch pieces, for the fish and cook it the same way. The texture of the daikon will mimic the texture of the fish—both will be soft and juicy. The fish will flake off your fork or chopsticks, and the daikon will gently break apart.

Set a large pot of unsalted water over high heat and bring to a boil. Peel the daikon deeply enough to remove the fibrous outer layer. (If you slice off one end of the radish, you will see a thick layer right beneath the outer skin; it is tough and lacking flavor, so it should be removed with the peel.) Slice the daikon into 1-inch-thick rounds.

(recipe continues)

Blanch the daikon in the boiling water for 10 minutes, or until soft and tender throughout; you'll know it's done if you can pierce it with a knife and there is no resistance. Using a slotted spoon or a spider, transfer the daikon to a wire rack set over a sheet pan and let cool. Add more water to the pot if needed, and bring it back to a boil. Prepare an ice bath. Add the yu choy or bok choy to the boiling water and blanch for 2 to 3 minutes, until just tender, then transfer to the ice bath to cool. Drain, pat dry, and reserve.

Use a mandoline or vegetable peeler to slice the ginger crosswise as thin as possible. Stack the slices and cut them into the finest threads you can manage. Put the ginger in a bowl of cold water and reserve. Soaking the ginger reduces its sharp taste; since it is served raw in this dish, it's helpful to mellow the flavor a bit.

To make the sauce, put the sake and mirin in a large straight-sided pan set over high heat. When it starts to boil, carefully light the liquid with a lighter or a long match, then let the flames die out, 1 to 2 minutes. (If you would rather not light the sake, let the mixture boil for 3 minutes to burn off the alcohol.) Add the soy sauce, sugar, garlic, minced ginger, onion, and gochugaru to the pan, reduce the heat to medium, and bring the mixture to a simmer.

Add the fish and daikon. Simmer for 6 minutes, uncovered, then flip the fish and daikon. Add the blanched yu choy or bok choy and cook for 2 minutes, or until the greens are hot and the fish is cooked through. Check to see if the fish is done by gently poking the thickest piece of a fillet with a fork; if the flesh springs back, it is done. By this time, the sauce should be reduced and thickened to the texture of a jus, lightly coating and clinging to the fish and daikon. If the sauce has thickened too much, add a bit of water to loosen it up. Or, if it has not thickened enough, plate the fish and vegetables, then put the pan back over high heat to finish the reduction, about a minute or two more.

Arrange the daikon in a shallow serving bowl, to use it as a base. Then pile the fish on top and lean the yu choy to the side. Pour the sauce over the fish and finish it off with the slivers of fresh ginger. Serve a bowl of rice alongside so your guests can use it to soak up all the extra sauce.

BRAISED SPICY HAIRTAIL
갈치조림 (Galchi Jorim)

½ pound Korean (mu) radish or daikon radish

2 medium onions

2 cups sake

2 cups Dashi (page 189), plus more if needed

6 garlic cloves, minced

1 teaspoon minced ginger

½ cup soy sauce

6 tablespoons gochugaru (Korean red chili flakes)

1 tablespoon sugar

1 teaspoon salt

1 large or 2 small hairtail (around 2 pounds total), cleaned, scaled, and cut into 5-inch fillets (see headnote)

1 medium red Korean chili pepper or other long hot chili, thinly sliced on a bias

1 bunch scallions, cut into 1-inch batons

There is a street inside Seoul's biggest market, Namdae-mun Sijang, that houses about twelve restaurants that specialize in this dish. The original galchi jorim restaurant has been there for more than twenty-five years. Its success inspired others to come and copy it, and eventually the entire block was overtaken by galchi jorim restaurants. People love it that much.

The best galchi, or hairtail, is from the island of Jeju, off the southern tip of Korea. It is silver with firm white flesh. Galchi is sold in the US at Korean markets, either in the frozen section or, thawed, in the fish section. The fish are two to three feet long and three to six inches wide, but only an inch or inch and a half thick. If you cannot find hairtail, you can use mackerel or pike mackerel instead. It is important that you use an oily fish with a strong flavor, as the sauce is fairly assertive, and a mild fish would be overpowered by it. It is impossible to fillet hairtail, because it is so thin and contains many tiny bones. It is traditionally cooked bones and all, and when it is done, diners use their chopsticks to pick the meat from the bones. It can get tricky to work your way around the bones, but it is well worth the effort.

Have the fishmonger remove the head, guts, scales, and fins from the hairtail. You can ask him to portion the fish into 5-inch fillets, or you can do it yourself. If you buy pre-packaged hairtail from the freezer section, it should be cleaned, portioned, and ready to go.

This recipe is very similar to the Soy-Poached Black Cod with Daikon (Eun-dae-gu Jorim, page 177). The big difference is that gochugaru is the highlight here, whereas in the black cod dish, it is one of several supporting flavors.

(recipe continues)

Peel the radish, being sure to remove the fibrous layer directly under the skin. (If you slice off one end of the radish, you will see a thick layer right beneath the outer skin; it is tough and lacking flavor, so it should be removed with the peel.) Slice the radish into ½-inch-thick rounds. (If it is very large in diameter, you can cut it lengthwise in half or even into quarters before slicing it.) Cut the onions lengthwise in half and then slice into ½-inch-thick half-moons.

Put the sake in a wide shallow straight-sided pan set over high heat. When it comes to a boil, carefully light the sake with a lighter or a long match, then let the flames die out, 1 to 2 minutes. (If you would rather not light the sake, let it boil for 3 minutes to burn off the alcohol.) Add the dashi and bring the mixture to a simmer. Add the onions, radish, garlic, ginger, soy sauce, gochugaru, sugar, and salt, reduce the heat to medium, and cook, uncovered, for 5 minutes.

Add the fish to the pan, making sure there is enough liquid to partially cover it. If not, add more dashi. Cover, bring to a low simmer, and cook for 5 minutes. Flip the fish and radish, cover, and cook for another 2 minutes. Add the chili peppers and scallions and stir well to mix them into the sauce. Cook for 5 minutes, uncovered. The liquid should be just thick enough to coat the back of a spoon; if it's too thin, cook for a few minutes more. Check the texture of the radish and make sure it gives no resistance when pierced with a sharp knife. Once the radish is done, the fish and other vegetables should be done too.

This is a dish that is best served directly from the pan. It can be the centerpiece of your dining table and everyone can help themselves.

OUPS AND
STEWS

Soups and stews are an essential part of a traditional Korean meal. Most older Koreans don't consider a meal complete unless there is a hot, savory broth on the table, regardless of the time of day. Stews, or *jjigaes*, are heartier and thicker than soups, or *guks*, so they can be served for lunch or dinner, whereas soups are almost always lunch or breakfast dishes.

A *guk* is sometimes a stand-alone dish, such as Tteok Guk (Rice Cake Soup, page 193). Most of the time, however, it requires rice as a complement. It is customary to eat your bowl of rice separately or to mix the rice into the soup and eat it all together. Unlike banchan, soups are served individually, so you can mix as much or as little rice as you like into your own soup.

Jjigaes are shared at the table. If you're just dining with family or close friends, it's typical to eat directly from the communal bowl, "double dipping" with your own spoon. In a more formal setting, or when you have guests over for dinner, you might serve the stew individually in small bowls.

I begin this chapter with a recipe for dashi, because the technique is absolutely crucial to achieving deep and intense flavors with layers of complexity in the broth. Dashi has a very subtle flavor, but it adds umami to other dishes and, more importantly, it has the power to enhance a wide variety of ingredients. It gives fish stews more depth, and in meat stews, it helps bind the flavors of the meat and vegetables together. It also enhances the broth's texture, making it silkier and softer. A good comparison would be the difference in mouthfeel of Evian water versus NYC tap water. A good dashi should not be as crisp and refreshing as the latter, but rather as soft, dense, and easy to swallow as Evian. The importance of dashi cannot be overstated. If there is one good habit that you pick up from this book, I hope it will be that of always using dashi rather than water in any Asian meal you cook.

Dashi while it's cooking.

DASHI

1 gallon cold water
One 6-inch square dashima
3 medium dried shiitake mushrooms
12 large dried anchovies (gutted and heads
  removed)

Dashi is a generic name for stock in Japanese; it is also a common term in Korea. While in Daniel Boulud's kitchen, I learned it was always best to use chicken, veal, or vegetable stock, not water, in cooking. In Masa's kitchen, the principle was the same, but we used dashi. There are as many different kinds of dashi as there are stocks. The main difference between the two is that dashi is made with dried vegetables and dried seafood while classic stocks are usually based on fresh vegetables and meat or fish bones. Most dashis use dried dashima seaweed. You can also add dried mushrooms or seafood, such as dried anchovies, shellfish, or bonito flakes.

Dashi has a very subtle flavor of the sea that makes everything you cook with it taste better. It is full of natural glutamates. While these are flavorless on their own, they amplify the flavors of all the other ingredients, enhancing them without masking their true nature. Instead of experiencing flavors that drop off immediately after hitting your tongue, the glutamates allow them to linger on your palate, even after you have swallowed that mouthful, creating a lasting finish.

The dashi recipe I've included in this book has earthiness (from shiitakes), depth (from dashima), and sea flavors (from both the dashima and dried anchovies). It's a very versatile version. It complements almost every Korean dish I can think of and enhances the flavors of both meats and seafood.

Since soup is mostly liquid, it benefits more than any other dish from the effects of dashi. The difference between a soup made with dashi and one made with water is like the difference between a 1982 Bordeaux and a Beaujolais Nouveau. One has structure, balance, character, dimension, and a long, memorable finish. The other might be

Note: Vegetarians can make a dashi from just dashima and dried shiitakes.

(recipe continues)

pleasant at first sip and have some character, but soon after that, the flavors fall away and you're left searching for depth and dimension where it doesn't exist.

Nowhere is this more apparent than when using dashi with a jang. When you've cooked a jang with dashi, the deep flavors of the jang will hit your palate and then continue to grow and develop. The impact of the jang will fully bloom over 10 to 20 seconds. But the impact of jang cooked with water disappears more quickly. This additional perception of flavor can elevate a dish and make it memorable. That is why when you cook a dish with jang and dashi, you have to taste it and then give the taste a minute to develop before deciding whether the seasoning is too bland or too salty. If you season it based on the initial taste, you will inevitably end up over-seasoning it. This is one of the first things that I teach new cooks at my restaurants, particularly those who have never cooked with jang or dashi. Once you've experienced what a difference it makes, dashi will become the most important ingredient in your kitchen.

We make dashi every day in both of my restaurant kitchens, and I do the same at home. The best (and fastest) way to make dashi is to combine all the ingredients in a large covered pot and let soak overnight at room temperature, then cook the broth the next morning. It takes 90 minutes or less of simmering time to get the flavor you want this way. If you do not soak it overnight, it can take more than 2 hours to cook. Some Koreans like to keep a container of water with dashi ingredients soaking in the fridge at all times. They replace the ingredients several times a week, adding more water as well whenever some of the dashi is used for cooking. This method doesn't provide the deepest or freshest flavor, but it means you always have dashi on hand, and it is still preferable to using plain water.

It's best to use dashi the same day you make it, though if you keep it refrigerated, you can use it for another day or two. By the third day, it will no longer taste fresh.

Put the water, dashima, shiitake mushrooms, and anchovies in a covered stockpot or other large pot and let stand at room temperature overnight, or for 8 to 12 hours.

Remove the lid, set the pot over high heat, and heat until the surface of the water begins to ripple; pay attention, and do not let it come to a boil. Lower the heat to maintain a very gentle simmer (the ideal temperature is a few degrees below a light boil) and simmer for 80 to 90 minutes. Taste the dashi every 20 minutes to monitor the changes in flavor and texture. You will notice the texture becoming softer. I describe it as having a slippery, slightly viscous texture compared to tap water. The sea flavor will become stronger, and the dashi will become darker, like pale Earl Grey tea. The sweetness will take a while to appear, but when it does, the dashi is almost ready. When you can taste the sweetness and deep sea flavors, and the dashi has a very soft texture, it is done. Be vigilant, because dashi will become bitter if cooked too long.

Strain the dashi into a covered container and store in the refrigerator for up to 2 days. After 24 hours, the dashi will begin to lose some of its flavor and it will turn slightly flat.

Rice Cake Soup with banchan:
Napa Cabbage Kimchi, page
96; Stewed Sweet Black Beans,
page 73; and Sweet Crispy Baby
Anchovies, page 79.

RICE CAKE SOUP
떡국 (Tteok Guk)

Serves 4

1 pound presliced frozen or fresh tteok (Korean rice cakes)

One ½-pound piece lean brisket (from the flat)

1½ quarts Dashi (page 189), plus more as needed

¼ cup soy sauce

4 garlic cloves, minced

Salt

2 pinches freshly ground black pepper

1 large egg

½ bunch scallions, cut into 1-inch batons

Gim (dried Korean seaweed) or nori, cut into thin strips, for garnish

Napa Cabbage Kimchi (Baechu Kimchi, page 96) for serving

Note: Old-school Koreans separate the eggs and cook the yolks and whites separately into omelets, then slice them into slivers, resembling fine noodles, to add to the soup. I like to just crack the egg directly into the soup, similar to Chinese egg drop soup.

Koreans traditionally eat this delicate soup on New Year's Day and at Lunar New Year. It is filled with soft, chewy sliced rice cakes and garnished with eggs and dried seaweed. It's tasty enough to enjoy throughout the year, though I do crave it more often in the wintertime.

If you are using frozen rice cakes, soak them in cold water for 1 hour; drain. Fresh rice cakes can be used immediately.

Put the brisket in a pot just large enough to hold it, add enough dashi to cover the meat, and set over high heat. Add 2 tablespoons of the soy sauce to the pot and heat until it comes to a simmer, then reduce the heat to maintain a low simmer. Cook for 2 hours, or until the brisket is tender. Use a shallow fine-mesh strainer to remove some of the residue that collects on top of the broth as it simmers.

Transfer the brisket to a bowl, cover tightly with plastic wrap so it doesn't dry out, and let it cool. Set the broth aside.

When the meat is cool enough to handle, about 15 minutes, use your hands to tear it into strips along the grain of the brisket, and then re-cover the meat and reserve.

Set another pot over high heat and add the broth, plus enough additional dashi to make 2 quarts. Bring it to a boil, then lower the heat to maintain a low simmer. Add the garlic and cook for 5 minutes. Add the tteok, the remaining 2 tablespoons soy sauce, 2 to 4 pinches of salt, and the pepper and cook for 4 to 5 minutes, until the rice cakes are very tender. Add the egg to the soup, stirring to break it up. Add the scallions and cook for 2 minutes more.

Ladle the soup into individual serving bowls. Add some of the brisket to each and lay a few strips of gim or nori over each portion. Serve immediately, with kimchi on the side.

A typical Korean breakfast table for two with Radish and Beef Soup, page 195; Sautéed Gray Squash, page 88; Spinach with Sesame, page 127; Spicy Bean Sprouts, page 126; and fried eggs.

RADISH AND BEEF SOUP

무국 (Mu Guk)

Serves 4

2 quarts Dashi (page 189)

4 garlic cloves, minced

2 large onions, cut into 1-inch dice

¼ cup soy sauce

¼ teaspoon salt, or to taste

1 small to medium Korean radish (mu) or
   daikon radish, cut into ¼-inch dice

¼ pound brisket or boneless sirloin, cut into
   ½-by-½-by-1-inch strips

1 block (18 ounces) silken tofu, cut into ½-inch
   cubes

½ bunch scallions, cut into 1-inch batons

2 pinches freshly ground black pepper

I love this soup for breakfast because it has such a soothing flavor and texture. I always like it with some rice and a bold banchan on the side, such as Mu Mallengi Muchim (Spicy Dehydrated Korean Radishes, page 115) and/or Myulchi Bokkeum (Sweet Crispy Baby Anchovies, page 79). As the radish cooks and softens, its texture changes from crisp to juicy, and the taste becomes mild and sweet. We serve this at Danji for lunch, and I've been told by diners that in addition to being delicious, it's a great hangover cure. This a great side dish for any of the Bibimbaps (pages 217, 219, and 222) and the Kimchi Chadol Bokkeum Bap (Kimchi-and-Brisket Fried Rice, page 228).

Put the dashi in a stockpot or other large pot set over medium-high heat and bring to a simmer. Add the garlic and simmer for 5 minutes. Add the onions, soy sauce, and salt and simmer for 5 minutes. Add the radish and simmer for 10 minutes more, or until tender.

Add the beef, tofu, scallions, and pepper and simmer until the beef is cooked through, about 5 minutes. Add salt to taste. Serve with rice and banchan or simply enjoy the soup on its own.

BEEF SHORT RIB SOUP
갈비탕 (Galbi Tang)

Serves 4

5 pounds beef short ribs, cut into 1½- to 2-inch pieces
3 quarts Dashi (page 189)

Aromatics
6 garlic cloves
A thumbnail-sized piece of ginger, peeled
1 medium onion, quartered
½ bunch scallions, trimmed

Salt
6 garlic cloves, minced
1 teaspoon minced ginger
2 tablespoons soy sauce
Freshly ground black pepper
½ bunch scallions, thinly sliced, rinsed, and dried as directed on page 45

Dipping Sauce
1 cup soy sauce
3 tablespoons rice vinegar
3 tablespoons mirin
1 teaspoon freshly ground black pepper

Napa Cabbage Kimchi (Baechu Kimchi, page 96) or Korean Radish Kimchi (Chongak or Kkak Dugi Kimchi, page 105)
Steamed Rice (page 212)

The dashi brings out the natural umami flavors of the beef short rib in this winter dish. The fat content of the meat is not a major factor in this soup, so I recommend that you use grass-fed natural beef; less-marbled grass-fed beef has more flavor than grain-fed. Add garlic, ginger, onion, and scallions, and you have an incredibly comforting, fortifying, and balanced soup.

I garnish it with fluffy thinly sliced scallions, which are a perfect counterpoint to the heavy broth. Served with rice and kimchi, this makes an ideal meal for a cold day. Many Koreans, including me, prefer to add the rice to their soup before eating. The practice is called *mara-muk-da*, which means to eat by adding rice to liquid.

Soak the short ribs in a large pot of cold water for 2 hours to extract the blood. The blood can darken the color of the soup and impart a bit of a gamey flavor. (If you prefer a beefier taste and don't mind a touch of the gaminess in the soup, you can skip this step.) Drain the ribs.

Put the dashi in a stockpot or other large pot set over medium-high heat and bring it to a simmer. Meanwhile, for the aromatics, wrap the garlic cloves, ginger, quartered onion, and scallions in a square of cheesecloth and tie securely so the contents won't escape.

Add the ribs, 2 pinches of salt, and the cheesecloth sac to the dashi, reduce the heat to low, and simmer slowly over low heat for 90 minutes, carefully skimming off the impurities as they rise to the top.

Note: For ease of serving, especially if you're feeding children, use kitchen scissors to cut the meat away from the bones and then into pieces before plating the soup in individual bowls.

Remove the cheesecloth sachet and discard. Add the minced garlic, ginger, and soy sauce to the soup and simmer for another 30 minutes, or until the ribs are tender, skimming as needed. Season with salt and pepper to taste.

Meanwhile, to make the dipping sauce, mix all the ingredients in a bowl. Reserve.

Transfer the ribs and broth to a large serving bowl (see Note above). Sprinkle the sliced scallions over the top. Serve the rice and kimchi on the side, along with individual bowls of the dipping sauce for the meat.

AGED-KIMCHI STEW
김치찌개 (Kimchi Jjigae)

Serves 4

1 teaspoon grape seed or canola oil

1 pound skinless pork belly, sliced ¼ inch thick (you can have the butcher slice it) and cut into 1-inch squares

2 pinches of salt, or to taste

6 garlic cloves, minced

1½ pounds aged kimchi (fermented for at least 3 weeks), store-bought or homemade (see page 100), cut into 1- to 2-inch-wide strips

1 tablespoon gochugaru (Korean red chili flakes)

4 cups Dashi (page 189)

1 pound silken or soft tofu, preferably homemade (page 67), cut into 1-inch cubes

1 bunch scallions, cut into 1-inch batons

Fish sauce (optional)

Gim (dried Korean seaweed) or nori, sliced into strips (optional; see headnote) for serving

If you were to ask a hundred Koreans what their favorite Korean dishes were, I bet a majority would name Kimchi Jjigae and/or Doenjang Jjigae (Fermented-Soybean Stew, page 205). Kimchi jjigae is a classic dish made with aged kimchi that has fermented for at least four weeks. If you don't have homemade aged kimchi on hand, store-bought kimchi is labeled with the date it was made, and the aged kimchi will be stored in the back of the store refrigerator. But be sure to get your aged kimchi from a trusted source; improperly aged kimchi can be too acidic and would overpower the other flavors in the stew and throw off the balance of the entire dish. If you don't have a source of good aged kimchi, when you're buying your favorite regular kimchi, you might want to get two jars so you can wrap one in foil and put it in the back of your fridge to use later for this stew.

The aged kimchi gives the stew depth and body. Properly aged kimchi is strong and pungent. It is also highly acidic, so that it cuts through the fattiness of the pork here. When making this dish, I reserve one-quarter of the kimchi to add at the end, because the kimchi that is added earlier will lose much of its texture and flavor as it simmers in the broth. The kimchi that is added at the end will still retain a bit of its bite and most of its flavor, so there is a nice contrast between the differently cooked kimchis.

Gim or nori makes an excellent complement to this dish. I cut it into strips with scissors and serve it on the side. Your guests can lay pieces of gim on top of their rice and spoon it up with the rice while eating the stew. Banchan such as Gyeran Jjim (Steamed Egg Custard with Salted Shrimp, page 89) and Myulchi Bokkeum (Sweet Crispy Baby Anchovies, page 79) are great choices, as they will help balance the acidity and spice of the kimchi jjigae.

(recipe continues)

In Jeju, aged-kimchi stew steams
in a traditional, open-fire pot
cemented into the ground.

Set a stockpot or other large pot over high heat and add the oil. When the oil begins to shimmer and just barely smoke, put the pork in the pot and season with the salt. Sear on one side until browned, 2 to 3 minutes. Stir the pork, reduce the heat to low, and cook for 5 minutes so some of the fat can render out. Add the garlic and cook, stirring constantly, for 1 to 2 minutes, making sure the garlic does not burn.

Raise the heat to medium, add three-quarters of the kimchi and the gochugaru, and cook for 7 minutes, or until lightly caramelized. Add the dashi and bring to a simmer, then reduce the heat slightly and simmer gently for 40 minutes.

Add the tofu, scallions, and the remaining kimchi and simmer for 5 minutes. Taste to check the seasoning. If you used a flavorful aged kimchi, you shouldn't need any additional salt. If stew is lacking in flavor or seasoning, you might want to add a few drops of fish sauce. Remember that this dish is eaten with rice, so the seasoning should be assertive enough to balance plain white rice. Serve immediately, with rice and, if desired, gim or nori on the side.

SPICY FISH BONE STEW
매운탕 (Mae-un Tang)

Serves 4

Fish Dashi

2 quarts Dashi (page 189)

Head and bones from 2 snapper, fluke, or other
white-fleshed fish

1 head garlic, separated into cloves, crushed,
and peeled

A 1-ounce piece of ginger, peeled and cut into
½-inch-thick slices

Soup

1½ quarts Fish Dashi (from above)

1 tablespoon gochujang (Korean red chili
paste)

3 tablespoons gochugaru (Korean red chili
flakes)

6 garlic cloves, minced

1 teaspoon minced ginger

2 medium onions, cut into 1-inch dice

3 tablespoons soy sauce

Salt

1 small Korean radish (mu) or daikon radish,
deeply peeled and cut into thin 1-inch squares

Leftover fish reserved from Hwe (page 161), or
a snapper, fluke, or other white-fleshed fish
fillet, cut into 2-inch pieces (optional; see
headnote)

2 red or green Korean chili peppers or other
long hot chilies, thinly sliced on the bias

½ bunch scallions, cut into 1-inch batons

½ bunch mugwort leaves (*sook*; sometimes
labeled chrysanthemum leaves in Korean
markets), trimmed of any thick stems
(optional)

This stew takes advantage of the bones and head left over after you fillet whole fish, as with the Hwe (Korean-Style Sashimi, page 161). I sometimes add some fresh fish too, because it makes the stew heartier and more flavorful. If you have any fish left over after serving Hwe, save it for this recipe; better yet, buy another fillet for this stew and cut it into 2-inch pieces to add to the stew. You can serve this stew with rice as a meal or as an anju (snack) to pair with ice-cold bottles of soju. I love to serve it that way for a circle of friends, with individual spoons so we can all dig into the pot placed in the center of the table. It's the essence of Korean eating: soju, close friends, and sharing.

To make the fish dashi, put the dashi in a large pot set over medium-high heat and bring to just below a simmer. Add the fish head and bones, garlic, and ginger and cook for 60 minutes at just below a simmer. Strain the dashi into a stockpot or other large pot; discard the solids.

Set the pot of dashi over medium-high heat and bring to a simmer. Add the gochujang, gochugaru, garlic, and ginger and simmer for 10 minutes. Add the onions, soy sauce, and salt to taste and cook for 5 minutes. Add the radish and simmer for 5 more minutes, or until the radish and onions are soft.

Add the reserved fish, if you have it, chilies, and scallions and cook for 5 more minutes. Season to taste with salt. If using mugwort, add to the pot, cover, and cook for 2 minutes, then turn off heat and let the soup stand, still covered, for 5 minutes to soften the leaves. The mugwort will add a subtle, herbal dimension to the soup.

Serve the soup immediately. Any leftovers can be refrigerated overnight (but no longer, because the flavor will slowly fade away) and reheated to serve the next day.

SPICY SOFT TOFU STEW WITH SEAFOOD

해물 순두부찌개 (Haemul Sundubu Jjigae)

Serves 4

4 cups Dashi (page 189)

8 large (U24) shrimp, peeled, shells reserved, and deveined

1 teaspoon salted shrimp

½ cup gochugaru (Korean red chili flakes)

8 garlic cloves, minced

1 teaspoon minced ginger

2 medium onions, cut into bite-sized dice

½ small Korean radish (mu) or daikon radish, peeled deeply and cut into ¼-inch-thick slices

2 medium zucchini, cut into ½-inch-thick slices

2 tablespoons soy sauce

1 teaspoon salt

4 littleneck clams, soaked in salt water for 30 minutes

4 mussels, soaked in salt water for 30 minutes

3 small squid, cleaned and cut into bite-sized pieces

1½ pounds extra-soft tofu (sundubu; available in Asian markets) or silken tofu, homemade (page 67) or store-bought

½ bunch scallions, cut into 1-inch batons

1 large egg (optional)

Soy sauce (optional)

This jjigae has become quite popular in both LA and NYC Koreatowns, spurring a phenomenon of restaurants that specialize exclusively in the dish. These restaurants let diners choose whether they'd like their stew mild, spicy, or very spicy. You can do the same at home by adjusting the amount of gochugaru in the recipe. The recipe below is spicy. My favorite part is the soft tofu, because it has such a comforting mouthfeel and it balances the effect of the spice. Just anticipating the flavor and texture of a spicy and tender sundubu jjigae warms you up. At restaurants, it is customary to mix a raw egg into the stew when it comes to your table still boiling in a clay pot. At home, simply add it to the pot at the last minute. The seafood called for in this recipe is often used in Korea and gives the broth a delicious sea flavor. The overall flavor of the stew is somewhat reminiscent of a French bouillabaisse—with a Korean kick of spice. Oee Muchim (Marinated Spicy Cucumbers, page 114) is a good counterpart to this stew.

Put the dashi in a large pot set over medium-high heat and bring to a simmer. Wrap the shrimp shells in a square of cheesecloth, tie it securely, and drop into the dashi. Cover and simmer for 30 minutes. Remove the shrimp shells and discard them.

Add the salted shrimp, gochugaru, garlic, and ginger to the dashi and simmer for 15 minutes. Add the onions and simmer for 5 minutes. Add the radish, zucchini, soy sauce, and salt and cook for another 5 minutes, or until the vegetables are just starting to soften.

(recipe continues)

203

Add the clams, mussels, and squid to the pot. When the broth comes back to a boil, add the tofu: Slide the tofu into the pot and use a spoon to break up the blocks into 2 or 3 pieces each; this helps the tofu heat faster and allows it to soak up the seasoning better. Add the scallions and bring to a boil again. Add the shrimp and simmer for 3 more minutes, then turn off the heat. If using the egg, add it now, stirring well. Let the stew rest for 3 minutes. The seafood will be cooked through, the mussels and clams should have opened and the vegetables will be tender.

Check the seasoning: The tofu will start absorbing salt as soon as it is added to the stew, and the flavor of the broth can change dramatically, so taste to see if the stew needs more salt or, possibly, a splash of soy sauce, if you'd like more depth. Serve with rice.

FERMENTED-SOYBEAN STEW
된장찌개 (Doenjang Jjigae)

Serves 4

4 cups Dashi (page 189)

¼ cup doenjang (Korean fermented soybean paste)

1 tablespoon gochujang (Korean red chili paste)

1 tablespoon gochugaru (Korean red chili flakes)

6 garlic cloves, minced

2 tablespoons soy sauce, or more to taste

2 medium onions, cut into 1-inch dice

2 medium green zucchini, cut into 1-inch chunks

1 red Korean chili pepper or other long hot chili, thinly sliced on the bias

1 green Korean chili pepper or other long hot chili, thinly sliced on the bias

½ pound brisket, sliced ⅛ inch thick (you can ask your butcher to slice it) and cut into 2- to 3-inch strips

1 pound soft or silken tofu, homemade (page 67) or store-bought, cut into 1-inch cubes

½ bunch scallions, cut into 1-inch batons

Doenjang jjigae is the quintessential representation of Korean jang. Because doenjang, the fermented soybean paste, is such a pungent ingredient, the best way to showcase its delicious flavor is to soften it. The soft tofu, the dashi, and the sweetness of the vegetables work together to mellow the intensity of the doenjang so that your palate can discern the different facets of flavor. If you buy artisanal natural doenjang, it will be quite sour in the beginning, but the sourness will turn to sweetness over time. Every traditionally made doenjang will take a different amount of time for this to happen.

Put the dashi in a stockpot or other large pot set over medium-high heat and bring to a simmer. Whisk in the doenjang and cook for 10 minutes to bring out its natural sweetness. Add the gochujang and simmer for 5 minutes. Add the gochugaru, garlic, and soy sauce and simmer for another 10 minutes.

Add the onions and simmer for 5 minutes. Add the zucchini and simmer for 5 minutes. (Adding the vegetables at different times will ensure that they will all be fully cooked at the end.) Add the chili peppers, beef, and tofu and simmer for 5 minutes. Taste and adjust the seasoning with more soy sauce if necessary.

Remove the pot from the heat, add the scallions, put on the lid, and let the stew rest for at least 30 minutes, and up to 2 hours, before serving. Serve with steamed rice and your favorite banchan, as any and all pair well with this stew.

(photos on following page)

Fermented-Soybean Stew cooked at home will be darker in color but just as delicious.

RICE

In most Korean meals, each person gets his or her own bowl of rice while sharing almost everything else on the table. Most of the recipes in this section are tasty one-bowl meals that contain all the starch, meat, and vegetables you need for a well-balanced meal. All you need is a spoon to enjoy them. In Korea, it is common to have leftover rice after most meals; fortunately, there are many great dishes that can be made with it. The reason why leftover rice is preferable for these recipes is that day-old rice contains less moisture, so it won't stick to the wok or pan while cooking.

Once you've mastered making Steamed Rice (page 212), every recipe in this book will taste better, from complex braised dishes to the simplest of banchans. Just as a well-made dashi enhances every dish it is used in, good rice highlights the flavor of anything that is served with it. Making perfect rice is much easier if you own a rice cooker. It's a worthwhile investment for your kitchen. I highly recommend the Cuckoo brand.

STEAMED RICE

Makes 8 cups

4 cups premium short-grain or medium-grain rice
4½ cups water

I love rice. A bowl of rice that blends perfect hydration, texture, and cooking temperature makes every banchan taste better. I think it's the most important element of a Korean meal. When Hanjan first opened, I had a hard time training cooks to make good rice consistently. I had to really work to convince them that rice is as important as every other dish on the menu. Six months in, I asked our dishwasher, Armando, if he knew how to cook. He said no, but he was eager to learn, so I decided to show him how to make rice. It took over a month of lessons and I checked every batch. Eventually, he mastered it. For three years, Armando made rice five times a day, every day, at Hanjan. The rice at Hanjan was never better than when Armando made it with heart and devotion, the *jung sung* that is an integral part of cooking Korean food.

Today at both Danji and Hanjan, only my chefs or sous chefs are allowed to make the rice. Even with seasoned cooks, it takes months to learn how to adjust the hydration step, calibrating both the amount of time and the amount of water necessary to perfectly cook each new bag of rice. Each bag is different, depending on how old and dry it is. As was clear in Armando's case, though, it's a task that can be mastered; all it takes is the willingness to pay attention to the small details.

Note: If your rice turns out too dry or too wet and overly sticky, it means the 4½ cups of water called for was either too little or too much for that specific bag of rice. At my restaurants, we make adjustments up or down in ¼-cup increments. Some batches of rice may need an additional full cup of water. This means that the bag of rice is older and the grains are brittle and dry. You will sometimes find a shiny label that says "New Crop" on Japanese and Korean brands of rice. These bags contain the freshest rice, and it will need less water to hydrate and cook. At both of my restaurants, we bring in 50-pound bags of rice. We use the first batches we cook as test runs to determine the correct rice-to-water ratio. Once we figure it out, usually after one or two batches, we write a label and plaster it on the bag. Starting with the next batch, every pot of rice is then perfect and consistent.

Put the rice in a large bowl and run cold water into it. Swirl your fingers through the rice, scooping up handfuls and gently rubbing the grains together to loosen the starch from the exterior. This is a meditative action; Masa used to say that this step "awakened the flavor molecules" of the rice. I believe the friction softens the exterior of each grain, allowing water to penetrate more easily during cooking. As you wash the rice, the water will become cloudy. Gently pour it out and add fresh cold water to the bowl. Repeat the process, rubbing the grains of rice together in each fresh batch of water, until the water remains

(recipe continues)

almost clear. This will take at least three and up to seven cycles. You'll know the rice is ready when you can see the details of your fingers through the water although it's still slightly cloudy. Drain the rice in a sieve and let air-dry for 20 minutes.

The rice will have absorbed some of the water that clings to it as it stands and the grains will be about 20 percent larger than their original size. The rice will appear brighter and whiter, and it should be almost dry. Check to see if the rice is ready for cooking by squeezing an individual grain. If it gives a little to the pressure of your fingertips, it is ready. If it's still rock-hard, or it breaks apart or flakes, then you will need to soak it for up to 5 minutes in the cooking water before you start cooking it.

Put the rice and the 4½ cups water in a rice cooker (or a heavy pot or stone bowl; see below). If necessary, soak for 5 minutes and then squeeze a grain of rice to check the texture. If you are unsure, squeeze an unsoaked grain of rice for comparison to feel the difference in texture.

Cook the rice using the "quick cook" setting; the regular setting incorporates a soaking period that is not necessary, since you have already soaked the rice. The quick-cook setting should take 15 to 20 minutes total. When it's done, leave the rice in the cooker for another 10 minutes to steam and rest. (If you don't allow the rice to rest for long enough, it will still be a bit wet and the kernels a bit al dente. If you leave it in the cooker for too long, it will be overcooked, overly soft, and too sticky.) After 10 minutes, open the lid and gently fluff the rice with a rice paddle. If the rice still seems wet and firm, close the lid and let it rest for another 5 minutes. Do not let the rice rest for more than 20 minutes. (Every bag of rice will have a different resting time.)

Alternatively, if you don't have a rice cooker, you can use a heavy-bottomed pot or, better yet, a flame-proof stone bowl (you can buy these in Korean supermarkets) with a tight-fitting lid. Put the rice and water in the pot or bowl, cover it, and set over high heat. Bring the water to a boil, then immediately reduce the heat to low. Let the rice cook until all the water is absorbed, about 15 minutes. Turn off the heat and let the rice rest and steam for 10 minutes before lifting the lid to fluff the rice.

Once the rice is ready, use a rice paddle or a flat wooden spatula to gently fold and fluff the rice up from the bottom of the cooker or pot, avoiding any grains that have stuck to the bottom. This should not be a problem in a rice cooker, because most of them are nonstick, but you may find a thin layer of rice stuck to the bottom of a pot or stone bowl. Ignore it for now and just fluff the cooked rice so it evens out from the bottom of the cooker or pot to the top. You are releasing some of the excess moisture and cooling off the rice as you do this. The rice will be slightly sticky and each grain should be intact, cooked all the way through with a consistent texture. Serve right away. (After you have scooped up most of the rice, you can pry off any rice stuck to the bottom of the pan.)

How to wash rice: (1) dry rice; (2) washing each grain; (3) the rice with its starch water; (4) rice drained and ready for cooking.

Note: You can store leftover rice in zip-top bags for later use. While it is still warm, put 1½-cup portions of the rice in separate zip-top bags and store in the refrigerator for up to 3 days. It will take just 1 minute in the microwave oven to have hot and steaming rice again.

DRY COOKED RICE

If you will be using cooked rice in recipes for fried rice, such as Omurice (Omelet Fried Rice, page 226), Kimchi Chadol Bokkeum Bap (Kimchi-and-Brisket Fried Rice, page 228), and Bacon Chorizo Kimchi Paella (page 230), allow the rice to cool to room temperature before portioning it. Put 1½-cup portions of the rice in zip-top bags and freeze overnight. The rice will dry out a bit in the freezer, because the moisture remaining in the rice will freeze and separate a bit from the grains of rice. Then microwave the rice for about 20 seconds before using, just enough so you are able to separate the grains of rice by hand.

RICE WITH BEEF AND VEGETABLES
비빔밥 (Bibimbap)

Serves 4

¼ cup grape seed or canola oil

1 medium carrot, peeled and cut into matchsticks

Salt

½ pound shiitake mushrooms, stems removed, caps cut into matchsticks

2 garlic cloves, minced

1 teaspoon soy sauce

Sauce

1 cup gochujang (Korean red chili paste)

¼ cup toasted sesame oil

¼ cup water

2 tablespoons sugar

2 garlic cloves, minced

½ pound (about 2 cups) bulgogi (page 142), or ½ pound ground beef *plus* 2 tablespoons soy sauce, 1 teaspoon minced garlic, and 1 teaspoon sugar

1 tablespoon grape seed or canola oil if using ground beef

2 tablespoons unsalted butter

4 large eggs

6 cups Steamed Rice (page 212), freshly cooked

¼ cup toasted sesame oil

¼ cup Spinach with Sesame (Sigeumchi Namul, page 127)

¼ cup Sautéed Gray Squash and Onion (Hobak Bokkeum, page 88)

¼ cup Spicy Bean Sprouts (Kong Namul, page 126)

4 teaspoons toasted sesame seeds

In Korean, *bibim* means mixed and *bap* means rice; hence the name for this classic dish, which is rice mixed with vegetables, gochujang (Korean red chili paste), and, occasionally, meat. Bibimbap is an iconic preparation, one that many Americans think of as a quintessential Korean dish. In Korea, it's considered a good alternative to salad, since it contains many vegetables.

Traditionally bibimbap is served in large bowls, with rice, four to eight different vegetables, and some ground beef, all topped with a sunny-side-up egg, and with gochujang on the side. You mix the contents yourself, adding enough gochujang to suit your palate. The texture will be very consistent because the vegetables are cooked separately. The egg and sesame oil enhance the flavor of the dish. I like to use bulgogi in my bibimbap recipe, because it gives it more flavor. If you are in a rush, you can substitute ground beef cooked and seasoned with soy sauce, minced garlic, and sugar, as described below. And if meat is not a part of your diet, the bibimbap will be delicious without it.

Don't hesitate to add other ingredients to your bibimbap— Korean cooks often throw together a bibimbap with whatever leftover banchan they have in the fridge. When the dish is served, the rice should be warm, the vegetables cold, the fried eggs hot, and the gochujang at room temperature. When everything is combined, the bibimbap will be roughly at room temperature.

Banchan are not necessary with bibimbap, but it's nice to serve kimchi (pages 96 to 109) on the side. I also like to serve a soup, such as Radish and Beef Soup (Mu Guk, page 195).

(recipe continues)

Set a large sauté pan over medium heat and add 1 tablespoon of the oil. When the oil begins to shimmer and just barely smoke, add the carrots and season lightly with salt. Cook, stirring for 5 minutes, or until the carrots are tender but not browned. Transfer to a plate to cool.

Set the pan back over medium heat and add the remaining 3 tablespoons oil. When the oil is hot, add the shiitake mushrooms, season lightly with salt, and cook, stirring, for 2 minutes, or until soft. Add the garlic and cook, stirring constantly, for 3 to 5 minutes, until golden brown. Add the soy sauce and cook for 1 minute more. Transfer to a plate to cool.

To make the sauce, put the gochujang, sesame oil, water, sugar, and garlic in a small bowl and mix well to blend. Set aside.

If using ground beef, set a medium skillet over medium-high heat and add the 1 tablespoon oil. Once the oil begins to smoke, add the ground beef and cook, stirring, for 5 minutes, or until the meat is lightly caramelized. Add the soy sauce, garlic, and sugar and cook, stirring for 2 to 3 minutes, until the garlic is softened. Transfer to a plate and set aside.

To fry the eggs, set a large sauté pan over medium heat and add the butter. When the butter melts, crack the eggs into the pan, leaving space between them. Season lightly with salt. Cook for 2 minutes, until the bottoms of the eggs are set, then reduce the heat to low and cook for 2 to 3 minutes more, until the whites are opaque and the yolks are golden yellow but still runny. Remove from the heat.

To assemble the bibimbap, put 1½ cups of hot rice in each bowl, drizzle with a tablespoon of the sesame oil, and slide an egg on top of the rice. Add one-quarter of the bulgogi or ground beef to each bowl and then arrange one-quarter of the carrots and mushrooms and 1 tablespoon of each of the different banchan on top of the egg whites so the yolks show in the center. Sprinkle 1 teaspoon of sesame seeds on top of each portion. Serve the sauce on the side.

To eat, add some of the sauce to your bowl, mix everything well, and enjoy with a spoon.

SIZZLING-HOT STONE BOWL BIBIMBAP

돌솥 비빔밥 (Dolsot Bibimbap)

This is my favorite lunch on a cold winter afternoon: The heated stone bowl keeps the bibimbap hot throughout my meal. When you order this at a Korean restaurant, the dish is sizzling and crackling when it's brought to the table. The best part is the delicious crust of rice, called *noo reung ji*, that forms on the bottom of the hot bowl. Not only does the crust give the rice a smoky, nutty flavor, it injects a crispy texture into the bibimbap. Be sure to scrape up the crust from the bottom of the bowl and mix it well with the rest of the bibimbap so you can enjoy a bit with each bite.

Stone bowls for bibimbap can be found in many Korean supermarkets. If you can't get them, small cast-iron skillets will do the job nicely. You can serve the dish in the skillets, as we do at Danji.

Prepare all the ingredients and components as directed on pages 217–18. To assemble the bibimbap: Brush 1 tablespoon of the sesame oil over the inside of each stone bowl (see headnote) or the bottoms of four small cast-iron skillets and scoop 1½ cups of the hot white rice into each one. Slide an egg on top of each bowl of rice. Add one-quarter of the bulgogi or ground beef to each bowl and then arrange one-quarter of the carrots and mushrooms and 1 tablespoon of each of the different banchan on top of the egg white so the yolk shows in the center. Heat each bowl or skillet over medium heat for 5 to 10 minutes, until you hear a crackling noise from the rice. Make sure to check after 5 minutes to ensure that the rice is not burning; it should turn light brown and crispy. Sprinkle 1 teaspoon of the sesame seeds on top of each portion. Use an oven mitt to transfer each bowl to its wooden base. Or, if using cast-iron skillets, set them on wooden or cork trivets. Serve with the sauce on the side. Let your guests know that it's important to scrape the rice from the bottom of the stone bowl or skillet and mix it well with all the rest of the bibimbap, as well as some of the sauce.

(photos on next page)

Sizzling-Hot Stone Bowl Bibimbap

To eat bibimbap, assemble, then mix together with sauce.

BIBIMBAP WITH BEEF TARTARE
육회 비빔밥 (Yukhwe Bibimbap)

Serves 4

¼ cup grape seed or canola oil

½ pound carrots, peeled and cut into matchsticks

Salt

½ pound shiitake mushrooms, stems removed, caps cut into matchsticks

2 garlic cloves, minced

1 teaspoon soy sauce

Sauce

¼ cup gochujang (Korean red chili paste)

2 tablespoons toasted sesame oil

2 tablespoons water

1 tablespoon sugar

1 garlic clove, minced

8 cups Steamed Rice (page 212), at room temperature

¼ cup Sigeumchi Namul (Spinach with Sesame, page 127)

¼ cup Hobak Bokkeum (Sautéed Gray Squash and Onion, page 88)

¼ cup Kong Namul (Spicy Bean Sprouts, page 126)

½ pound Yukhwe (Beef Tartare with Soy and Korean Pear, page 139)

4 large egg yolks

Jeonju, which is in the province of Jeolla in southwestern Korea, is known throughout the country for its passion for food. Its bibimbap is legendary, and many people, myself included, travel to Jeonju just to have this bibimbap with beef tartare.

If you ever visit Korea, be sure to spend a day in Jeonju to visit the markets, and the family-run restaurants inside these markets, where several generations of women rule the kitchen. Each restaurant has been serving the same food for decades, and it is simple, inexpensive, and incredibly delicious. The flavors are soulful and surprisingly complex. Some of my best meals in Korea have been at these market restaurants.

Jeonju bibimbap is very similar to classic bibimbap, but it contains beef tartare rather than cooked beef and raw egg yolks instead of fried eggs. These two small changes result in a completely different dish. To serve, the rice should be at room temperature and the beef tartare and banchan cold, so the dish will end up on the cooler side after you mix all the ingredients together. The raw egg both adds a wonderful texture and acts to bind all the ingredients. The tartare transforms a simple bibimbap into a luxurious experience.

Set a large sauté pan over medium heat and add 1 tablespoon of the oil. When the oil begins to shimmer, add the carrots and season lightly with salt. Cook, stirring constantly, for 5 minutes, until the carrots are tender but not browned. Transfer to a plate to cool.

(recipe continues)

**Bibimbap with
Beef Tartare and
Bibimbap sauce**

Set the pan back over medium heat and add the remaining 3 tablespoons oil. When the oil begins to shimmer, add the shiitake mushrooms, season lightly with salt, and cook, stirring constantly, for 2 to 3 minutes, until soft. Add the garlic and cook for about 3 minutes, until golden brown. Add the soy sauce and cook for 1 minute more. Transfer to a plate to cool.

To make the sauce, put the gochujang, sesame oil, water, sugar, and garlic in a small bowl and mix well to blend. Set aside.

To assemble the bibimbap, put 2 cups of the rice in each of four cold serving bowls and arrange the banchan, carrots, and shiitake mushrooms around and over the rice. Mound one-quarter of the beef tartare in the middle of each bowl, making a small depression in the center of the tartare for the egg yolks. Place an egg yolk in the center of each mound of tartare, sprinkle the bibimbap with the sesame seeds, and serve with the sauce on the side.

To eat, you add some of the sauce to your bowl, mix everything well, and enjoy with a spoon.

MARINATED RICE WITH SASHIMI SALAD

회덮밥 (Hwe Deop Bap)

Serves 4

Marinated Rice

½ cup mirin

½ cup rice vinegar

2 teaspoons sugar

1 teaspoon salt

6 cups Steamed Rice (page 212), freshly
 cooked

2 tablespoons toasted sesame seeds

1 pound sashimi-grade fish fillets or steaks,
 any combination of bluefin tuna, hamachi,
 salmon, and/or any white fish, cut into
 ½-inch cubes

1 pound mixed salad greens

1 bunch watercress, thick stems removed and
 cut into 2-inch pieces

1 medium red onion, quartered and sliced very
 thin

¼ cup toasted sesame oil

½ cup Chojang (page 58), or more to taste

Micro-watercress for garnish (optional)

Toasted sesame seeds for sprinkling

Imagine a Japanese chirashi with lots of fresh vegetables mixed with a spicy, sweet, and tangy gochujang dressing. The marinated rice pairs wonderfully with the raw fish, and mixed greens and watercress provide a fresh, crispy texture that contrasts with the soft rice and silky fish. Hwe deop bap is delicious, healthy, and surprisingly easy to make. During the summer, I try to eat it for lunch at least once a week. It is featured on the menus at both Danji and Hanjan.

A simple soup like Mu Guk (Radish and Beef Soup, page 195), or even Japanese miso soup, goes very well with this dish.

For the marinated rice, put the mirin, rice vinegar, sugar, and salt in a small bowl and whisk to blend. Gently fold in the marinade with the rice, stirring constantly so the rice slowly soaks up all the marinade. Fanning the top of the rice in between the folds will help the liquid evaporate. After the rice has absorbed all the marinade, about 5 minutes, add the sesame seeds and mix well.

Divide the rice evenly among four large bowls (using large bowls will make it easier to mix all the ingredients together later) and set aside to cool to room temperature.

When ready to serve, put the fish, mixed greens, watercress, red onion, sesame oil, and chojang in a large bowl and mix gently to blend. Add more chojang if you want more spice. Divide the fish into 4 equal portions and arrange one portion over each serving of rice. Garnish with sprigs of micro-watercress, if desired, and sprinkle with toasted sesame seeds.

To eat, mix the ingredients well and enjoy with a spoon.

OMELET FRIED RICE
오므라이스 (Omurice)

Serves 2

3 cups Dry Cooked Rice (page 216)

3 tablespoons grape seed or canola oil

⅓ pound ground beef (sirloin or short rib)

Salt and freshly ground black pepper

1 small onion, cut into small dice

1 small carrot, peeled and cut into small dice

3 medium shiitake mushrooms, stems
 removed, caps cut into small dice

1 cup frozen green peas, thawed

3 tablespoons soy sauce

½ bunch scallions, thinly sliced, rinsed, and
 dried as directed on page 45

3 large eggs

1 tablespoon unsalted butter

Ketchup

This simple dish of fried rice wrapped inside a classic French omelet is a popular lunch food in both Korea and Japan. I like to stuff my omelet with the fried rice and eat the first half plain, then enjoy the rest of it with a healthy dousing of ketchup to keep things interesting. Kimchi also pairs well with this dish.

The most important part of this recipe is the technique of frying the rice. If you can master this dish, you will be able to make hundreds of other equally delicious fried rice variations; the ingredients listed below can be varied according to your own preferences. You must use slightly dried day-old rice, because the moisture in fresh rice will cause it to stick to the wok or pan and make it difficult to achieve a fluffy texture. The fried rice should be done in less than 7 minutes from the time you start cooking, because the success of the dish hinges on high heat and fast cooking; overcooking fried rice will make it dry rather than fluffy.

Put the rice in a large bowl and add 1 tablespoon of the oil. Crumble the rice with your hands to separate all the grains; there should not be any clumps, or the rice will not absorb the seasoning properly.

Set a wok or large cast-iron skillet over high heat and add the remaining 2 tablespoons oil. When the oil is hot, add the ground beef, a pinch each of salt and pepper, and cook, stirring with a wooden spoon, for 1 minute, or until the beef is just barely cooked and still quite rare. Add the onion, carrots, shiitakes, and 2 pinches of salt, and cook, stirring, for 2 minutes. Stir in the peas. Then move the beef and vegetables to the edges of the pan and add the rice to the center. Season with a pinch each of salt and pepper and stir the rice for 30 seconds. Put the meat and vegetables on top of the rice and let cook without stirring for a minute to dry out the rice and crisp it up. Then toss so the rice is thoroughly mixed in.

If you're using a wok, pour the soy sauce in around the sides of the wok; it will reduce as it trickles down the sides. If you're using a skillet, move the rice to one side, tilt the skillet, and add the soy sauce to the empty part of the pan; allow the soy sauce to reduce by two-thirds. Once the soy sauce has reduced, mix everything together. Remove from the heat, add the scallions, toss once or twice, and set aside.

Whisk the eggs in a bowl with a pinch each of salt and pepper. Set a 10-inch nonstick sauté pan over medium heat, add the butter, and heat until it melts. Add the eggs to the hot pan, tilting and turning it as you add them so the eggs fully coat the bottom of the pan. Let cook until the omelet is just set, about 1 minute.

Put the fried rice on one half of the omelet and flip the other half over to cover the rice. Transfer to a plate and serve with ketchup.

KIMCHI-AND-BRISKET FRIED RICE
김치 차돌 볶음밥 (Kimchi Chadol Bokkeum Bap)

Serves 2

2 cups Dry Cooked Rice (page 216)

3 tablespoons grape seed or canola oil

⅓ pound thinly sliced brisket, with about 25% of the fat left on (you can ask your butcher to slice the meat)

Salt and freshly ground black pepper

1 medium onion, cut into small dice

1 cup Napa Cabbage Kimchi (Baechu Kimchi, page 96), cut into small dice

1 cup Korean Radish Kimchi (Chongak or Kkak Dugi Kimchi, page 105), cut into small dice

½ bunch garlic chives, chopped

2 tablespoons soy sauce

1 tablespoon toasted sesame oil

1 teaspoon toasted sesame seeds

3 scallions, thinly sliced

1 tablespoon unsalted butter

2 large eggs

I had this dish for the first time on a trip to Seoul right before we opened Hanjan. Typically, it is made with baechu (cabbage) kimchi and pork. This version was made with kkak dugi (Korean radish) kimchi and beef brisket instead of pork. I have loved traditional kimchi-and-pork fried rice since I was a kid. I was delighted to find that substituting brisket for pork resulted in a great balance between the acidity of the kimchi and the rich, slightly fatty meat. In this recipe, I use both traditional cabbage kimchi and Korean radish kimchi. It is one of our best-selling dishes at Hanjan.

To make this recipe, you will need to cook the rice a day in advance. This will yield fantastic fried rice that is dry and fluffy. You can taste each ingredient individually, yet they all combine to make a harmonious whole, and the flavor of the dish lingers on your palate. I love the initial crispy texture of the fried rice and then that moment where you break the egg yolk and it mixes into the rice to make everything creamy and soft.

Put the rice in a large bowl and add 1 tablespoon of the grape seed or canola oil. Use gloved hands for the rice, or it will stick: Crumble the rice to separate all the grains; there should not be any clumps, or the rice will not absorb the seasoning properly.

Set a wok or large cast-iron skillet over high heat and heat for 3 to 4 minutes, until it just starts to smoke. Add the remaining 2 tablespoons oil and the beef and season with a pinch each of salt and pepper. Do not toss or stir the beef at first, just let it sit and sear on the first side. This will take about 30 seconds. Add the onion and toss/stir for about 30 seconds using a wooden spoon. Add the two kimchis and toss and stir for 1 minute. Add the garlic chives and toss and stir for 30 seconds. Push the mixture to the edges of the pan and add the rice, flattening it gently against the bottom of the pan. Season the rice lightly with salt and pepper and then flip the kimchi mixture on top of it. Leave the rice alone for 1 minute, then toss and mix everything together.

If you're using a wok, pour the soy sauce in around the sides of the wok; it will reduce as it trickles down the sides. If you're using a skillet, move the rice to one side, tilt the skillet, and add the soy sauce to the empty part of the pan; allow the soy sauce to reduce by two-thirds. Once the soy sauce has reduced, mix everything together. Add the sesame oil and sesame seeds and toss for 1 minute to mix well. Then gently flatten the rice in the pan and let cook for 1 minute, or until the rice on the bottom of the pan crisps to form a crust. Sprinkle on the scallions and set aside.

To fry the eggs, set a medium nonstick skillet over medium heat and add the butter. When the butter melts, crack the eggs into the pan, leaving space between them. Season lightly with salt. Cook for 2 minutes, until the bottoms of the eggs are set, then reduce the heat to low and cook for 2 to 3 minutes more, until the whites are opaque and the yolks are golden yellow but still runny. Remove from the heat.

Transfer the fried rice to two bowls, place an egg on top of each portion, and serve immediately.

BACON CHORIZO KIMCHI PAELLA WITH FRENCH SCRAMBLED EGGS

Serves 4

4 cups Dry Cooked Rice (page 216)

2 tablespoons grape seed or canola oil

¼ pound bacon, cut into medium dice

¼ pound Spanish chorizo, skin removed and crumbled

2 medium onions, cut into medium dice

3 cups aged kimchi (fermented for at least 3 weeks), store-bought or homemade (see page 100), cut into medium dice

½ bunch garlic chives, chopped

Salt and freshly ground black pepper

1 cup juice from the kimchi

1 tablespoon soy sauce

2 tablespoons toasted sesame oil

1 bunch scallions, thinly sliced

2 tablespoons toasted sesame seeds

2 tablespoons unsalted butter

4 large eggs

This was one of the twelve dishes on Danji's opening menu. It has gone through more than twenty transformations since then. You can replace the chorizo with other pork such as bacon or pancetta, or even Spam. The rich flavor and the fattiness of pork pair beautifully with the acidity of aged kimchi. It's a traditional Korean combination that always tastes delicious.

I call this dish paella, though the technique and ingredients are similar to fried rice. I have a very high standard for fried rice, and when we opened Danji, we did not have enough gas power in our range to get the wok as hot as I wanted. Without the super-high heat, the fried rice turned out soggy. So we changed things up, added kimchi juice to give the dish more moisture and flavor, and served it on a cast-iron hot plate that formed a delicious crust on the bottom, reminiscent of the soccarat in paella. Thus our fried rice became Korean-flavored paella. When I opened Hanjan, I made sure we had enough gas power to make real fried rice (see Kimchi-and-Brisket Fried Rice/Kimchi Chadol Bokkeum Bap, page 228). Funny thing, Danji's paella is more popular than the fried rice at Hanjan.

Put the rice in a large bowl and add 1 tablespoon of the grape seed or canola oil. Crumble the rice with your hands to separate all the grains; there should not be any clumps, or the rice will not absorb the seasoning properly.

Set a large cast-iron skillet over medium heat and add the remaining 1 tablespoon oil and the chopped bacon. Cook for about 10 minutes, stirring occasionally, until the bacon has turned golden brown. (You can remove some of the fat from the pan at this point, but I never do; it adds a lot of flavor to the finished dish). Add the chorizo, increase the heat to high, and

(recipe continues)

cook, stirring occasionally, for 5 to 7 minutes; you want a little color to develop on the meat. Add the onions and sauté for 3 to 5 minutes, until they are just slightly tender. Move the meat and onions to the sides of the pan and spread the kimchi out in the middle, then put the meat and onions on top of the kimchi. This way, the meat will gently steam on top while the kimchi caramelizes below. Add the garlic chives and mix well.

Move everything to the sides of the pan and add the rice to the center of the skillet. Season lightly with salt and pepper and mix well. Flip the kimchi mixture on top of the rice and let the rice dry out a bit without browning, about 1 to 2 minutes. Start mixing everything together as you add the kimchi juice, soy sauce, and sesame oil. Spread the rice out evenly in the skillet, reduce the heat to medium-low, and cook for 5 to 8 minutes to give the rice a nice crust, then sprinkle the scallions and sesame seeds on top.

While the crust is forming, set a medium nonstick pan over low heat and add the butter. Whisk the eggs in a bowl and season with salt and pepper. When the butter has melted, add the eggs and stir well with a rubber spatula, scraping the bottom of the pans so the eggs don't overcook. When the scrambled eggs are creamy and loosely cooked, pour them on top of the paella.

Serve right away, directly from the skillet.

MUSHROOM PORRIDGE

버섯죽 (Beoseot Juk)

Serves 4 as an appetizer or side dish

½ pound cremini mushrooms or white button
    mushrooms
½ pound hen of the woods mushrooms

Porridge
1 cup sweet glutinous rice
2 tablespoons unsalted butter
1 tablespoon olive oil, plus more if needed
1 medium onion, cut into small dice
1 small carrot, peeled and cut into small dice
Salt
1 cup sake
6 to 8 cups Dashi (page 189), heated until hot
2 tablespoons soy sauce

1 tablespoon unsalted butter
1 tablespoon olive oil
1 small shallot, minced
Salt
½ bunch chives, thinly sliced

Mushrooms are one of my favorite cold-weather foods. Full of umami and earthiness, they warm your body. Another of my favorite cold-weather foods is juk, also known as congee or Asian porridge. We serve this dish at Danji as a first course in the winter months. In Europe, it's more customary to start a meal with something acidic and bright to whet your palate. In Korea, we like to serve food that is easily digestible, like a soft and mellow juk, to prepare the stomach for the rest of the meal. It's a gentle way to wake up your digestive tract, and that's exactly what I had in mind when I came up with this dish. Kimchi (pages 96 to 109) makes a great accompaniment.

Clean the cremini or button mushrooms: The best way to do this is to fill a large bowl with cold water and add the mushrooms. Move them around a bit with your hands and then leave them for a minute so all the dirt settles to the bottom. Using your hands, transfer the mushrooms to a colander and rinse out the bowl. Refill with fresh water and repeat 3 or 4 times, until the water remains clear of debris. Dry the mushrooms with paper towels and remove and discard the stems. Cut the mushrooms into small dice, cover, and reserve in the refrigerator.

Separate the "fleurettes" from the thick stems of the hen of the woods mushrooms; discard the stems. Save half of the fleurettes, the nicest-looking ones, to sauté for the garnish. Roughly dice the remaining fleurettes and set aside.

To make the porridge, put the rice in a large bowl of cold water and swirl it around with your hands. Rinse the rice several times, changing the water, until the water remains clear. Transfer the rice to a strainer to drain.

(recipe continues)

Set a large pot over medium-high heat and add the butter and oil. Once the butter melts, add the onion, carrots, cremini or button mushrooms, and diced hen of the woods mushrooms. Add a large pinch of salt and cook for 8 to 10 minutes, until the onions are tender and translucent. Add the rice and cook, stirring, for 5 minutes. If the mixture seems a little dry, add another tablespoon of oil. Add the sake and reduce until the pan is almost dry.

Add 2 cups of the hot dashi to the pan and cook, stirring, until the rice has absorbed the broth. Then add 4 more cups dashi 2 cups at a time, letting the rice absorb each addition before adding more.

Meanwhile, set a medium sauté pan over medium-high heat. Add the butter and olive oil. Once the butter has melted and the oil is shimmering, add the hen of the woods mushroom fleurettes and sauté for 2 minutes. Add the shallots, season lightly with salt, and cook for 3 to 5 minutes, stirring, until the mushrooms are tender and fully cooked. Add the chives and remove from the heat.

Once you've added about 6 cups of the dashi to the rice, the rice should be cooked all the way through, with no bite in the center. You may need to add another cup or two of dashi, stirring until the rice absorbs the broth. When the rice is done, the texture should be like that of a thick porridge but still runny like lava; it should be looser than a risotto but thicker than a soup. But even Koreans differ in textural preferences in a juk, so ultimately it's what you like to eat. Add 2 pinches of salt and the soy sauce and mix well. Taste and season with more salt if necessary.

Divide the porridge among four bowls. Spoon an equal amount of the sautéed mushroom fleurettes over each bowl and serve immediately.

SPICY SALTED COD ROE OVER RICE
명란 덮밥 (Myung Lan Deop Bap)

Serves 1

3 ounces frozen spicy cured cod or pollack roe (see headnote)

2 cups Steamed Rice (page 212), freshly cooked

2 tablespoons toasted sesame oil

A pinch of thinly sliced scallions (sliced, rinsed, and dried as directed on page 45)

Pinch of toasted sesame seeds

1 sheet toasted gim (dried Korean seaweed) or nori, cut into thin strips

---

Note: Use the best sesame oil you can—it makes a huge difference in this dish. My favorite brand is NH. It can be found at H Mart across the country and online. Or go to kimcmarket.com or gothamgrove.com for high-quality artisanal sesame oil.

While I was a line cook at Daniel, I tasted a lot of buttery French sauces all day long. When I got home, I craved something easy with spicy Asian flavors to counteract the rich food at work. During that time, I ate this dish more than any other. It's the perfect 5-minute midnight meal, as long as you have an electric rice cooker full of warm rice.

Cod roe, or *myung-lan jeot*, is a huge delicacy in both Korea and Japan (where it is called mentaiko). The typical way to eat it in Korea is to cut it into bite-sized pieces with scissors and drizzle some toasted sesame oil over them. We serve the cured roe cold as a banchan with a hot bowl of rice. The sharp and aggressively spicy, salty, fishy roe is gently smothered by the warmth of the rice to create the ultimate umami experience from the sea.

There are two types of cod roe and there is a huge difference in quality and flavor between the two. The kind I prefer and use at my restaurants is referred to as *sun-dong* in Korean, which means the roe was extracted from the cod on the boat before it was frozen. It tastes less fishy and is usually cured using less salt and fewer of the other flavorings sometimes used to mask the fishy flavor. However, the majority of cod roe is harvested after the fish have been frozen with the roe still intact. The fish are thawed later when being packaged or sold, and that is when the roe is extracted. This inferior roe is called *yook-dong* in Korean. Cured cod roe or cured pollack roe (a common substitute) are found in the freezer section of most Asian markets. As always, look for the best quality when you purchase cured cod roe.

(recipe continues)

Peel the skin off the frozen roe sacs and then carefully cut the roe into ½-inch pieces. You can use scissors and cut them inside a bowl if they seem to be too slippery for a knife. Or use a paper towel to get a better grip on the sacs as you cut them. Transfer the roe to a small serving bowl. Cover with the hot rice and leave for 3 minutes, or until the roe melts.

Drizzle the sesame oil over the top of the rice and mix everything together. Garnish with the scallions, sesame seeds, and strips of toasted gim or nori. Eat immediately.

Chinese-Korean food at Shin Heung Gwan, a 65-year-old restaurant in Haeundae, Busan.

NOODLES

If rice is a staple in the Korean diet, noodles are more of a passion. As in most other Asian cultures, Koreans are serious about their noodles. The variety of noodles seems endless and there is one for every palate. For me, hands down, my favorite noodle dish is Bibim Naengmyeon (Spicy Cold Buckwheat Noodles, page 246). It is one of the first dishes I seek out when I visit Korea and one of the last dishes I eat before my trip ends. There are many restaurants in Korea that specialize in just this one dish, and I've probably been to too many of them: I have more pictures of bibim naengmyeon on my Instagram feed than any other dish. Just thinking about the fiery, vinegary red sauce makes my mouth water—I am a bibim naengmyeon addict. When you try the recipes in this chapter, I'm sure you will soon discover your favorite noodle dish as well.

Unlike Italian pasta, which is mostly made with wheat flour, Korean noodles vary not only in terms of size and shape, but also, more important, in terms of the ingredients from which the noodles are made. The technique and method of making the noodles will vary depending on the base ingredient, which may be wheat, buckwheat, sweet potato, arrowroot, or mung bean. I have not included recipes for making these different kinds of noodles in this book, as it is very labor intensive to make them at home, and you can buy sufficiently good-quality noodles at most Asian supermarkets.

While Koreans sometimes eat noodles instead of rice, noodles do not replace rice in most meals. When there is banchan, fish, meat, and/or stew at a meal, these are almost always served with rice. Noodles are eaten when you don't want to bother with all those other items. A bowl of noodles will have a well-seasoned sauce or broth that will complement the neutral flavor of the pasta. These are one-bowl meals that can be enjoyed for breakfast, lunch, or dinner. The recipes I share with you are some of the most popular noodle dishes in Korea—and they're also my personal favorites.

BUCKWHEAT NOODLES IN CHILLED BROTH

물냉면 (Mul Naengmyeon)

Serves 10

Broth

4 pounds lean beef brisket

One 2-pound boneless pork shoulder roast

3 gallons water

One 10-inch square of dashima

3 dried shiitake mushrooms

2 pounds boneless chicken breasts

3 medium onions, peeled, halved, and charred on the cut sides on a grill or in a cast-iron skillet

1 pound Korean radishes (mu) or daikon radishes, deeply peeled and cut into ⅛-inch-thick slices

2 bunches scallions, trimmed

2 heads garlic, cut horizontally in half

½ cup sugar

Salt

Cucumber and Radish Pickle

1 cup water

1 cup rice vinegar

1 tablespoon sugar

2 teaspoons salt

2 Kirby cucumbers, sliced paper-thin (use a mandoline if you have one)

½ pound Korean radish (mu) or daikon radish, peeled deeply and cut into matchsticks

Mul naengmyeon, from North Korea, is the most popular cold noodle dish in Korea. There is a restaurant that specializes in mul naengmyeon in almost every small neighborhood all across the country. It is insanely popular and it is one of the few foods Koreans will wait in line for during the hot summer months. Most Korean barbecue restaurants also serve naengmyeon, as the last savory course after the meat.

In Korea, mul naengmyeon isn't usually made at home because it involves so many different ingredients and the cooking process is very tedious. And it's quite affordable at restaurants, because most places charge less than $15 a bowl. With so much meat going into a broth that takes over a day's cooking time, you may wonder how it can be so cheap. Because the dish is so popular and has long been considered an inexpensive lunch or snack, there is intense pressure on restaurants to keep their prices low. So practically every naengmyeon restaurant in Korea, and the US, uses MSG and bouillon cubes instead of meat to flavor their broth. I've spent more than ten years trying to find a naengmyeon restaurant in Korea that does not use MSG and I haven't yet succeeded.

So I decided to make mul naengmyeon myself to serve at Hanjan in the summer months. Our broth is all natural and intensely flavorful. I am very proud of this mul naengmyeon, and I honestly believe that it is the most delicious bowl of mul naengmyeon you can get whether here in New York City or in Korea.

To Serve

3 tablespoons Korean mustard powder

2 tablespoons water

10 portions naengmyeon (buckwheat) noodles (my favorite brand is Chung Soo)

5 hard-boiled eggs, peeled and sliced lengthwise in half

Gochugaru (Korean red chili flakes)

Toasted sesame seeds

Rice vinegar

Note: This recipe makes enough broth for 10 servings. You will need 1½ to 2 cups of broth for each serving. Because you freeze the broth to serve it, if you want to serve just 2 or 4 or 6 people, you can simply keep the extra broth frozen for another meal. Simply reduce the garnish amounts accordingly.

To make the broth, put the beef and pork in a large bowl filled with cold water. Let rest for 2 hours in the refrigerator, until most of the blood has drained into the water. Rinse the meat, pat it dry, and refrigerate in a covered container until you are ready to use it.

Pour the 3 gallons of cold water into a large stockpot or other pot set over high heat and add the dashima and dried shiitake mushrooms. When the water comes to boil, add the beef brisket and lower the heat to maintain a simmer. Simmer for 1 hour, skimming off the impurities that rise to the surface.

Add the pork shoulder and simmer for another hour, skimming, then add the chicken breasts and simmer for another 30 minutes, skimming. Transfer the beef brisket to a large bowl and allow to cool to room temperature, 30 to 45 minutes, then cover tightly with plastic wrap and refrigerate.

Once you removed the brisket, add the onions, radish, scallion, and garlic to the broth and simmer for 1½ hours (4 hours in total). Strain the broth into a large bowl or another pot and discard the solids (the pork and chicken will be spent at this point). Remove as much of the fat floating on top of the broth as possible with a ladle. You should have 5 to 6 quarts of broth, depending on evaporation. Add the sugar to the hot broth, then add 1 teaspoon salt per quart of broth, or to taste. Check the seasoning once more and add more salt if necessary. Let the broth cool to room temperature, then remove any surface fat with a paper towel. Transfer to quart containers, being sure to leave some room at the top of each container, and freeze overnight.

Meanwhile, to make the cucumber and radish pickle, put the water, rice vinegar, sugar, and salt in a small pot set over medium heat and cook, stirring constantly, until the sugar and salt have dissolved. Remove from the heat.

(recipe continues)

Buckwheat Noodles in Chilled Broth

Put the cucumbers and radish in a container and pour the vinegar mixture over them. (If you like, you can pickle the cucumbers and radish separately and add a pinch of gochugaru to the radish to achieve a beautiful pinkish hue.) Stir gently to combine, cover, and refrigerate overnight.

The next day, an hour or two before you're ready to serve the noodles, pull the broth from the freezer and let it thaw until it is half-liquid with a slushy texture. You can microwave it in 1-minute intervals to speed up the process. If you don't want the slushy texture, you can thaw the broth completely, but make sure it's icy cold when you serve it.

Set a large pot of water over high heat and bring to a boil.

Meanwhile, thinly slice the chilled beef brisket against the grain into bite-sized strips.

Make Korean mustard by mixing the mustard powder with the water in a small cup, stirring until it rehydrates and forms a paste. Reserve to serve with the noodles.

Cook the naengmyeon noodles in the boiling water following the directions on the package. Set up a generous ice water bath to chill and rinse the noodles. The noodles are very starchy, so they need to be rinsed very well. When they are cooked, transfer the noodles to the ice bath. Drain the noodles and squeeze to remove as much of the water as possible, then discard the ice water and add fresh ice water to the bowl. Repeat the rinsing process 2 more times to rid the noodles of most of their starch.

Divide the noodles among individual serving bowls. Pour 1½ to 2 cups of the slushy broth into each bowl. Add a spoonful of the drained cucumbers and radish, some sliced brisket, and half a hard-boiled egg to each bowl. (When serving this in the colder months, I also add a few slices of sweet Asian pear.) Add a sprinkle of gochugaru to give it a nice kick, followed by a pinch of toasted white sesame seeds. Serve with the prepared mustard and a small container of rice vinegar on the side.

SPICY COLD BUCKWHEAT NOODLES
비빔냉면 (Bibim Naengmyeon)

Serves 6

Sauce

4 cups broth from Buckwheat Noodles in Chilled Broth (Mul Naengmyeon, page 242) or Dashi (page 189)

½ small Vidalia or other sweet onion

1 small Korean or Asian pear

1 small Fuji apple

1¾ cups sugar

1 head garlic, separated into cloves, peeled, and minced

4 teaspoons minced ginger

⅔ cup gochugaru (Korean red chili flakes)

¾ cup rice vinegar

2 tablespoons soy sauce

1 tablespoon fish sauce

2 tablespoons plus 2 teaspoons salt

1½ tablespoons toasted sesame seeds

6 portions naengmyeon (buckwheat) noodles (my favorite brand is Chung Soo)

To Serve

1¼ cups sauce (above)

¾ cup toasted sesame oil

3 cups chilled broth from Mul Naengmyeon or Dashi

¾ cup Cucumber and Radish Pickle (page 242)

18 thin slices beef brisket from Mul Naengmyeon

18 thin slices Korean or Asian pear (from 1 to 2 pears)

3 hard-boiled eggs, peeled and sliced lengthwise in half

Like Mul Naengmyeon (Buckwheat Noodles in Chilled Broth, page 242), bibim naengmyeon is from North Korea, but these noodles are very aggressively seasoned with a sweet, salty, spicy, and tangy thick dark red sauce that is mixed in with the noodles with chopsticks right before eating. The intricate balance between the complex flavors of the sauce and the cold, chewy noodles make the dish very addictive. Even on the hottest of summer days, when I have zero appetite, I will still crave a bowl of these noodles. It is one of my favorite Korean dishes, and it's difficult to find a good version outside of Korea. Be sure to make the sauce at least 24 hours in advance; for best results, make it two full days ahead so the sharp flavors can mellow a bit and harmonize with each other. I would also suggest that you make this dish after you have made mul naengmyeon, because it has many of the same garnishes and makes good use of any leftover broth.

To make the sauce, put the broth or dashi in a pot set over medium heat and bring to a boil. While the broth is heating, thinly slice the onion and peel and core the pear and apple.

When the broth comes to a boil, add the onion, pear, apple, sugar, garlic, and ginger, bring to a simmer, reduce the heat slightly, and cook at a gentle simmer for 20 minutes, or until all the vegetables and fruit are fully cooked. Remove from heat and let cool to room temperature.

Transfer the broth mixture to a blender and puree until smooth (you may need to work in batches), then add the gochugaru, rice vinegar, soy sauce, fish sauce, salt, and sesame seeds and blend well. The texture will be like a thick soup or Texas-style chili. Transfer to a covered container and refrigerate for at least 24 hours, and up to 48 hours, so the flavors can settle and harmonize.

When ready to serve, set a large pot of water over high heat and bring to a boil. Add the naengmyeon noodles and cook following the directions on the package. Set up a generous ice water bath to chill and rinse the noodles. The noodles are very starchy, so they need to be rinsed very well. When they are cooked, transfer the noodles to the ice bath. Drain the noodles and squeeze them to remove as much of the water as possible, then discard the ice water and add fresh ice water to the bowl. Repeat the rinsing process 2 more times to rid the noodles of most of their starch.

Divide the noodles among six chilled bowls. Garnish each one with 3 tablespoons of the sauce, 2 tablespoons sesame oil, and ½ cup chilled mul broth or dashi. Put 2 tablespoons of the cucumber and radish pickle and 3 slices of brisket on top of the noodles in each bowl, add 3 slices of pear and half of a hard-boiled egg, and serve. Tell your guests to mix the noodles well to distribute the sauce and garnishes before they eat the noodles.

SPICY COLD NOODLES
비빔국수 (Bibim Guksu)

Serves 4

1 cup soy sauce

One 3-inch square dashima

2 dried shiitake mushrooms

1 head garlic, cut horizontally in half

1 medium onion, cut into small dice

4 cups water

1 pound beef brisket

2 large eggs

1 tablespoon salt

1 teaspoon baking soda

1 tablespoon vinegar

Bibim Sauce

2 cups Chojang (page 58)

¼ cup toasted sesame oil

¼ cup BKO (Bacon Kimchi Onion) Sauce (page 60)

4 quarts water

4 portions dried buckwheat, soba, or somyeon noodles

1 cup kimchi (store-bought or homemade, page 96), cut into matchsticks

1 medium English cucumber, unpeeled, cut into matchsticks

4 teaspoons toasted sesame seeds

This is a spicy cold noodle preparation that is best served in the summer to wake up the palate with its intense flavors. When I'm not up for making naengmyeon (page 242 or 246) at home, this is the dish I turn to. The sauce is seasoned with a condiment I call BKO (Bacon Kimchi Onion) Sauce (page 60). It provides an exciting kick of flavor, with the slightly nutty, smoky taste of the bacon, the sweetness of the onion, and the sour, spicy kimchi. I top the chilled noodles with more kimchi, tender braised brisket, crunchy cucumber, and cold soft-boiled eggs. Even if you think you're not that hungry, you'll be amazed by how quickly this dish disappears once you start slurping up the flavor-packed noodles.

The temperature of this dish is not important—the noodles can be enjoyed hot, cold, or at room temp. But there is the question of when to eat the egg. Some say you should eat it first so it can coat your stomach lining, readying it for the spicy noodles. Some say you should eat it last, to satiate you, because the spicy and tangy noodles will not be enough for your taste buds to be content. I eat it with the noodles to balance the spiciness.

Preheat the oven to 325°F.

Put the soy sauce, dashima, dried shiitakes, garlic, onion, and water in a Dutch oven or other large ovenproof pot set over medium-high heat. Bring the mixture to a simmer and add the brisket. Make sure it is completely submerged in the liquid; weight it down with a clean plate if necessary.

Cover the pot with the lid, transfer to the oven, and braise the brisket for 2½ hours, or until the meat is fork-tender. Remove from the oven and let the meat cool in the braising liquid.

(recipe continues)

When the meat is cool enough to handle, remove it from the braising liquid and pull it apart into matchstick-sized pieces, discarding any chunks of fat and gristle that you find. Strain the braising liquid, discard the solids, and pour into a covered container. Add the brisket and refrigerate until ready to use.

Set a small pot of water, enough to cover the 2 eggs, over medium-high heat. Set up a small ice bath. Once the water comes to a boil, add the eggs, salt, baking soda, and vinegar and bring back to a boil. (The baking soda makes it easier to peel the soft-boiled eggs, and the vinegar will help center the yolks.) Adjust the heat to maintain a gentle boil and cook for exactly 6 minutes. Transfer the eggs to the ice bath and chill for 5 minutes. Drain the eggs, carefully peel them, and slice lengthwise in half. Reserve.

To make the bibim sauce, put the chojang, sesame oil, and BKO in a large bowl and stir to blend. Set aside.

Set a large pot of water over high heat and bring to a boil. Add the noodles to the boiling water and cook following the directions on the package. Drain the noodles in a colander and rinse very well under cold running water to chill the noodles and remove all the exterior starch. Drain, transfer to a lint-free kitchen towel, and pat dry.

Add the noodles to the bowl with the bibim sauce and mix well to coat the noodles. Divide the noodles among four large bowls and top each with an equal amount of the kimchi, cucumber, and cold brisket. Then add half a soft-boiled egg to each bowl. Sprinkle the toasted sesame seeds on top and serve immediately. Tell your guests to mix the garnishes and noodles together before eating.

SOMYEON NOODLES IN ANCHOVY BROTH
잔치국수 (Janchi Guksu)

Serves 4

2 quarts Dashi (page 189)

4 garlic cloves, minced

8 medium fresh shiitakes, stems removed, caps thinly sliced

2 medium carrots, cut into matchsticks

2 medium onions, thinly sliced

¼ cup soy sauce

1 teaspoon salt, or to taste

1 teaspoon freshly ground black pepper, or to taste

4 portions somyeon noodles

1 bunch scallions, thinly sliced, rinsed, and dried as directed on page 45 (optional)

Toasted gim (dried Korean seaweed) or nori, cut into thin strips (optional)

If you've only ever tasted cured anchovies sold in jars or cans or marinated fresh anchovies served in restaurants, you will be surprised by how delicate this anchovy broth is. It is a light, clear broth redolent of subtle ocean flavors. This dish is widely served at celebrations and weddings, hence its name: *janchi* means party.

Koreans also consider this dish a hangover remedy—one to be eaten *before* you go to sleep, not when you wake up. For that reason, it is offered in many of the pojang machas, roadside tents that open in the early evening and serve food and drinks until dawn. Pojang-machas used to be ubiquitous in Seoul. Now they are mostly found in the older neighborhoods and outside the city. Most of the time, there's just one cook manning a gas stove, with the ingredients spread out on a counter in front of him or her. Diners can pick and choose their ingredients to order a variety of dishes. These roadside tents are popular drinking spots, where guests can gather around wooden benches and tables.

Pour the dashi into a large stockpot or other pot set over medium-high heat and bring to barely a simmer. Meanwhile, bring a large pot of water for cooking the noodles to a boil over high heat.

Add the garlic, mushrooms, carrots, and onions to the simmering dashi. Cook, stirring occasionally, for 10 minutes, or until all the vegetables are just cooked through and tender. Add the soy sauce, salt, and pepper and stir to blend; the broth will be quite peppery. Adjust the seasoning to taste if necessary. Turn off the heat and cover to keep warm.

(recipe continues)

Cook the noodles in the boiling water for 3 to 4 minutes, until just tender. Transfer to a colander and rinse with hot water to remove the exterior starch. Drain thoroughly.

Divide the noodles evenly among four large bowls. Ladle 2 cups of the hot broth over each portion. Top with the sliced scallions and seaweed and serve immediately, with banchan, if you like.

NOODLES IN BLACK BEAN SAUCE
자장면 (Jajangmyeon)

Serves 4

½ cup plus 2 tablespoons grape seed or canola oil

1 cup Korean black bean paste (jajang or choonjang, found in Korean markets)

1 pound pork belly, cut into ½-inch dice

Salt and freshly ground black pepper

5 garlic cloves, minced

A 1-ounce piece ginger, peeled and minced

3 medium onions, cut into ½-inch dice

2 medium zucchini, cut into ½-inch dice

½ cup sugar

1 tablespoon gochugaru (Korean red chili flakes)

4 cups Dashi (page 189) or low-sodium chicken stock

2 tablespoons cornstarch

3 tablespoons cold water

1½ cups frozen green peas, thawed

¾ pound fresh or 1 pound dried jajang or kalguksu noodles

½ medium English cucumber, cut into matchsticks

This Chinese-Korean dish is the most popular hot noodle dish in Korea, across all ages—kids love it as much as their grandparents do. It's the ultimate comfort food. You won't find this dish anywhere in China, but every single one of the thousands of Chinese restaurants in Korea serves it. The technique used in this recipe for slowly cooking the black bean paste is similar to the way Indian curry spices are cooked with ghee to open up their flavors. The paste is fried in oil for at least 20 minutes to bring out its nutty flavors. You can serve any leftover sauce over rice with a fried egg and have a brunch dish to be proud of.

Set a medium sauté pan or skillet over low heat and add ½ cup of the oil. When it is warm, add the black bean paste and cook for 20 to 25 minutes, stirring constantly with a heatproof spatula to prevent scorching, until the bean paste and oil have emulsified and the flavor has become sweet. Transfer the paste to a bowl and reserve.

Set a large pot over medium heat and add the remaining 2 tablespoons oil. When it begins to shimmer, add the diced pork belly. Season the meat with salt and pepper and cook, stirring constantly, for 5 minutes, or until the pork is crispy and golden brown. Add the garlic, ginger, and onions and cook for 5 minutes, stirring. Add the zucchini and cook for another 5 minutes. Add the reserved black bean paste, the sugar, and gochugaru and cook for another 5 minutes, stirring constantly.

Add the dashi or stock and bring to a simmer. Cook for 8 to 10 minutes, until all of the vegetables are tender. Make a slurry by whisking the cornstarch and cold water in a small bowl until the cornstarch is dissolved. Pour the slurry in a stream into the simmering sauce, moving the bowl around the pot as you add it

(recipe continues)

and whisking so the starch does not clump up. Simmer for 5 more minutes, or until the sauce has thickened and turned glossy, then turn off the heat and stir in the peas.

Meanwhile, set a large pot of water over high heat and bring to a boil. Drop the noodles into the boiling water and cook following the package direction until completely tender. While the noodles are cooking, prepare a large ice bath and set a colander in it. Use a strainer to transfer the cooked noodles to the colander and cool the noodles for 1 minute. ("Shocking" the noodles like this gives them an elastic texture that makes them more fun to eat.) Lift the colander of noodles from the ice bath and return them to the boiling water for 15 to 20 seconds to reheat them.

Drain the noodles in the colander, shake off the excess water, and divide them evenly among four large bowls. Ladle about 1½ cups of sauce over each portion of noodles and top with an equal amount of the cucumber matchsticks. Serve immediately.

NOODLES IN SPICY SEAFOOD BROTH
짬뽕 (Jjamppong)

Serves 4

Chicken Stock
1 small chicken, with fat intact
3 quarts water

Broth
½ cup grape seed or canola oil
1 small green cabbage, cut into bite-sized
  pieces
2 onions, cut into bite-sized pieces
6 garlic cloves, minced
A ½-ounce piece of ginger, peeled and minced
¼ cup gochugaru (Korean red chili flakes)
2 quarts Chicken Stock (above) or canned low-
  sodium chicken broth

2 medium fresh squid (4 to 6 ounces), cleaned
16 bay scallops
8 mussels, cleaned and debearded if necessary
8 colossal (U14–16) shrimp, peeled and
  deveined
2 tablespoons soy sauce
1 tablespoon fish sauce
2 teaspoons salt, or to taste
¾ pound fresh or 1 pound dried jajang or
  kalguksu noodles

Garnish
1 bunch scallions, sliced into thin rounds,
  rinsed, and dried as directed on page 45
1 red Korean chili pepper or other long hot
  chili, thinly sliced

Jjamppong is served in the same restaurants that serve Jajangmyeon (Noodles in Black Bean Sauce, page 255). While it was originally created by Chinese immigrants in Korea, it has evolved into a dish that is uniquely Korean. Jjamppong is the counterpoint to jajangmyeon. Its hot, spicy, seafood-laden broth is the opposite of the thick, sweet, porky jajangmyeon sauce. I used to have a hard time deciding whether to order jajangmyeon or jjamppong noodles. Fortunately, these days you can order half and half, in a dish called jjam ja myeon. Many Koreans crave jjamppong after a night of drinking because its sharp, spicy flavor can awaken a palate dulled by alcohol and the hearty, spicy broth makes you break out in a nice sweat.

More so than any other recipe, high quality, homemade chicken stock is integral to the flavor of the broth in this dish. While you can opt to use store-bought chicken broth, I highly recommend that you make it using the method given here. You won't regret it.

If making the chicken stock, rinse the chicken under cold water. Put the water and chicken in a large pot set over medium-high heat and bring to a boil, then lower the heat to maintain a gentle simmer and cook for 1½ hours. Remove from the heat and cool to room temperature.

Remove the chicken from the pot and reserve for another use, such as chicken salad. Strain the stock (do not skim off the fat) into a covered container and refrigerate until you are ready to use it. You will need 2 quarts stock for this recipe; reserve the extra stock for another use.

(recipe continues)

To make the broth, set a large wok or deep skillet over high heat and heat until it is very hot. Add the oil, and when it is smoking, add the cabbage and onions. Sauté the vegetables for 5 minutes, stirring constantly and gently tilting the pan toward the flame so it hits the oil inside and it flares up; Koreans call this *bul-mat*, or fire taste, and the slight bitterness it creates is a nice addition to the overall flavor profile of this dish. As soon as the oil flares set the pan flat on the burner again, add the garlic and ginger, and cook for 5 minutes, stirring constantly. Add the gochugaru and cook for another 5 minutes, stirring constantly. Add the 2 quarts chicken stock, bring it to a boil, and add the seafood, soy sauce, fish sauce, and salt. Reduce the heat, bring the mixture to a low simmer, and cook for 4 minutes, or until all of the mussels have opened and the seafood is cooked through. Taste the broth; depending on how salty your fish sauce and soy sauce are, you may need to add more salt.

While the broth is cooking, set a large pot of water over high heat and bring to a boil. Just before serving, cook the noodles as directed on the package. It usually takes 6 to 8 minutes for dried noodles and 4 minutes for fresh. While the noodles are cooking, prepare a large ice bath and set a colander in it. Use a strainer to transfer the cooked noodles to the colander and cool for 1 minute. ("Shocking" the noodles like this gives them an elastic texture that makes them more fun to eat.) Lift up the colander of noodles and return them to the boiling water for 15 to 20 seconds to reheat them.

Use a strainer to remove the noodles from the pot, shake off the excess water, and divide them evenly among four large bowls. Add some of the hot broth and an equal portion of the seafood to each bowl. Put a pile of the scallions in the middle of each bowl, add a few red pepper slices, and serve immediately.

SWEET POTATO NOODLES WITH VEGETABLES

잡채 (Japchae)

Serves 4

¾ pound dried dangmyeon noodles

1 pound spinach, washed and thick stems removed

6 tablespoons grape seed or canola oil

2 medium onions, thinly sliced

Salt

1 green bell pepper, cored, seeds and ribs removed, and cut into matchsticks

1 red bell pepper, cored, seeds and ribs removed, and cut into matchsticks

¼ cup toasted sesame oil

½ pound shiitake mushrooms, stems removed, caps thinly sliced

6 garlic cloves, minced

½ cup plus 2 tablespoons soy sauce

Freshly ground black pepper

2 cups Dashi (page 189) or water, plus more if needed

2 tablespoons sugar

1 tablespoon toasted sesame seeds

Japchae is made with dangmyeon, clear noodles made from sweet potato starch; the overall flavor of the dish is sweet and salty, with a touch of nuttiness from the sesame oil. This dish is very popular in Korean restaurants in the US, where it is served as an appetizer. Like Scallion Pancakes (Pajeon, page 285), japchae has become an American favorite in Korean restaurants all over the country. Dangmyeon noodles are fun to eat because they have a stringy and stretchy texture. The noodles are versatile because they easily absorb the flavors of the other ingredients. You can add 1½ to 2 cups of bulgogi (page 142) to this recipe for a heartier dish.

This dish requires a lot of knife work, and I highly suggest buying a Japanese mandoline with a julienne cutter, because it will save you a lot of time. These are relatively inexpensive and, if you cook regularly, you will find yourself using yours all the time.

Japchae is best served warm, although in the summertime you can serve it at room temperature. My favorite way to use up the leftovers is to make fried rice the next day. I mix 2 parts japchae with 1 part cold Dry Cooked Rice (page 216) and a touch of soy sauce for seasoning. Fry it up in a large sauté pan, and you get two good meals from one delicious dish.

Soak the dangmyeon noodles in cold water for 1 hour.

Meanwhile, set a large pot of salted water over high heat and bring to a boil. Prepare an ice bath. Blanch the spinach in the boiling water for 2 minutes, then transfer to the ice bath to cool. Drain in a colander and then squeeze all the water out of the leaves.

Set a 12-inch sauté pan over medium-high heat and add 2 tablespoons of the grape seed or canola oil. When the oil begins to shimmer and just barely smoke, add the onions and a pinch of salt and cook for 3 minutes, stirring constantly. Add the green and red bell peppers and a pinch of salt and cook for about 3 minutes, stirring, until all of the vegetables are cooked through and tender. Transfer to a medium bowl.

Wipe the pan clean, set it over medium-high heat, and add the remaining ¼ cup grape seed or canola oil and 2 tablespoons of the sesame oil. When the oil begins to shimmer and just barely smoke, add the mushrooms, three-quarters of the minced garlic, and 1 tablespoon of the soy sauce and season with salt and pepper. Cook, stirring constantly to keep the mushrooms from sticking to the pan; they will release some of their liquid and turn golden brown. When the mushrooms are cooked through and tender, about 5 minutes, transfer them to the bowl with the other vegetables.

Put the dashi or water, the remaining ½ cup soy sauce, the sugar, the remaining garlic and 1 tablespoon sesame oil, and 1 teaspoon salt in a large straight-sided pan and bring to a simmer. Add the noodles and cook for about 5 minutes, until they are just tender but still stretchy and chewy; you may need to add more dashi or water. Add all of the vegetables, mix well, and cook for another 2 minutes, or until everything is hot. All the liquid should have been absorbed by the noodles or evaporated in the cooking process so all you see is sesame oil coating the ingredients. If there is any liquid left, increase the heat to high and cook until it has all evaporated.

Transfer the noodles to a large platter and sprinkle the toasted sesame seeds over the top. Serve immediately.

SPICY PORK AND GOCHUJANG BOLOGNESE NOODLES

Serves 4

1 tablespoon grape seed or canola oil

1 pound ground pork

Salt and freshly ground black pepper

2 tablespoons gochugaru (Korean red chili flakes)

1 medium onion, cut into small dice

4 garlic cloves, minced

2 tablespoons soy sauce

¼ cup BKO (Bacon Kimchi Onion) Sauce (page 60)

1 cup gochujang (Korean red chili paste)

1 tablespoon sugar

¾ pound fresh or 1 pound dried jajang or kalguksu noodles

About 1 cup Dashi (page 189; optional)

1 medium English cucumber, cut into matchsticks

This is a fun dish that came about because of my love of gochujang and Italian food. The sauce has similar ingredients to a traditional Italian Bolognese, but instead of tomatoes, I use gochujang as the base. Although the flavors are undeniably Korean, the appearance of the dish brings to mind an Italian red sauce pasta. I serve this at Danji for lunch in the winter as something spicy and flavorful that will warm people up from the inside out.

Set a large pot of water over high heat and bring to a boil. Meanwhile, set a medium pot over medium heat and add the oil and ground pork. Cook for 2 minutes, stirring gently with a wooden spoon to break up the pork. Season with 2 pinches each of salt and pepper. Add the gochugaru and stir to blend. Add the onion and garlic and cook, stirring, for 10 minutes, or until the vegetables have softened and become fragrant. Add the soy sauce, BKO, gochujang, and sugar and mix well. Remove from the heat.

Drop the noodles into the boiling water and cook until they are just tender, about a minute less than what the package suggests, because you will finish cooking them in the sauce. Prepare a large ice bath and set a colander into it. Transfer the cooked noodles to the colander in the ice bath to stop the cooking process and remove exterior starch. ("Shocking" the noodles like this will enhance their stretchy, chewy texture.)

Lift up the colander, shake gently to drain the noodles, and transfer to the pot with the sauce. Set over high heat and stir gently until the noodles are hot and have absorbed some of the sauce, 3 to 4 minutes. Add a cup or so of dashi or hot water from the noodle cooking pot if the mixture is too dry. When done, these noodles should be completely tender, not al dente.

Divide the noodles evenly among four bowls. Serve with the cucumber matchsticks on top.

HANJAN'S 12-HOUR KOREAN RAMYEON
라면

Serves 8

Broth

3 pounds pork bones (ask your butcher or
  supermarket to save the pork and chicken
  bones for you)
2 pounds chicken bones
4 gallons water
2 pounds fish bones and heads (or substitute 1
  pound large dried anchovies)
Two 6-inch squares dashima
8 dried shiitake mushrooms
2 heads garlic, cut horizontally in half
2 onions, halved
1 leek, halved
½ head Napa cabbage, quartered
½ cup gochugaru (Korean red chili flakes)
½ cup soy sauce
2 tablespoons minced garlic
Salt

Soft-Boiled Eggs

4 large eggs
1 tablespoon salt
1 teaspoon baking soda
1 tablespoon vinegar (any kind will do)

Four 7-ounce portions fresh ramen noodles
  (sold in Korean, Japanese, and other Asian
  supermarkets)
1 bunch scallions, thinly sliced, rinsed, and
  dried as directed on page 45

This dish was inspired by the hand-pulled Chinese noodles called *lamian*. The Japanese translated *lamian* to *ramen*, and their version of the noodles is the most famous here in the US; Koreans call them *ramyeon*. As opposed to Japan, where they have restaurants and counters that serve ramen made from scratch, in Korea, the word *ramyeon* refers only to the instant variety that you can make in less than five minutes with fried dried noodles and packets of soup base powder. The most popular Korean brand is Shin Ramyeon. In this recipe, I tried to re-create the flavors of that ramyeon with all natural ingredients (and more advanced cooking techniques). While the flavor of the two may be similar, in my homemade ramyeon, you can taste the intensity of the pork, the lightness and sweetness of the vegetables, and the heat of the spice; all the ingredients have their own distinctive flavors, unlike the instant version, where the MSG is dominant. This dish provides a delicious—and healthier—alternative using the natural glutamates in the dashi.

The dish takes a very long time to make, and you may wonder if it's worth making from scratch when Shin Ramyeon costs about $2 and takes barely any time to cook. The answer is definitely yes. This is a dish for those who feel that the journey is as important as the destination. To see and taste the ramyeon broth as it takes shape will teach you a lot about the ingredients that go into it. It's fascinating to watch as water is transformed into an intense meaty broth, then fish and vegetables are added to lighten the flavor, and the spices to give the broth a new dimension. Before I opened my restaurants, I would sometimes throw a blind-tasting wine party and

(recipe continues)

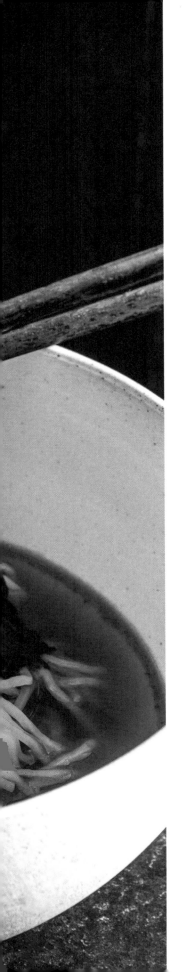

invite a bunch of friends over while this broth simmered on the stove. We would drink into the wee hours, until the ramyeon broth was done, and finish off the night with each person slurping away at an intense bowl of pure umami. I hope that one day when you're feeling ambitious, you will make this recipe and invite a few friends over to share it (and perhaps some wine) with you.

I like to serve this with any appropriate garnish among the leftovers I have in my fridge. One of my favorites is leftover strips of bossam (page 145); I freeze them for an occasion just as this. Also delicious are Seaweed Sashimi (Miyeok, page 87) and Spicy Bean Sprouts (Kong Namul, page 126). Be creative, and top off the dish with anything you like!

Preheat the oven to 500°F.

To make the broth, put the pork and chicken bones on two sheet pans and roast, turning occasionally, for 25 to 30 minutes, until browned. Remove the chicken bones from the pans, let cool slightly, and refrigerate (you'll use them later). Transfer the roasted pork bones to a large stockpot or other large pot set over medium-high heat, add the water, and bring to a boil. Lower the heat to maintain a very gentle simmer and simmer for 6 hours.

Add the roasted chicken bones to the pot and gently simmer for another 4 hours. Then add the fish head and bones, dashima, shiitake mushrooms, garlic, onions, leeks, and Napa cabbage and gently simmer for 90 minutes. You should end up with about a gallon of broth. If the liquid seems to be evaporating too quickly, you can add another quart or two of water when you add the chicken bones, but it's better to keep the temperature low enough so that it simmers gently without overreducing. As long as you keep the stock at a very gentle simmer, it should be fine. Strain the broth and discard the solids.

(recipe continues)

Shortly before you're ready to serve, pour 2 quarts water, or enough to submerge the 4 eggs, into a small pot and bring to a boil over high heat. When it comes to a fast boil, add the salt, baking soda, and vinegar. (The baking soda makes it easier to peel the soft-boiled eggs, and the vinegar will help center the yolks.) Bring the water back to a boil and add the eggs. When the water comes back to a boil, set a timer for 6 minutes. Prepare an ice bath. When the timer goes off, transfer the eggs to the ice bath and let them cool for 5 minutes, then drain the eggs and peel right away; reserve. Just before serving, cut each egg lengthwise in half.

To cook the noodles, set a large pot of water over high heat and bring to a boil. Meanwhile, put the broth in a separate pot, bring to a simmer, and add the gochugaru, soy sauce, minced garlic, and salt to taste.

Open the noodle package and separate the noodles a little, using your hands, so they will not stick together while cooking, add them to the boiling water, and cook for 3 minutes. Meanwhile, prepare a large ice bath and set a colander in it. Transfer the cooked noodles to the ice bath to chill, stirring gently, until they are completely cold, about 1 minute. ("Shocking" the noodles like this gives them more elasticity and chew.) Return the noodles to the boiling water for 30 seconds to rewarm them. Drain the noodles thoroughly.

Divide the noodles evenly among individual serving bowls and add 2 cups of the hot ramyeon broth to each bowl. Garnish each bowl with half a soft-boiled egg and some sliced scallions.

Early morning in Bukchang-dong, Seoul, a pojang macha (tent food stall) is closing shop for the night.

ANJU AND SNACKS

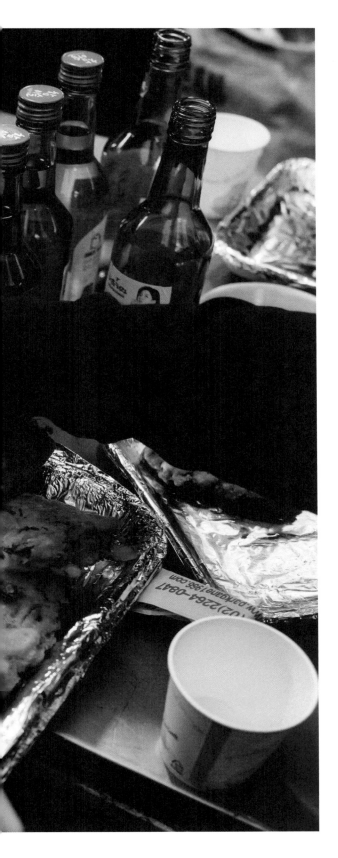

In Korea, it's traditional to always serve food with alcohol. Foods that are specifically paired with certain alcoholic drinks are called *anju*. Koreans like to have some soju or beer mixed with soju (*so-mek*) at a barbecue restaurant and then move on to a bar to drink more, while snacking on anju. Unlike a French wine pairing, where the wine is chosen to suit the food, for anju, appropriate food is chosen to suit a specific alcohol.

The three most popular alcoholic drinks in Korea are soju, beer, and makgeolli, an unfiltered rice beer. All three are served at most Korean restaurants, both in Korea and in the US. Korean supermarkets will sell some of these alcoholic beverages, depending on the laws of your state. For instance, in New York City, you can purchase beer and makgeolli at a market but you must go to a liquor store to find soju.

Anjus are almost never served with rice. The alcohol is intended to replace the rice, so as not to fill you up, so you are able to drink more. Some of my favorite Korean dishes are anjus. I firmly believe that when the two are well matched, alcohol enhances your dining experience by making food taste better. Although I give you some specific food pairings with Korean alcoholic beverages in this chapter, there are no hard-and-fast rules. These are my personal favorites, but please experiment and find your own favorite combinations.

SOJU

Soju is the most popular alcoholic beverage in Korea. It is a clear liquor that is around 16 to 25% ABV. Traditionally soju was distilled from rice, but these days, sweet potatoes, potatoes, and tapioca are also used. Natural soju brands sold in the US include Tokki Soju, which is made with organic rice and artisanally brewed and distilled in Brooklyn, NY, and Yobo Soju, a unique version made with grapes that is distilled in upstate New York. You can find cheaper alternatives to these, which are usually sold in green bottles for a fraction of the price of natural sojus. These sojus are mass-produced without the benefits of traditional fermentation.

Soju has a neutral flavor that reminds me of vodka with a mild hint of sweetness. It is served in the bottle, as cold as possible, and then poured into shot glasses. You can drink it straight, but soju cocktails are not uncommon. Since it has a crisp taste, soju is an excellent complement to Korean barbecue and grilled pork belly. The relatively high alcohol content of soju also means that it is ideally paired with stews and soupy dishes. And after a shot of soju, it's nice to have a flavorful soup or stew, such as Budae Jjigae (Spicy DMZ Stew, page 273) to counteract the slight burn from the alcohol.

SPICY DMZ STEW
부대찌개 (Budae Jjigae)

Serves 4

1 tablespoon toasted sesame oil

1 tablespoon grape seed or canola oil

1 pound pork belly, cut into 1-by-1-by-¼-inch
squares

1 teaspoon minced ginger

6 garlic cloves, minced

1 pound aged kimchi (fermented for at least 3
weeks), store-bought or homemade (see page
100), cut into 1- to 2-inch-long strips

2 quarts Dashi (page 189)

1 tablespoon gochujang (Korean red chili
paste)

1 cup gochugaru (Korean red chili flakes), or to
taste

1 package instant ramen noodles, preferably
Shin Ramyun (optional)

4 hot dogs, sliced ½ inch thick on a bias

1 can Spam, cut into 1-by-1-by-¼-inch squares

1 package silken tofu (about 1 pound), cut into
1-inch cubes

2 slices American cheese (such as Kraft Singles)

1 bunch scallions, cut into 2-inch batons

There are hundreds of restaurants in Seoul that specialize in this dish, which is often served with grilled sausages on the side. It was invented during the Korean War. When the American military shared processed meats, such as Spam, ham, and hot dogs, with the local civilians. The Koreans made them into a stew similar to kimchi jjigae, and served it with packaged ramen. The dish originated in a city just north of Seoul called Uijeongbu, which housed one of the largest US army bases—and is still home to the nation's best budae jjigae restaurants. The Koreans named it budae jjigae (literally, army stew).

As much as I believe in the importance of using the best ingredients and not taking shortcuts, when it comes to certain dishes like budae jjigae, it is impossible to replace the Spam or American cheese with healthier options without losing the inherent character of the dish.

A great-tasting budae jjigae balances the fat and salt content of the processed meats—in this recipe, Spam and hot dogs—with the spiciness of traditional Korean seasonings. The broth should have a hearty texture and a spicy, garlicky flavor, aggressive enough to chase away the harsh finish of a shot of soju. The meats and noodles should be soft and fully cooked.

Spam is still very popular in Korea. Every household keeps a stock of Spam in the pantry and it is used as a very popular banchan, simply panfried in an egg batter. At department stores, you will find gift boxes with sets of a dozen cans of Spam, beautifully packaged for the holidays. The Spam sold in the US is different from that sold in Korea; I much prefer Korean Spam, because it is more flavorful.

(recipe continues)

Spicy DMZ Stew assembled and ready to cook.

In keeping with the spirit of the dish, you can add any other ingredients you like. Some other popular ingredients in Korea are bologna, baked beans, canned tuna, and any kind of mushrooms. And if you have a portable burner, it's fun to just put all the ingredients in a pot on the burner in the middle of the table, add the dashi, and cook the dish right in front of your guests. The textures will be different than if you cook it on the stove, because the ingredients will cook at different rates, but the pleasure of the presentation is more than worth it.

Put the oils in a large Dutch oven or other large pot set over medium-high heat. Once the oil begins to shimmer and just barely smoke, add the pork belly and let it sear on one side for 3 to 5 minutes, until it turns golden brown on the bottom. Add the ginger and garlic and stir-fry for 3 minutes, being careful not to let the garlic burn. Remove the pork and aromatics and put them in a shallow bowl.

Add the kimchi to the hot fat and stir-fry for 5 minutes. Add the dashi, gochujang, gochugaru, and the packet of the ramen noodle soup base if you like; traditional recipes use the soup base, but I find it unnecessary if the kimchi is good. Add the hot dogs and Spam and cook for 5 minutes. Add the ramen noodles and tofu and cook for 2 minutes, stirring occasionally to help separate the noodles. Add the cheese and scallions and cook for 1 minute more. The noodles should be springy and tender but not too soft.

Serve immediately, so the noodles do not overcook. Put the pot in the middle of the table with individual bowls for your diners.

Let everyone dig in and help themselves. I recommend eating the noodles while they're still al dente and then savoring the rest of the stew. Ice-cold soju is a must because the broth can become quite aggressive due to the salt content of the processed ingredients.

Spicy DMZ Stew, page
273, served with Perilla
Dumplings with Pork and
Shrimp, page 293; Fried
Chicken Wings with Two
Sauces, page 296; and Spicy
Cold Noodles, page 249.

WARM TOFU WITH KIMCHI AND PORK BELLY STIR-FRY
두부김치 (Dubu Kimchi)

Serves 4

1 medium leek

2 tablespoons grape seed or canola oil

1 pound pork belly, sliced ¼ inch thick (you
can have the butcher slice it for you)

Salt and freshly ground black pepper

4 garlic cloves, minced

½ teaspoon minced ginger

1 pound aged kimchi (fermented for at least 3
weeks), store-bought or homemade (see page
100), cut into 1-inch squares

2 tablespoons toasted sesame oil

1 teaspoon sugar

1 pound silken tofu

½ bunch scallions, thinly sliced, rinsed, and
dried as directed on page 45

Toasted sesame seeds for garnish

Kimchi and pork are the ultimate classic combination in Korean cuisine. The strong, sour, fermented spiciness of the kimchi is nicely balanced by the fatty, gentler flavors of the pork. The two help each other bring out their best attributes while muting the aggressiveness of the spice. Usually this combination is served with rice, because it is very intense; here I use tofu. The soft warm bean curd, with its silken texture, provides a wonderful contrast to the strong flavors of the kimchi. The only thing that could be better is to wash it down with a chilled shot of soju.

This is my favorite dish when I'm drinking soju at a pojang macha, street-side tent restaurants that are only open at night. These are where locals go to drink close to home or work while munching on anju. Pojang machas are often romanticized in Korean movies and television shows. If you ever travel to Korea, consider visiting a pojang macha and ordering this anju and a bottle of soju. The chef/matron and the other diners will welcome you as a true local.

Set a large pot half-filled with water over medium-high heat. Once it comes to a boil, lower the heat to maintain a simmer.

Meanwhile, cut off the green tops of the leek and trim the bottom, leaving the root intact. Slice lengthwise in half; the two halves will be held together by the root. Rinse the leek under cold running water, separating the layers to remove any dirt. Rub the leek with your hand to make sure there is no dirt remaining between the layers. Pat the leek dry with paper towels. If your leek is large, you may need to cut it lengthwise in half again; you want the parts attached to the root to be about 1 inch wide. Then cut each half or quarter of the leek into 1-inch squares and discard the root ends. Set aside.

(recipe continues)

Set a large sauté pan over medium-high heat. Add 1 tablespoon of the grape seed or canola oil, and when it begins to shimmer and just smoke, add the pork belly and season with a pinch each of salt and pepper. Cook for 4 to 5 minutes, until the underside turns a deep golden brown. Flip the pork and add the ginger and garlic. Cook, stirring constantly so the garlic doesn't burn, for 1 to 2 minutes, until the ginger and garlic have softened and are fragrant. Transfer the pork and aromatics to a plate.

Wipe out the pan, set it back over the heat, and add the remaining 1 tablespoon oil. When the oil begins to shimmer and just smoke, add the leeks and stir-fry for 3 to 5 minutes, until they soften and release their fragrance but do not brown. Add the kimchi and increase the heat to high. Add the sesame oil and sugar and continue stir-frying for 5 minutes, or until the kimchi starts to soften slightly. Add the pork belly and stir-fry for another 3 to 5 minutes, or until the meat is hot.

While the kimchi is cooking, slide the tofu into the pot of simmering water. Let it cook for 5 minutes, or until it is heated through. Use a large skimmer to lift it out onto a plate, letting any excess water drain back into the pot. Cut the tofu into 16 rectangular pieces.

Arrange the tofu around the circumference of a large serving plate. Mound the pork belly and kimchi mixture in the center. Generously sprinkle the scallions and toasted sesame seeds over everything. Serve immediately, with chilled soju.

FISH CAKES IN DASHI BROTH
어묵탕 (Eomuk Tang)

Serves 4

1 pound frozen fish cakes (see headnote), defrosted overnight in the refrigerator

1½ quarts Dashi (page 189)

1 large onion, cut into 1-inch dice

1 small Korean radish (mu) or daikon radish, peeled deeply and cut into ¼-inch-thick 1-inch squares

1 tablespoon soy sauce

Salt and freshly ground white pepper

1 green Korean chili pepper or other long hot chili, thinly sliced

½ bunch scallions, sliced, rinsed, and dried as directed on page 45

To Serve

¾ cup soy sauce

2 teaspoons wasabi paste

Special Equipment

Bamboo skewers

Whenever I'm in Korea in the colder months, I love drinking soju at an *odeng* bar that specializes in fish cakes (*odeng* is the Japanese word for fish cake). Korean fish cakes are available in different shapes; I like making this soup with thin rectangular ones that have a soft texture. I cut the fish cakes into wide strips and then thread them onto bamboo skewers. Depending on the shape and size of the fish cakes you buy, you can leave them whole or cut into strips that you can slide onto the skewers accordion-style. Just make sure that you leave enough space free at the end so you can easily pick up the skewers.

This dish is served with the skewers of fish cakes in the communal pot or bowl of the broth, with the ends of the skewers peeking out of the top so you can grab them with your hands. Serve small individual dishes of soy sauce with a mound of wasabi on the side, like the ones you get with sushi in Japanese restaurants. Then lift a skewer out of the soup and dip each bite into the soy sauce before eating. Soju pairs well with both the fish cakes and, especially, the broth.

If using flat rectangular fish cakes, cut them into long strips about 1 inch wide. You want 16 pieces total. If you buy thicker pieces or round balls, you may need to adjust the size, or leave them whole and adjust the cooking time.

Put the dashi in a medium pot set over high heat and bring to a boil. Add the onion and daikon. Simmer for 5 minutes, or until the vegetables are translucent and softened. Add the fish cakes and simmer for 3 minutes. Add soy sauce, salt to taste and about 5 pinches of pepper. Remove from the heat.

(recipe continues)

Using a slotted spoon, remove the fish cakes from the dashi, then put them on skewers. I like to form curves with the fish cakes so they make an S-shape with the skewer running through the middle. You can also cut each strip into 3 pieces and thread them onto the skewer so it's easier to pull them off with your teeth. Put all the skewers in the pot, making sure the ends of the skewers stay above the dashi, and bring it to a simmer, then add the sliced chili and sprinkle the scallions over the top.

Bring the whole pot to the table, with a ladle on the side. Set out four bowls and ladle about 6 ounces of the soup into each one. (I like to give everyone their own bowl of soup so they can double-dip.) Then diners can take the skewers straight from the pot and eat the fish cakes over their bowls of soup. Serve each diner a small bowl of soy sauce and wasabi alongside for dipping. Finally, don't forget the ice-cold soju.

MAKGEOLLI 막걸리

Makgeolli is a Korean rice beer brewed from white rice and not filtered. It has a cloudy appearance and texture from the remaining rice starch. It is slightly sweet, with a milky texture and a slight carbonation. It tastes very similar to nigori sake, but at 6% ABV, it goes down like a beer. Historically makgeolli was the filtered residue left over from making more refined alcoholic beverages for the noble class. Since it was cheap and readily available, it was a popular drink for farmers and other laborers.

In Korea, makgeolli is served the same way it was a hundred years ago: in a communal wooden bowl with a ladle. I think it tastes best when it's as cold as possible, so at Hanjan, we serve it in frosted mugs. Makgeolli pairs well with fried or panfried dishes, because the mild natural carbonation helps to wash away the fat on your palate. It also works well with spicy dishes, as its starchy texture mutes the sharpness from the spices.

SCALLION PANCAKES
파전 (Pajeon)

Makes 4 or 5 pancakes

Batter

2 cups all-purpose flour

½ cup cornstarch

2 teaspoons baking powder

2 teaspoons sugar

1 teaspoon doenjang (Korean fermented
    soybean paste)

½ teaspoon freshly ground black pepper

2 cups ice-cold club soda

1 medium egg yolk

2 teaspoons minced garlic

3 bunches scallions, cut into 2-inch batons
    (if the scallions are thick, cut the white
    parts lengthwise in half before cutting into
    batons)

About 5 tablespoons grape seed or canola oil
    for frying

Pajeon Sauce (page 59)

Pajeon are thin savory scallion pancakes traditionally paired with makgeolli. With their crispy exterior and soft insides, they make makgeolli taste that much more refreshing. To get the pancakes crispy enough, make sure the batter is very cold and the pan very hot, with plenty of oil. In fact, we keep the batter in the freezer, rather than the refrigerator, during service so it is as cold as possible. We also use soda water to lighten up the batter with the carbonation. This prevents the pancakes from becoming too dense.

While this recipe features scallions, Korean pancakes can be filled with almost anything. Instead of or in addition to the scallions, you could use garlic chives, ramps, or chrysanthemum leaves. Add thin slices of Korean hot pepper if you want an extra kick, or julienned carrots and onions for more sweetness. If you want something a little more substantial, you can easily turn this recipe into *hamul pajeon*, or seafood pancakes, by adding 6 ounces raw squid or shrimp, cut into small bite-sized pieces, to the batter.

To make the batter, combine the flour, cornstarch, baking powder, sugar, doenjang, and pepper in a medium bowl and mix well to blend. Add the club soda, egg yolk, and garlic and mix gently using a whisk. Do not whisk too much, or extra gluten will form in the batter, making it too thick and doughy. Whisk about 10 times, then let the batter rest for 10 minutes in the freezer so any remaining small clumps of flour can dissolve and blend into the mixture by themselves.

When you're ready to make the pancakes, line a sheet pan with paper towels and set aside. Fold the scallions into the cold batter.

(recipe continues)

Scallion Pancake, page 285, with
Korean Radish Kimchi, page 105,
and Scallion Dressing, page 59.

Set a 10-inch nonstick sauté pan over high heat and add about 1 tablespoon of the oil. When the oil begins to shimmer and just barely smoke, add 1 cup of the scallion batter to the center of the pan. Using a spatula, spread it out to form a 7-inch pancake. (You don't want the pancake to touch the sides of the pan, or the edges may burn before the center is cooked through.) Reduce the heat to medium and cook for 4 to 5 minutes, until the bottom of the pancake has set. Once it has set, gently slide your spatula under the edges of the pancake and lift them, tilting the pan, so some of the hot oil runs underneath the pancake. Then cook for 2 to 3 minutes more, until the bottom is a deep golden brown and crisp. You can check the color by gently lifting an edge of the pancake with your spatula. Flip the pancake and cook on the other side for 3 to 4 minutes, until it is golden brown on the second side and cooked through. Transfer to the prepared sheet pan to drain. Wipe out the pan, set it back over high heat, add another tablespoon or so of oil, and repeat until all of the pancakes are cooked. The finished pancakes can be kept in a low (200°F) oven on a clean sheet pan while you cook the remaining batches, but it's best to eat them right away.

Cut each pancake into quarters and serve with small bowls of the sauce and ice-cold makgeolli.

HANJAN'S SPICY RICE CAKES
떡볶이 (Tteokbokki)

Serves 4

1 pound precut frozen rice cakes, or 1 pound fresh rice cakes, cut into 2- to 3-inch-long batons

2 large eggs

1 teaspoon baking soda

1 teaspoon salt, plus more to taste

1 tablespoon vinegar (any kind will do)

Sauce

2 cups Dashi (page 189), plus more if needed

½ medium onion, minced

3 garlic cloves, minced

1 cup gochugaru (Korean red chili flakes)

2 tablespoons sugar

1 tablespoon gochujang (Korean red chili paste)

Salt if needed

½ cup grape seed or canola oil

½ pound fish cakes, cut into batons the same size as the rice cakes

1 medium onion, thinly sliced

½ bunch scallions, cut into 1-inch batons

These rice cakes are Korea's most famous street food. I fell in love with them for the first time when I was four years old and we visited Busan to see my maternal grandmother. I still think Busan has the best tteokbokki (as pictured). Kristin, my photographer, says that they were the best bites she experienced during her entire Korean trip.

Tteokbokki are not traditionally considered an anju, but my version pairs exceedingly well with ice-cold makgeolli. The rice cakes are spicy and salty, with a crispy texture that screams for a carbonated drink to wash it down. And the soothing milky texture of makgeolli neutralizes a bit of the spice. Usually these rice cakes are stewed for an extended period of time in a liquid sauce so the texture becomes very soft. Mine have an extremely crispy texture and a more concentrated spicy flavor.

If you are using frozen rice cakes, soak them in cold water for 1 hour after cutting. Fresh rice cakes can be used straight from the package.

To prepare the soft-boiled eggs, add enough water to a small pot to cover the 2 eggs. Set over high heat, add the baking soda, salt, and vinegar, and bring to a boil. (The baking soda makes it easier to peel the soft-boiled eggs, and the vinegar will help center the yolks.) Add the eggs and wait until the water starts to boil again, then lower the heat to maintain a gentle boil and cook for 6 minutes. While the eggs cook, prepare an ice bath. When they are cooked, immediately transfer the eggs to the ice bath. Chill for 5 minutes, or until they are cool enough to peel. Carefully peel the eggs. Slice lengthwise in half, sprinkle the yolks lightly with salt, and set aside.

(recipe continues)

To make the sauce, put the dashi in a medium pot set over high heat. Bring to a boil and boil to reduce the volume by half, 15 to 20 minutes. Add the onion, garlic, gochugaru, sugar, and gochujang, reduce the heat to medium, and cook for 15 to 20 minutes, until the onions are tender and the flavors have come together. Taste and add salt if necessary. Remove from the heat and reserve.

Add the oil to a large skillet set over medium heat, and when it just begins to smoke, add the rice cakes. Cook, turning the rice cakes occasionally, until they are crispy on all sides but have not browned much, 8 to 10 minutes; lower the heat if necessary. Add the fish cakes, onions, and scallions, increase the heat to high, and toss with a wooden spoon for about a minute or two, until everything is heated through. Add the sauce and stir for 2 or 3 minutes so the oil emulsifies with the sauce. The sauce should be thick enough to coat the rice cakes, but you may need to add a little more dashi or water if it reduces too much and starts to burn.

Serve the rice cakes family-style on a large plate, garnished with the soft-boiled eggs. Enjoy with cold glasses of makgeolli.

BEER

Beer has become increasingly popular in Korea as new microbreweries have begun making craft beers using Western traditions and techniques. Just ten years ago, all Korean beer tasted pretty much the same. Your typical Korean beer was a light lager, low on flavor and high on acid, like Budweiser or Coors. It had less flavor than soju, and it was more expensive. And, because Koreans like to eat while drinking, as mentioned earlier, beer was too filling to drink during or after a substantial meal.

But now these microbreweries are producing flavorful dark beers with local hops, wheat, and malts and, most important, a higher ABV than traditional Korean beers. These beers have spurred a brand-new culinary pairing of beer and fried chicken, especially during the summer months, and at sporting events such as the FIFA World Cup and Korean professional-league baseball games.

Korean microbrews have their roots in German style beers, because the original techniques used were borrowed from that country. Quite a few Korean microbrew pioneers learned their craft in Germany. Today you can find all types of beers in Korea: lagers, ales, malts, pilsners, dark, wheat, you name it. You can even find pub-style bars that mostly serve beer and foods that go with beer.

Whether you like the new full-flavored beers or the traditional light lagers, the recipes in this chapter will make them taste better. The recipes are fairly simple and straightforward, easy to prepare just before an afternoon of watching football or baseball. The accompanying sauces are incredibly versatile, and they can be made ahead and used over and over again. Eating these beer anjus is easy, because they are finger foods that do not require cutlery or even chopsticks.

CRISPY CALAMARI

Serves 4

2 teaspoons gochugaru (Korean red chili flakes)
1 teaspoon salt

Wasabi Dip
¼ cup mayonnaise
1 tablespoon soy sauce
1 tablespoon wasabi paste

Canola oil for deep-frying
2 cups potato starch
2 pounds fresh squid, cleaned and cut into bite-sized pieces
Lemon wedges for serving

Fresh squid is absolutely essential for this dish. If you use packaged frozen calamari, you will get a mushy texture without much real flavor. I use potato starch rather than flour or bread crumbs to bread the calamari. It both makes it extra crispy and allows the flavor of the squid to shine. The wasabi dip gives your tongue (and sinuses) a swift kick that will leave it begging for ice-cold beer.

Put the gochugaru and salt in a small bowl and mix well. Reserve.

To make the wasabi dip, combine the mayonnaise, soy sauce, and wasabi paste in a small bowl and whisk until smooth. Reserve.

Pour the oil into a deep-fat fryer and heat to 375°F. Or pour 3 inches of oil into a large pot and heat to 360°F over medium-high heat

Line a sheet pan with paper towels. Put the potato starch in a medium bowl. Make sure the squid is cold before you dredge it, because that will increase the level of crispiness when fried.

Working in batches to avoid crowding the deep fryer or pot, one at a time, dredge the pieces of calamari in the potato starch, shake off the excess, and drop into the oil. Fry the squid until crisp and just tender, 1 to 2 minutes, then transfer to the prepared sheet pan. After about 10 to 15 seconds, transfer the squid to a bowl and season with the salt and gochugaru mixture: I teach my cooks to toss the squid inside the bowl with one hand and season with your other hand held high, at least 18 inches above the bowl. This helps to distribute the seasoning evenly, as having clumps of it stuck onto a piece of squid can be very unpleasant. Serve the first batch immediately, with lemon wedges and the wasabi dip on the side, then cook and serve the remaining batches.

PERILLA DUMPLINGS WITH PORK AND SHRIMP

깻잎전 (Kkaennip Jeon)

Makes 16 dumplings

16 perilla leaves

Filling

7 ounces ground pork

3¼ ounces peeled shrimp, finely chopped

2 garlic cloves, minced

1 teaspoon minced ginger

4 garlic chives, thinly sliced

1 shallot, minced

½ medium carrot, peeled and finely diced

2 scallions, thinly sliced

2 teaspoons soy sauce

¾ teaspoon salt

½ large egg (lightly beat a whole egg and then measure out half)

Batter

2 cups tempura flour or Korean buchim garu

1 cup water

1 large egg yolk

2 teaspoons rice vinegar

1 gallon canola oil for deep-frying

3 large egg yolks

2 cups all-purpose flour

Pajeon Sauce (page 59)

These are not your typical flour-based half-moon-shaped dumplings. Instead, I use Korean perilla leaves as wrappers, giving the dumplings a fresh, aromatic touch. Then I crisp them up by coating them in tempura batter and frying them quickly. With the tangy dipping sauce, they are a wonderful complement to makgeolli.

The stuffing is a mixture of pork, shrimp, and vegetables. After you make the filling, it is important to cook one dumpling and taste it to see if it is to your liking. Once all the dumplings are stuffed, it's too late to tweak the seasoning.

Soak the perilla leaves in cold water for about 15 minutes to wash off any dirt, refresh the leaves, and tame the occasionally aggressive aroma. Drain, pat dry, and reserve.

To make the filling put the ground pork, shrimp, garlic, ginger, chives, shallot, carrot, scallions, soy sauce, salt, and egg in a large bowl and use your hands or a rubber spatula to mix well so that everything is evenly distributed throughout. Cook a teaspoon of the filling in a lightly oiled small sauté pan over medium heat and taste for seasoning, then make any necessary adjustments to the rest of the filling. Set aside.

To make the batter, put the tempura flour, water, egg yolk, and rice vinegar in a small bowl and whisk until smooth. Cover and refrigerate until needed.

Pour the oil into a deep-fat fryer and heat to 360°F. Or pour 5 inches of oil into a large deep pot and heat to 360°F over medium to medium-high heat.

(recipe continues)

Fried Chicken Wings with Two Sauces, page 296, and Perilla Dumplings with Pork and Shrimp, page 293

To assemble and fry the dumplings, whisk the 3 yolks in a small bowl until smooth. Put a perilla leaf on a cutting board with the shiny side down and the stem to the left. Put 1 tablespoon of the filling on the bottom half of the leaf, flattening it slightly, leaving a ½-inch border all around the edge. Dip a fingertip in the egg yolk and rub it along the bottom edge of the leaf. Fold the top half down over the filling and press the edges together to seal the dumpling. Roll it in the all-purpose flour. Lay it on a large plate or sheet pan and repeat with the remaining leaves and filling.

Line a large plate with paper towels. Working in batches of 4 or 5, dip the dumplings one by one in the batter, rub off the excess batter on the edge of the bowl, and gently slide into the hot oil. Do not crowd the fryer or pot, or the temperature will drop and you will have soggy dumplings. Cook for 3 minutes. Flip and cook for 1 minute more, until they are golden brown on both sides and the oil is no longer bubbling around them. Transfer the cooked dumplings to the prepared plate to drain.

Serve immediately, with the Pajeon Sauce on the side and ice-cold makgeolli.

FRIED CHICKEN WINGS WITH TWO SAUCES

Makes about 30 wings

2 cups soy sauce

2 cups sake

1 head garlic, separated into cloves and peeled

One 2-inch piece ginger, peeled and sliced

5 pounds medium chicken wings

1 pound (about 4½ cups) potato starch

2 to 4 quarts canola oil

2 cups Spicy Asian Sauce or Soy Garlic Sauce
   (recipes follow)

The wing is my favorite part of the chicken. It has enough fat and bone to keep the meat very moist during the cooking process. Of course, frying wings gives you the best-tasting result, and either of these variations will make a delicious anju for beer. The wings stay super crispy, even when you coat them with the thick, flavorful Spicy Asian or Soy Garlic Sauce. Marinating the wings before frying gives the flavors a longer finish and accentuates the sauces. Which sauce you choose is a question of whether you're in the mood for spicy or sweet.

Put the soy sauce, sake, garlic, and ginger in a blender and puree for 30 seconds to blend everything together.

Divide the wings between two gallon-sized zip-top bags and divide the marinade evenly between them. Seal the bags and put them in a bowl in the refrigerator for 1 to 2 hours. (If left for longer than 2 hours, the salt in the marinade will start to pull the moisture from the wing meat, leaving you with dry chicken.)

Transfer the wings to a large colander and let them drain for 10 minutes. Line two sheet pans with wire racks; reserve one for later. Put the potato starch in a large bowl. One at a time, dredge the wings in the starch, shake off the excess starch, and lay on the first prepared pan. Refrigerate the wings for 30 minutes, uncovered, to allow the starch to dry. Reserve the extra potato starch.

Pour the oil into a deep-fat fryer and heat to 330°F. Or pour 4 inches of oil into a large pot and heat to 330°F over medium-high heat. You will be frying the wings twice. The first fry is at a lower temperature to cook them all the way through, and the second time will be at 360°F to get them really crispy.

Put the sauce you have chosen in a large bowl and set aside.

Remove the tray of wings from the refrigerator. Shake off the wings, dredge them in the reserved potato starch once more, and return to the same sheet pan. Working in batches of 6 to 8, add the wings to the deep fryer or pot, being careful not to overcrowd it, and fry for 6 to 8 minutes, until they are fully cooked through and golden in color. Transfer the cooked wings to the reserved sheet pan.

Increase the temperature of the oil to 360°F. Working in batches of 6 to 8 wings again, drop them into the hot oil and cook for 4 more minutes, or until golden brown and crispy. Remove the finished wings and return them to the rack.

When all the wings are cooked, add them to the bowl with the sauce and toss to coat them thoroughly. Serve immediately, with ice-cold beer.

SPICY ASIAN SAUCE

Makes 6 cups

1 tablespoon grape seed or canola oil
1 medium onion, cut into small dice
Salt
12 garlic cloves, minced
A 1-inch piece ginger, peeled and minced
2 cups sake
3 tablespoons sugar
1 cup Sriracha
⅔ cup sambal oelek chili paste
1 cup ketchup
½ cup soy sauce
1 cup rice vinegar
¼ pound cold unsalted butter, cubed
½ bunch cilantro, leaves only, coarsely chopped

You will only need 2 cups of this sauce for Fried Chicken Wings (page 296), but I like making it in big batches to keep in my fridge. It is a great hot sauce or stir-fry sauce base, and it is wonderful with other deep-fried or crispy foods. It will keep for up to a month in the refrigerator.

Put the oil in a wide medium pot set over medium heat. When the oil begins to shimmer and just smoke, add the onion, season with a pinch of salt, and turn the heat to low. Cook, stirring occasionally, for 8 minutes, or until the onion is soft and translucent. Add the garlic and ginger and cook, stirring occasionally, for 3 to 4 minutes, until soft and fragrant. Add the sake, bring it to a boil, and carefully light it with a lighter or a long match, then let the flames die out, 1 to 2 minutes. (If you would rather not light the sake, let it boil for 3 minutes to burn off the alcohol.)

Lower the heat to medium and stir in the sugar, Sriracha, sambal oelek, ketchup, and soy sauce and bring to a simmer, then reduce the heat to low and simmer for 20 minutes, stirring occasionally so the sauce does not stick to the bottom of the pot or burn. Stir in the vinegar and remove from the heat. (The sauce can be made ahead and kept in the refrigerator for up to a month. Reheat before proceeding with the recipe.)

Add the diced butter a few pieces at a time, whisking constantly to emulsify it. If the sauce breaks, you can whisk in a few tablespoons of cold water to re-emulsify it. Add the cilantro and serve, or set aside in a warm spot until ready to use.

SOY GARLIC SAUCE

Makes about 4½ cups

1 tablespoon grape seed or canola oil
12 garlic cloves, minced
A 1-inch piece ginger, peeled and minced
Salt
2 cups sake
1 cup mirin
1 teaspoon gochujang (Korean red chili paste)
1 tablespoon gochugaru (Korean red chili flakes)
2 tablespoons dark brown sugar
2 tablespoons honey
½ cup rice vinegar
1 tablespoon cornstarch
1 cup cold water
2 tablespoons toasted sesame seeds

Again, this makes more sauce than you need for the chicken wings (page 296), but it keeps well and is so delicious that I'm sure you will find many uses for it once you have it in your pantry. You can use it in all of the same ways that you would use classic barbecue sauce, but with a Korean flair.

Put the oil in a large deep sauté pan set over low heat. Once it begins to shimmer, add the garlic and ginger with a pinch of salt and cook, stirring, for 3 minutes, or until the garlic and ginger have softened but not browned. Add the sake and mirin, turn the heat up to high, and bring to a boil, then carefully light the liquid with a lighter or a long match and let the flames die out, 1 to 2 minutes. (If you would rather not light the sake, let it boil for 3 minutes to burn off the alcohol.)

Lower the heat to medium and whisk in the gochujang, gochugaru, brown sugar, and honey. Simmer for 5 minutes, whisking occasionally, to blend the flavors. Add the vinegar. Then make a slurry by combining the cornstarch with the cold water in a small bowl and whisk until smooth. Slowly drizzle the slurry into the sauce, whisking constantly. Cook, whisking, until it comes to a simmer and thickens. Turn off the heat and stir in the sesame seeds.

The sauce can be made ahead and kept in the refrigerator for up to a month.

COCKTAILS

When I opened Danji in 2010, I thought it was important to have a cocktail program and to make each cocktail distinctly Korean. In doing so, I was faced with a challenge: In Korea, it is very uncommon to have a cocktail before your meal. Korean restaurants don't have bars where you can grab a predinner drink or eat dinner alone. There wasn't much of a cocktail culture until recently, so there is no single traditional cocktail like a French 75 or a Gin and Tonic that I would call authentically Korean. Even in the US, most Korean restaurants don't have a cocktail menu or a full-service bar.

While we lack a cocktail culture in restaurants, the cocktail bar scene in Korea is as progressive as you can get. Korea has embraced the idea of bespoke cocktails and cocktail chefs. My favorite cocktail bars are in Gangnam and Seoul, and as you can see from the photos, they don't kid around.

Every cocktail in this book is unique and original, created by either me or my bartenders specifically for Danji or Hanjan. I love collaborating with my bartenders to come up with new drinks that have both Korean and seasonal influences. Diners who have come to us from Korea tell us that even the cocktails in Korea aren't as "Korean" as the cocktails we serve.

This chapter begins with several recipes for the simple syrups we use to sweeten our cocktails. I generally prefer using flavored syrups over plain simple syrup because they add more concentrated flavors without diluting the cocktail, which is important when you are serving a 4- or 5-ounce drink in a glass filled with ice. All of the syrups will keep for at least a few weeks in the refrigerator.

SIMPLE SYRUP

Makes about 1½ cups

1 cup water
1 cup sugar

This syrup is so versatile it should be in every fridge. Not only do we use it at the bar for cocktails, we also use it in the kitchen every time we need to sweeten up a dish that is not hot enough to dissolve sugar. It's perfect for iced coffee, iced tea, and fresh-squeezed juices where the fruits aren't sweet enough on their own, such as lemonade or grapefruit juice.

Put the water and sugar in a small saucepan set over medium-high heat and bring to a boil, stirring until all of the sugar has dissolved. Cool and transfer to a covered container. The simple syrup will keep for up to 4 weeks in the refrigerator.

SPICY SIMPLE SYRUP

Makes about 1½ cups

1 cup water
1 cup sugar
2 dried red Thai chili peppers (including seeds)

This is simple syrup with a kick. We use whole dried chili peppers so the heat creeps up on you slowly. It can get intense, depending upon on the peppers you use. I use this syrup in certain special drinks at my restaurants. That said, it could go with many classic cocktails. If you like spice, try replacing classic simple syrup with this in your favorite cocktail recipe. Or, if you want to make some refreshing nonalcoholic drinks, this pairs well with fresh juices and seltzer.

Put the water, sugar, and chili peppers in a small pot set over medium-high heat and bring to a boil, stirring until all of the sugar has dissolved. Reduce the heat and simmer for 3 to 4 minutes to infuse the peppers in the syrup. Turn off the heat and let the syrup rest for 30 minutes.

Strain the syrup and transfer to a covered container. The spicy simple syrup will keep for up to 4 weeks in the refrigerator.

CINNAMON SIMPLE SYRUP

Makes about ¾ cup

1 cup water
1 cup sugar
4 cinnamon sticks

This cinnamon syrup adds a warm, spicy flavor to many cocktails. It works well with both light- and dark-colored spirits. It's perfect for fall and winter cocktails because the cinnamon imparts a feeling of warmth and celebration. I also like to add it to coffee and hot chocolate.

Put the water, sugar, and cinnamon sticks in a small saucepan set over medium-high heat and bring to a boil, stirring to dissolve the sugar. Reduce the heat and simmer for about 20 minutes, until the syrup has reduced by half. Remove from the heat, cover, and set aside to infuse for 60 minutes.

Remove the cinnamon sticks and transfer to a covered container. The syrup will keep for up to 4 weeks in the refrigerator.

CINNAMON AND STAR ANISE SIMPLE SYRUP

Makes about 1½ cups

The addition of star anise gives the cinnamon simple syrup an Asian flair. The cinnamon is nicely balanced by the fragrant earthiness of the star anise, giving it a more exotic flavor. The result is quite subtle and works well in both cocktails and hot chocolate.

Add ½ piece star anise along with the cinnamon sticks. Proceed as directed above, but do not simmer the syrup to reduce it. Remove from the heat, cover, and let steep for at least 2 hours, and up to 6 hours. Strain and store as directed.

SU JEONG GWA COCKTAIL (COLD OR HOT)

Makes 1 drink

1½ ounces Old Overholt rye whiskey

3 ounces Su Jeong Gwa Tea (recipe follows)

¼ ounce fresh lemon juice

2 dashes Angostura bitters

An orange twist for garnish

Su jeong gwa is a traditional Korean drink made from dried persimmons, cinnamon, and ginger. It was this drink that inspired me to introduce a Korean-influenced cocktail menu at Danji. I knew there were authentic Korean flavors that would pair well with Western spirits like whiskey and rum.

When we opened, I was living in Williamsburg, Brooklyn, and my favorite bartender was Vincent Favella at The Counting Room on Berry Street. One day, I brought Vincent a container of su jeong gwa and asked him which spirit would go best with its flavor profile. In five minutes, he came up with this cocktail. It was inspiring to see Vincent create such a delicious drink based on the flavors of something uniquely Korean that he had just tasted for the first time. Because he knows so much about spirits, he was able to divine that it would pair perfectly with rye whiskey. Vincent still doesn't really know how to pronounce su jeong gwa (for reference, it's *soo-jung-gwah*), but he gave me the confidence to create Korean cocktails at my restaurants.

Rye whiskey can be quite raw and aggressive on its own. The sweet cinnamon in the su jeong gwa mutes the strong flavors, while the spicy ginger distracts the tongue from the sharp pinch of the alcohol. You can serve this on the rocks, for a refreshing drink in the summertime, or hot, like a hot toddy, in the cooler months.

(recipe continues)

For a cold drink, fill a cocktail shaker with ice and add the rye, tea, lemon juice, and bitters. Cover and shake vigorously for 10 seconds. Fill a rocks glass with ice and strain the cocktail into the glass. Add the orange twist and serve.

For a hot drink, pour the rye, tea, lemon juice, and bitters into a microwave-safe glass or other container and microwave on high for 40 seconds. Pour into a snifter. Twist the orange peel, squeezing its oil into the drink, and garnish the drink with the twist. Serve immediately.

SU JEONG GWA TEA

Makes about 3 cups

¼ pound ginger, peeled and sliced ¼ inch thick
1½ cinnamon sticks
2 jujubes
¼ cup sugar
¼ teaspoon pine nuts
3 cups water

Combine all of the ingredients in a medium saucepan set over high heat and bring to just under a boil, stirring to dissolve all the sugar. Reduce the heat and simmer for 20 minutes. Remove from the heat, cover, and let steep at room temperature for 2 hours.

Strain the tea into a container, cover, and reserve in the refrigerator until ready to use.

SUMMER SOJU SANGRIA

Makes 32 ounces; serves 8

3 ripe peaches, halved, pitted, and cut into
    ½-inch cubes
4 ripe plums, halved, pitted, and cut into
    ½-inch cubes
½ pound strawberries, cut into ½-inch cubes
Two 375-ml bottles soju (preferably Jinro 24;
    make sure that the soju you buy is over 20%
    ABV)
4 cups sparkling rosé
2 cups San Pellegrino Aranciata or Orangina
    soda

On a trip to Spain the summer before I opened Danji, I discovered a new favorite drink, the Tinto de Verano, which can be found at every tapas or pintxos bar. The name of this refreshing cocktail, which is a mix of red wine and lemon-lime soda, translates as "red wine of summer," and it is very similar to sangria. I was inspired to create a similar drink with a Korean twist by adding soju. The soju in this delicious fruity cocktail packs a very subtle punch. This is best served in the summer, when the stone fruit and berries are ripe and at their sweetest. Seasonal local fruits will always taste best.

Divide the fruit between two quart-sized Mason jars. Pour 1 bottle of soju into each jar. Cover and let the fruit infuse for at least 48 hours, at room temperature or in the refrigerator. (The fruit will keep almost indefinitely if submerged in the soju.)

To serve, pour the fruit and soju into a large pitcher. Add the sparkling rosé and the orange soda. Stir well to blend and pour into eight glasses filled with ice. Alternatively, you can divide the punch between two ice-filled pitchers and pour into empty glasses. Serve immediately.

WINTER SOJU SANGRIA

Makes 32 ounces; serves 8

2 Fuji apples, cored and cut into ½-inch cubes

1 Korean or Asian pear, peeled, cored, and cut into ½-inch cubes

2 seedless oranges, peeled and cut into ½-inch cubes

Two 375-ml bottles soju (preferably Jinro 24; make sure that the soju you buy is over 20% ABV)

4 cups sparkling Shiraz

2 cups San Pellegrino Aranciata or Orangina soda

This soju sangria takes advantage of two of my favorite fall fruits. I combine apples and Korean pears with cubes of oranges to brighten their sweet, subtle flavors. I use a sparkling Shiraz to deepen the flavor of the punch. While certainly refreshing, this sangria is perfect for the colder winter months. And again, using local seasonal fruits will achieve the best results.

Divide the fruit between two quart-sized Mason jars. Pour 1 bottle of soju into each jar. Cover and let the fruit infuse for at least 48 hours, at room temperature or in the refrigerator. (The fruit will keep almost indefinitely if submerged in the soju.)

Pour the fruit and soju into a large pitcher. Add the sparkling Shiraz and orange soda. Stir well to blend and pour into eight glasses filled with ice. Alternatively, you can divide the punch between two ice-filled pitchers and pour into empty glasses. Serve immediately.

KOREAN PEAR COCKTAIL

Makes 1 drink

1 Korean or Asian pear

2 ounces Ketel One vodka

¾ ounce Cinnamon and Star Anise Simple
   Syrup (page 306)

⅓ ounce fresh lemon juice

I love Asian pears, especially Korean pears, which tend to be larger and sweeter than American pears, with a crisp texture, lots of refreshing juice, and an addictive light floral taste. I use a Korean pear puree for marinating meats, balancing the richness in braises and sauces, and naturally sweetening Yukhwe (Beef Tartare with Soy and Korean Pear, page 139). The pear is such a classic ingredient in Korean cuisine that I had to share its special flavor in a cocktail too. The cocktail has a unique fibrous texture because of the unstrained pear puree. As you chew on the pear fibers, the flavor blooms in your mouth.

To make the pear puree, peel the pear and cut it into quarters; remove the core. Cut one quarter into slices and reserve for garnish.

Place the remaining pear quarters in a food processor or blender and puree until smooth. The puree should be used the same day it is made, or it will start to discolor.

Put the vodka, 1½ ounces of the Korean pear puree, the syrup, and lemon juice in a cocktail shaker filled with ice. Cover and shake for 10 seconds, then strain into a rocks glass filled with ice. Garnish with 1 or 2 of the reserved pear slices. (You can enjoy the remainder of the pear on its own or make a few more cocktails.)

Korean Pear Cocktail and Red Sky at Night (page 314)

RED SKY AT NIGHT

Makes 1 drink

2 ounces Gosling dark rum
1 ounce Cranberry Mix (recipe follows)
2 drops orange bitters
About 6 ounces Fever Tree ginger beer
A few cranberries for garnish

This is our Thanksgiving cocktail. Its beautiful ruby color makes me think of the dusky fall sky in Hell's Kitchen, where Danji is located. As the sun sets, the sky over the Hudson River glows a vibrant dark red, reminding you of the cold weather to come. This drink is bright with fruity notes from the cranberry and orange, with a little kick from fresh chili pepper and a hint of ginger beer to round things out.

Fill a cocktail shaker with ice and add the rum, cranberry mix, and orange bitters. Cover and shake vigorously to blend. Fill a tall glass with ice and strain the drink into it. Top off with ginger beer. Garnish with the fresh cranberry on a toothpick and serve immediately.

CRANBERRY MIX

Makes about 2 quarts

One 12-ounce bag frozen cranberries
2 cups packed dark brown sugar
4 cups water
2 red Korean chili peppers or other long hot
　　chilies, thinly sliced

Put the cranberries, brown sugar, and water in a medium pot set over medium-high heat. Bring to a boil, stirring to dissolve the sugar. Remove from heat, cover, and let cool completely, then transfer the mixture to a covered container and refrigerate for 24 hours.

Put the cranberry mixture in a blender and add the chilies. Puree until smooth, and strain. The cranberry mix will keep in a covered container in the refrigerator for up to a week, or you can freeze it in 1-ounce portions in an ice cube tray and keep the cubes in a zip-top bag in the freezer for up to a month.

YAKULT COLADA

Makes 1 drink

2 small (100-ml) bottles yakult, frozen

1½ ounces Fleur de Cana white rum

¼ ounce Simple Syrup (page 304)

½ ounce pineapple juice

¼ ounce fresh lemon juice

1 Drunken Cherry (recipe follows) for garnish

Yakult is a sweet, milky probiotic drink that's a favorite of children across Korea and Japan. I used to love drinking it on my summer visits to Korea, and whenever I taste yakult, it takes me back to that time. Fortunately, it's now readily available in Asian supermarkets here in the US. Since it's such an iconic beverage, I thought it would be fun to make it into a cocktail. You'll have to pick up the yakult at least a day in advance of when you want to make this so you can freeze it. This drink tastes very similar to a piña colada, so it's appealing to all of my customers. But it's also a way for me to share my own memories with Korean customers who remember yakult from their own childhoods.

Fill a piña colada glass with ice and water and set it aside to chill.

Place the 2 frozen yakult bottles in a large bowl of warm water. They will take about 3 minutes to turn into slush.

Meanwhile, fill a cocktail shaker with ice and add the rum, simple syrup, pineapple juice, and lemon juice. Cover and shake vigorously for 10 seconds. Pour out the ice water in the chilled glass and strain the cocktail into the glass. Pour the slushy yakult into the glass and garnish with the drunken cherry. Serve immediately.

(continues)

Yakult Colada, page 315, garnished with a Drunken Cherry

DRUNKEN CHERRIES

Makes about 1 cup

1 cup fresh Bing cherries
12 ounces dark rum

Cut a small slit in the bottom of each cherry to allow the rum to penetrate them. Remove the pits if you prefer. Put the cherries in a pint-sized container with a lid and cover them with the rum.

Let the cherries marinate for at least 2 days before using. The cherries will improve with age and will keep indefinitely at room temperature as long as they are completely submerged in the rum.

SPICY GINGER MARGARITA

Makes 1 drink

1½ ounces Herradura Silver tequila
¾ ounces fresh lime juice
⅓ ounce Spicy Simple Syrup (page 304)
½ teaspoon Ginger Puree (recipe follows)
1 teaspoon honey
About 6 ounces San Pellegrino Aranciata soda
1 lime

Who doesn't love a margarita? This is the most popular drink at Danji, created by our Mexican bartender, Ricky. He incorporated simple syrup infused with dried chili peppers and a ginger puree into a classic margarita to "Koreanize" it with a spicy, exotic kick.

Fill a cocktail shaker with ice. Add the tequila, lime juice, simple syrup, ginger puree, and honey, cover, and shake vigorously to blend. Fill a rocks glass with ice and strain the cocktail into the glass. Top off with Aranciata soda. Using a Microplane, grate some lime zest over the top of the drink for garnish.

GINGER PUREE

Makes about ½ cup

½ pound ginger, peeled and thinly sliced
¼ cup tequila (a simple tequila is fine here; it will take on the flavor of the ginger), or as needed

Put the ginger and tequila in a blender and puree until smooth. Add more tequila if needed to create a smooth puree. The ginger puree will keep for 10 to 14 days in a covered container in the refrigerator. If it starts to turn brown and oxidize, cover the puree with more tequila.

PERILLA JULEP

Makes 1 drink

1 perilla leaf, plus another leaf for garnish
2 ounces Bulleit rye whiskey
⅓ ounce Simple Syrup (page 304)
⅓ ounce fresh lemon juice
1 drop Angostura bitters
1 drop orange bitters

The minty quality of the perilla leaf inspired me to try a perilla julep, a Korean-American twist on the classic American cocktail. As it happens, the Kentucky Derby falls right at the peak of perilla season in May, when the leaves are fragrant and fresh. If you can't find perilla leaves, you can substitute Japanese shiso in this cocktail.

Rip the perilla leaf into ¼-inch pieces and drop them into a cocktail shaker. Muddle them well to release the natural oils. Add ice cubes, the rye, simple syrup, lemon juice, Angostura bitters, and orange bitters, cover, and shake for 10 seconds.

Fill a rocks glass with ice and strain the cocktail into the glass. Garnish with the perilla leaf on the side and serve immediately.

VESPER'S S(E)OUL

Makes 1 drink

1 ounce Wodka vodka (or any other vodka)
1 ounce Bulldog gin
¾ ounce Bekseju (Korean herbal soju)
½ ounce yellow Chartreuse
A strip of lemon peel for garnish

This drink was inspired by the classic Vesper Cocktail made famous by the James Bond film *Casino Royale*. Instead of Lillet Blanc, I use Bekseju, a very mild, herbal brand of soju that tastes like ginseng. This is one of the few cocktails at either of my restaurants where the main flavor profile comes from a flavored alcohol, rather than a seasonal fruit. It's herbal and refreshing, which makes it perfect as both an aperitif and a digestif.

Fill a coupe glass with ice water to chill; set aside.

Fill a cocktail shaker with ice. Add the vodka, gin, Bekseju, and Chartreuse, cover, and shake vigorously to blend. Pour the ice water out of the coupe glass and strain the cocktail into it. Garnish with the lemon peel and serve immediately.

PERFECT DATE

Makes 1 drink

1½ ounces Bourbon Date Mix (recipe follows),
    plus ½ jujube from the mix for garnish
½ ounce dry vermouth
½ ounce sweet vermouth
15 drops Angostura bitters

This drink is a unusual take on a Manhattan with a little Korean flair. It uses the Korean jujube, a dried red date called *daechu*. It tastes somewhat like a dried raisin or prune, with a similar jam-like texture and a slight medicinal tinge. I wanted to showcase it as the main ingredient in a cocktail to bring out its subtle flavor. The sweetness of the bourbon pairs perfectly with the jamminess of the jujube.

Fill a martini glass with ice water and set aside to chill.

Fill a cocktail shaker with ice and add the bourbon date mix, dry vermouth, sweet vermouth, and bitters. Cover and shake vigorously to blend. Pour out the ice water from the martini glass and strain the cocktail into the glass. Put the jujube on a toothpick and drop it into the glass. Serve immediately.

BOURBON DATE MIX

Makes about 3 cups

½ pound jujubes (daechu)
24 ounces Bulleit bourbon

Remove the pits from the jujubes and put them in a 2-quart Mason jar. Add the bourbon and close the lid. Set aside for at least 48 hours to infuse. (This will keep indefinitely at room temperature as long as the jujubes are submerged in the bourbon.)

Strain the jujubes through a sieve set over a bowl, pressing on them gently with a wooden spoon to squeeze out as much liquid as possible. Transfer the jujubes to a covered container and store in the refrigerator for up to a week. Strain the liquid into a jar, cover, and refrigerate; it will keep almost indefinitely.

MAKGEOLLI MADE EASY

Makes 1 drink

1½ ounces Bulldog gin
½ ounce Cucumber Puree (recipe follows)
½ ounce fresh lime juice
½ ounce Ginger Syrup (recipe follows)
1½ ounces makgeolli
1 cucumber slice for garnish

Fruity makgeollis (Korean rice beers) are very popular in Korea. They're often flavored with blueberry, strawberry, peach, or lemon. Some are brewed with real fruit, but in other cases, an establishment will add fruit juice. Since makgeollis are about 6% alcohol, similar to beer, I decided to make a fruit-flavored makgeolli that was a bit more potent by adding gin, instead of simply diluting it with fruit juice. The result is a deliciously refreshing summer drink.

Fill a cocktail shaker with ice and add the gin, cucumber puree, lime juice, and ginger syrup. Cover and shake vigorously to blend. Fill a highball glass with ice and strain the cocktail into the glass. Pour the makgeolli on top. Garnish with the slice of cucumber.

CUCUMBER PUREE

Makes about ½ cup

½ English cucumber, peeled and cut into chunks

Puree the cucumber in a blender. Transfer to a covered container and refrigerate. Use within 48 hours.

GINGER SYRUP

Makes about 1 cup

1 cup water
1 cup sugar
One 4-inch piece ginger, peeled and sliced

Put the water, sugar, and ginger in a small saucepan set over medium-high heat and bring to a boil, stirring to dissolve the sugar. Reduce the heat and simmer for about 20 minutes, until the syrup has reduced by half. Remove from the heat, cover, and set aside to infuse for 60 minutes.

Strain the syrup and transfer to a covered container. It will keep for up to 4 weeks in the refrigerator.

DESSERTS

Fruit is the most popular dessert in Korea. In Korea and Japan, most fruits are cultivated with a focus on developing sweetness and, as a result, they are much more expensive than in the US. A high-quality Korean pear may cost as much as $15. After a meal at home, the mother will bring out fruit, often ripe apples, pears, or melons, and will start peeling or slicing it as the family converses. After a meal in a restaurant, fruit is sometimes served free. You will rarely see a dessert menu except at fine dining or hotel restaurants.

But Koreans sometimes serve sweet drinks for dessert, such as Sikhye (Sweet Rice Drink, page 332) and Su Jeong Gwa (Cinnamon-Ginger Tea, page 331). Sikhye is made from white rice; the natural sweetness and soft texture of the cooked rice make it a very comforting drink. Su jeong gwa is a cinnamon-flavored drink that can be served hot or cold, and it is a perfect pick-me-up after a meat-heavy meal. I love these drinks not only as dessert, but at any time of the day, especially in summer. I have also included several recipes for ice creams based on traditional Korean flavors. Because ginger acts as a palate cleanser, the ginger sorbet is an ideal end to a heavy meal.

My absolute favorite Korean dessert is Patbingsu (Shaved Ice with Sweet Red Beans, page 338). It is similar to Hawaiian shave ice and Taiwanese baobing. The Korean version includes stewed sweet red beans, rice cakes, and condensed milk, and it is a comforting and delicate finish to any meal. Patbingsu is served in bakeries, cafés, and dessert shops along with cakes, ice cream, and other typical Western desserts. It's rarely served at restaurants in Korea. It's more of a treat to seek out after dinner, or for a snack in between meals.

Seolbing is a chain store in South Korea that specializes in these shaved ice desserts called *bingsu*.

CINNAMON-GINGER TEA

수정과 (Su Jeong Gwa)

Serves 6

1 pound ginger, peeled and cut into ½-inch
cubes
2 quarts water
6 cinnamon sticks
1 dried persimmon (available in Korean
markets)
3 jujubes (daechu)
¾ cup sugar, or more to taste
¼ teaspoon salt
¼ cup pine nuts

Su jeong gwa is a traditional Korean dessert drink made of cinnamon, ginger, jujubes, dried persimmons, and pine nuts. It is served cold in the summer and hot in the winter. It is an incredible palate cleanser after a garlicky or spicy meal. The spicy ginger balances out the strong fragrance of the cinnamon, while the earthy pine nuts, jujubes, and sweet dried persimmon gives it a subtle, nuanced finish. See page 307 for a boozy cocktail version of this traditional drink.

Put the ginger and 4 cups of the water in a medium pot set over high heat and bring to a simmer, then lower the heat and simmer for 45 minutes. Turn off the heat, cover, and let steep for 1 hour.

Meanwhile, put the cinnamon sticks, persimmon, jujubes, and the remaining 4 cups water in another medium pot set over high heat and bring to a boil, then lower the heat and simmer for 20 minutes. Add the sugar and salt and stir until they dissolve. Turn off the heat, cover, and let steep for 1 hour.

Strain the ginger mixure through a fine-mesh sieve into a bowl; discard the ginger. Strain the cinnamon mixture into the same bowl; discard the solids. Taste to make sure the sweetness level is balanced with the flavors of the ingredients; if you'd prefer the drink to be a little bit sweeter, add a bit more sugar now, while the liquid is still hot, and stir to dissolve the sugar. Serve hot or refrigerate until chilled before serving.

Pour the drink into cups and garnish with the pine nuts.

SWEET RICE DRINK

식혜 (Sikhye)

Serves 4 to 6

1½ cups short-grain or medium-grain white
    rice
1¾ cups filtered water, or as needed
4 cups barley malt syrup
1½ cups sugar
½ teaspoon salt
5 quarts Evian (or other very low pH water)

Sikhye is sometimes called "floating rice drink." I learned this particular version from my mother-in-law. She used to make it for my son and me in the summertime. The drink is sweet and refreshing, and the rice is soft and wonderfully chewy. To Americans, rice floating in a drink may seem strange at first; once you get used to it, though, the rice will probably be your favorite part. It is cooked down to bring out its natural sweetness, which is further enhanced by the malt syrup. While you can find sikhye in cans or bottles in Korean supermarkets, when freshly made, it is far more delicious and subtle.

Put the rice in a large bowl and run cold water into it. Swirl your fingers through the rice, then carefully pour out the water and add fresh water. Repeat as many times as necessary (probably 5 to 8 times) until the water is only barely cloudy. You should be able to see the rice clearly through the water. Put the rice in a medium bowl and add the filtered water. The rice should be completely immersed; add more water if necessary. Let the rice soak for 30 minutes.

Cook the rice in a rice cooker using the quick cook setting, or steam it in a small heavy pot. If you are using a pot, bring the rice and soaking water to a simmer, cover the pot, reduce the heat to low, and steam for 20 minutes; remove from the heat.

When the rice is done, combine the malt, sugar, salt, and 1 quart of the Evian in a medium pot set over medium heat and cook, stirring, until the sugar dissolves. Transfer to a large bowl and add the remaining 4 quarts Evian, which will cool the mixture down to room temperature. Stir in the cooked rice, making sure it does not clump together. Cover and refrigerate overnight before serving. (The sikhye will keep for up to a week in a covered container in the refrigerator.) The drink should be served very cold. Stir before pouring it into glasses.

HYDRANGEA TEA SORBET
수국차 소르베 (Suguk Cha Sorbet)

Makes about 1½ quarts

4 cups water
1½ cups sugar
½ teaspoon salt
6 tea bags hydrangea tea (my preferred brand is Haeoreum)
1 teaspoon fresh lemon juice

Hydrangea tea is one of the most popular teas in Korea. Made with Korean Hydrangea serrata leaves, it is mildly floral with a sweet flavor. It is believed to aid digestion and to help wash away any strong flavors lingering on your palate. We do not offer a tea service at Hanjan, so I thought of using the tea in a sorbet for a dessert.

Put the water in a medium pot set over medium-high heat and bring to a boil. Add the sugar and salt and stir until completely dissolved. Remove from the heat and add the tea bags. Steep for exactly 2 minutes (any longer, and the tea will become quite bitter), then remove the bags.

Add the lemon juice and stir to blend. Transfer the tea to a covered container and let cool, then cover and refrigerate for 2 hours to chill.

Freeze in an ice cream machine according to the manufacturer's instructions. Transfer to a freezer container and freeze until ready to serve.

GINGER SORBET
생강 소르베 (Saenggang Sorbet)

Makes about 5 cups

4 cups water
2 cups sugar
¼ teaspoon salt
1 piece star anise
1 pound ginger, peeled
1 tablespoon fresh lemon juice

I love serving desserts made with ginger because it acts as both a palate cleanser and a digestive aid. It warms your stomach at the end of the meal and wakes you up a bit so you can enjoy the rest of your evening. It is spicy enough to provide a strong contrast to the sweetness of the sugar in this sorbet. This recipe also features star anise, which adds an exotic accent to the clean ginger flavor.

Put the water, sugar, salt, and star anise in a medium pot set over medium heat and bring to a simmer, stirring to dissolve the sugar, then remove from heat and cool the simple syrup in an ice bath.

If you have a juicer, juice the ginger and measure out 1¾ ounces (3½ tablespoons) ginger juice. If you don't have a juicer, chop the ginger and puree in a food processor, then wrap the ginger in a square of cheesecloth and squeeze the juice out into a bowl to get 1¾ ounces (3½ tablespoons).

Whisk the ginger and lemon juices into the syrup. Freeze in an ice cream machine following the manufacturer's directions. Transfer to a freezer container and freeze for at least 4 hours, and up to 24 hours, before serving.

SWEET GLUTINOUS RICE ICE CREAM
찹쌀 아이스크림 (Chapsal Ice Cream)

Makes about 1 quart

1 quart whole milk
1 quart heavy cream
4 cups sweet glutinous rice
2 cinnamon sticks
5 large egg yolks
1½ cups sugar
1 teaspoon salt

Chapsal, sweet glutinous rice, is used to make traditional Korean rice cakes for dessert. It contains more starch and is slightly sweeter than regular Korean short-grain rice. After a large meal, rice cakes can be a bit heavy, so I turned glutinous rice into an ice cream instead. It is refreshing and surprisingly light, and a very comforting finish to a meal.

Combine the milk, cream, and rice in a medium pot set over medium-low heat and slowly bring to a boil. Adjust the heat to maintain a very gentle simmer and simmer for 6 to 7 minutes, or until the rice starts to absorb the milk and the liquid thickens.

Immediately strain the milk mixture into a clean pot and discard the rice. Add the cinnamon sticks to the hot milk mixture, cover, and let steep for 15 minutes, then remove and discard the cinnamon.

Whisk the egg yolks, sugar, and salt in a bowl until doubled in volume and pale. Whisk in the milk mixture. Return to the same pot, set over low heat, and cook, stirring constantly with a heatproof spatula, until the mixture is thick enough to coat the back of a spoon and has reached 170°F; be sure to scrape the bottom corners of the pot so the custard doesn't settle there and start to scorch. Strain the custard through a fine-mesh sieve into a stainless steel bowl set over an ice bath and let cool, stirring frequently. Once it is chilled, transfer the custard to a covered container and refrigerate for at least 3 hours.

Freeze the ice cream base in an ice cream machine according to the manufacturer's directions, then transfer to a freezer container and freeze until ready to serve.

SEVEN-GRAIN ICE CREAM

미숫가루 아이스크림 (Misugaru Ice Cream)

Misugaru is made from a powdered mix of seven (or more or less) roasted seeds, grains, and beans, such as sesame seeds, brown rice, black beans, and barley. It makes a great summer drink when mixed with cold water and sugar and served over ice. Misugaru is a very traditional drink that my grandmothers used to enjoy as children. The grain mix was a basic household staple. Misugaru powder, which is gray in color, is only found in Korean supermarkets or online; it has yet to catch on in Japan or China. Used to flavor my chapsal ice cream base, it makes for a uniquely Korean ice cream.

Add 7 tablespoons misugaru powder to the strained custard (page 335), cool, and continue as directed.

(Top to bottom): Hydrangea Tea Sorbet, page 333, and Seven-Grain Ice Cream

SHAVED ICE WITH SWEET RED BEANS

팥빙수 (Patbingsu)

Serves 4

Red Beans

¾ cup dried red azuki beans or ¼ cup canned
    sweet red beans
¼ teaspoon salt
3 cups water
1 cup sugar

½ cup condensed milk
Vanilla ice cream for serving
¼ cup small mochi (specifically for shaved ice;
    available in Asian markets)
¼ cup seasonal fruit cut into small bite-sized
    cubes

Special Equipment
Ice shaver (see Note below)

Note: You will need an ice shaver to make this dessert. The specialty shops in Korea use a special snow machine that costs thousands of dollars and produces ice as smooth as snow. For home use, Hawaiian and Cuisinart are two reasonably priced brands I can recommend, available on Amazon or in Asian supermarkets.

You will need to freeze water in the tray that comes with the ice shaving machine the night before making this dessert.

This shaved ice dessert topped with sweet red beans and condensed milk is incredibly popular in Korea, as well as in many other Asian countries. It's a fine balance of rich, sticky condensed milk and fluffy shaved ice that reminds me of snow. There are many cafés that specialize in just this dish. It's made with seasonal fruits such as strawberries and peaches and topped with ice cream or frozen yogurt. Although it is excellent after a meal, I prefer to serve it as a snack in the hot summer months. Traditionally this dish is served in one large bowl and shared by everyone.

If you are making the sweet red beans from scratch, soak the beans overnight in water that covers them by 2 inches.

Drain the soaked beans and transfer to a medium pot. Add the salt and water, set over high heat, and bring to a simmer. Adjust the heat to maintain a simmer and cook for 1 hour, stirring often. Add more water if the beans start to get too dry. When the water is reduced and the beans are fully cooked, add the sugar and stir well so all the sugar is dissolved; set aside to cool.

Transfer the cooled beans to a covered container and refrigerate until needed, preferably overnight, because the sugar will slowly penetrate the insides of the beans over time. (The beans will keep in the refrigerator for up to a week.)

To serve, put 2 tablespoons of the condensed milk in the bottom of each of four chilled bowls. Shave some ice and arrange over the condensed milk in each bowl in the shape of a dome. Put a scoop of vanilla ice cream on top of each serving and scatter 1 tablespoon of the red beans on top or around the sides. Sprinkle 1 tablespoon each of the mochi and fruits on top or around the sides of each bowl and serve.

ACKNOWLEDGMENTS

Many thank-yous to:

Daniel, JFK, Chef Eddy, who showed me nothing is impossible in a kitchen.
Marco at Tocqueville, who gave me my first kitchen experience.
Masa, who showed me cooking is art.

Sharon Bowers, who convinced me I should write this book.
Maria Guarnaschelli, who wouldn't let me publish just an okay one.
Melanie Tortoroli, who carried us to the finish line.

Kristin, who traveled around Korea with me to take all the pics.
Nidia, for the beautiful backgrounds, tables, and props.
Kay and Daniel, whose amazing cooking made our studio pics so real and delicious.
Catharine, who gave my stories life.
Aki and Alex, who put those stories into words.

The entire W. W. Norton family for making this *My Korea* dream come true.
Ingsu L. and James C., for making this book beautiful and timeless.
Anna O. and Susan S., for managing this seven-year project to the end.
The amazing Judith S., who performed magic on this book that had seven years of edits.
Bob B. and Elizabeth P., who had to learn a bit of Korean while proofing and indexing this book.
Will S., for working patiently with me to help share this book with as many as possible.

Steve, Soomin, Hank, John L., Dan P., Kevin, my old friends whom I don't see as much as I like but I know they'll always be there when I need them.

The Hwang family in Jeju, who have almost adopted me in Korea. They continue to teach me Korean food is medicine and also the most delicious food in the world.

My friends who keep me safe and sane while in Korea: Hino, HaPD, ImPD, BaeYK, JangHJ, Sejin & SJ, DJ, Gayeon, Yuna, Minji, Jitae, Gia, Yongin, Alice, Jane, Somin, Yoosuk, Prof YJ, MoonK, Yankie.

The Yori Chunsa chefs who cook for our orphans every Tuesday in Seoul.
The children at Sionwon that inspire us to cook for and train them so they can become happy chefs just like us.
Sunjin and Minjae in Seoul and Chantal in New York, who run Yori Chunsa with me.
Brian Choi, Ms. Doolittle, Prof Park, for all their generosity to Yori Chunsa.

My friends in this tough and rough industry we call hospitality: Soogil, Mel, Matteo, Brandon, Haksoo, Jin, SK, Simon, John M, Esther, Kalynn, Tom & Mary, Taka, Jihan, Bobby & Joe, Seojin, SJL, Austin.

Friends who make it happy to come to work: Lina & Kenny, Jung, Kyung, Jungsun, Julia, Yohan, Goldenbergs, Sunny, Jen & Davey, Vero, Eunah, Meena, Boomi, Emmy, Diane, Chris.

Jook Jang Yeon, whose jangs make Danji and Hanjan special.
Yido Pottery, for many of the beautiful traditional Korean plates and bowls in this book.

And my biggest thank you to the former and current staff at Danji and Hanjan, who bring *My Korea* alive every day.

INDEX

Note: Page references in *italics* indicate photographs.

Korean (or Asian) pears
about, 46, *47*
Beef Tartare with Soy and Korean
Pear, 139–40
buying and storing, 46
Korean Pear Cocktail, 312, *313*
Soy-Marinated Raw Blue Crabs, 84–86
Spicy Cold Buckwheat Noodles,
246–47
uses for, 46
Winter Soju Sangria, *310*, 311
Korean radish. *See* Mu
Korean red chili flakes. *See* Gochugaru
Korean soy sauce. *See* Ganjang
Korean-Style Sashimi, *160*, 161–64

L

Lettuce Salad, Spicy, 121

M

Mackerel, Grilled Salted, 169–71, *170*
Maemilmyeon noodles
about, *40*, 41
Spicy Whelk Salad with Soba
Noodles, 167–68
Mae-un Tang (Spicy Fish Bone Stew),
172, 201
Makgeolli
about, 284
Makgeolli Made Easy, 324
Margarita, Spicy Ginger, 318, *319*
Mayo, Spicy, *56*, 61
Meat. *See also* Beef; Pork
sourcing, 130
Mirin
about, *49*, 50
buying and storing, 50
Chojang, *56*, 58
Scallion Dressing, *56*, 59
Soy Garlic Sauce, *294*, 299
uses for, 50
Misugaru Ice Cream (Seven-Grain Ice
Cream), 336, *337*
Miyeok (dried seaweed)
about, 34, *35*
buying and storing, 34
Seaweed Sashimi, 87
uses for, 34

Mochi (rice cakes)
about, 41, *42*
buying and storing, 41
Shaved Ice with Sweet Red Beans,
338, *339*
uses for, 41
Mu (Korean radish)
about, 46, *47*
Braised Spicy Hairtail, 181–82
Buckwheat Noodles in Chilled Broth,
242–45, *244*
buying and storing, 46
Korean Radish Kimchi, *104*, 105–7
Radish and Beef Soup, *194*, 195
Spicy Dehydrated Korean Radishes,
115–17, *116*
Spicy Fish Bone Stew, *172*, 201
uses for, 46
White Water-Radish Kimchi, 108, *194*
Muchim
about, 113
Marinated Spicy Cucumbers, 114, *253*
Spicy Bean Sprouts, *76*, 126
Spicy Brussels Sprouts, 122, *123*
Spicy Dehydrated Korean Radishes,
115–17, *116*
Spicy Garlic Chives, *118*, 119–20
Spicy Lettuce Salad, 121
Spinach with Sesame, 127, *194*
Steamed Eggplant, *124*, 125
Mu Guk (Radish and Beef Soup), *194*, 195
Mul Naengmyeon (Buckwheat Noodles
in Chilled Broth), 242–45, *244*
Mu Mallengi Muchim (Spicy Dehydrated
Korean Radishes), 115–17, *116*
Mushrooms. *See also* Dried shiitake
mushrooms
Bibimbap with Beef Tartare, 222–
24, *223*
Mushroom Porridge, 233–34
Omelet Fried Rice, 226–27
Somyeon Noodles in Anchovy Broth,
251–53, *252*
Sweet Potato Noodles with
Vegetables, 260–61
Mussels
Noodles in Spicy Seafood Broth,
257–58, *259*
Spicy Soft Tofu Stew with Seafood,
202–4, *203*

Myulchi Bokkeum (Sweet Crispy Baby
Anchovies), *76*, 79–80
Myung Lan Deop Bap (Spicy Salted
Cod Roe over Rice), 235–36, *236*

N

Naengmyeon noodles
about, 39–41, *40*
Buckwheat Noodles in Chilled Broth,
242–45, *244*
Spicy Cold Buckwheat Noodles,
246–47
Noodles
Buckwheat Noodles in Chilled Broth,
242–45, *244*
buying and storing, 39–41
dangmyeon, about, 39, *40*
Hanjan's 12-Hour Korean Ramyeon,
263–66, *264*
jajangmyeone, about, *40*, 41
Korean, about, 241
maemilmyeon, about, *40*, 41
naengmyeon, about, 39–41, *40*
Noodles in Black Bean Sauce, *254*,
255–56
Noodles in Spicy Seafood Broth,
257–58, *259*
somyeon, about, *40*, 41
Somyeon Noodles in Anchovy Broth,
251–53, *252*
Spicy Cold Buckwheat Noodles,
246–47
Spicy Cold Noodles, *248*, 249–50
Spicy DMZ Stew, 273–75, *276*
Spicy Pork and Gochujang Bolognese
Noodles, 262
Spicy Whelk Salad with Soba
Noodles, 167–68
Sweet Potato Noodles with
Vegetables, 260–61
Nori. *See* Gim

O

Oee Muchim (Marinated Spicy
Cucumbers), 114, *253*
Ojingeo Bokkeum (Spicy Stir-Fried
Squid), 174–76, *175*
Omelet Fried Rice, 226–27

Squid
    Crispy Calamari, 292
    Noodles in Spicy Seafood Broth,
        257–58, *259*
    Spicy Soft Tofu Stew with Seafood,
        202–4, *203*
    Spicy Stir-Fried Squid, 174–76, *175*
Sriracha
    Spicy Asian Sauce, *294*, 298
    Spicy Mayo, *56*, 61
Ssak Yang Bechu Muchim (Spicy
    Brussels Sprouts), 122, *123*
Ssamjang, *45*, 57
Star anise
    Cinnamon and Star Anise Simple
        Syrup, 306
    Ginger Sorbet, 334
Suguk Cha Sorbet (Hydrangea Tea
    Sorbet), 333, *337*
Su Jeong Gwa (Cinnamon-Ginger Tea),
    330, 331
Su Jeong Gwa Cocktail (Cold or Hot),
    307–8
Su Jeong Gwa Tea, 308
Syrups
    Cinnamon and Star Anise Simple
        Syrup, 306
    Cinnamon Simple Syrup, 306
    Ginger Syrup, 324
    Simple Syrup, 304
    Spicy Simple Syrup, 305

T

Tartare
    Beef Tartare with Soy and Korean
        Pear, 139–40
    Bibimbap with Beef Tartare, 222–24,
        223
Tea
    Cinnamon-Ginger Tea, *330*, 331
    Hydrangea Tea Sorbet, 333, *337*
    Su Jeong Gwa Cocktail (Cold or Hot),
        307–8
    Su Jeong Gwa Tea, 308

Tequila
    Ginger Puree, 318
    Spicy Ginger Margarita, 318, *319*
Toasted sesame oil. *See* Sesame oil
Toasted sesame seeds. *See* Sesame seeds
Tofu
    about, 43, *43*
    Aged-Kimchi Stew, 198–200, *199*
    buying and storing, 43
    extra soft, about, 43, *43*
    Fermented-Soybean Stew, 205, *206*,
        207
    firm, about, 43, *43*
    Fried Tofu with Pajeon Sauce, *70*,
        71–72
    Radish and Beef Soup, *194*, 195
    silken, about, 43, *43*
    soft, about, 43, *43*
    Spicy DMZ Stew, 273–75, *276*
    Spicy Soft Tofu Stew with Seafood,
        202–4, *203*
    uses for, 43–45
    Warm Tofu with Kimchi and Pork
        Belly Stir-Fry, 278–80, *279*
Tteok (rice cakes)
    about, 41, *42*
    buying and storing, 41
    Hanjan's Spicy Rice Cakes, *288*,
        289–90
    Rice Cake Soup, *192*, 193
    uses for, 41
Tteokbokki (Hanjan's Spicy Rice Cakes),
    288, 289–90

V

Vegetables. *See also specific vegetables*
    choosing, for kimchi, 95
    Rice with Beef and Vegetables, 217–18
    Sizzling-Hot Stone Bowl Bibimbap,
        219, *220*, 221
    Sweet Potato Noodles with
        Vegetables, 260–61
Vermouth
    Perfect Date, 322, *323*

Vesper's S(e)oul, 321
Vinegar. *See* Rice vinegar
Vodka
    Korean Pear Cocktail, 312, *313*
    Vesper's S(e)oul, 321

W

Walnuts
    Ssamjang, *45*, 57
    Sweet Crispy Baby Anchovies, *76*,
        79–80
Wasabi Dip, 292
Watercress
    Marinated Rice with Sashimi Salad,
        225
    Spicy Whelk Salad with Soba
        Noodles, 167–68
Whelk Salad, Spicy, with Soba Noodles,
    167–68
Wine
    Summer Soju Sangria, 309
    Winter Soju Sangria, *310*, 311

Y

Yakult Colada, 315, *316*
Yangnyeom Galbi (Soy-Marinated BBQ
    Beef Short Ribs), *132*, 133–34
Yangnyeom Gejang (Spicy Raw Blue
    Crabs), 81–83, *82*
Yukhwe (Beef Tartare with Soy and
    Korean Pear), 139–40
Yukhwe Bibimbap (Bibimbap with Beef
    Tartare), 222–24, *223*

Z

Zucchini
    Fermented-Soybean Stew, 205, *206*,
        207
    Noodles in Black Bean Sauce, *254*,
        255–56
    Spicy Soft Tofu Stew with Seafood,
        202–4, *203*